Carrol's Conversion: A Story Of Life...

Helen Van-Anderson

CARROL'S CONVERSION

A Story of Life

HELEN VAN-ANDERSON

AUTHOR OF

"THE RIGHT KNOCK," "VICTORIA TRUE; OR, THE JOURNAL OF A
LIVE WOMAN," "STORY OF TEDDY," "TEMPLE TEACHINGS.
"HEART TALKS," ETC., ETC.

"All things are possible to him that
believeth."—*Jesus.*

"I can do all things through Christ
which strengtheneth me."—*Paul.*

THE NEW YORK MAGAZINE

OF MYSTERIES
22 NORTH WILLIAM STREET
NEW YORK CITY

DEDICATED

TO

ALL SEARCHERS AFTER THE HIGHER LIFE.

"What we are to expect is an awakening of the soul; the rediscovery and rehabilitation of the genuine and indisputable religious instinct. Such a religious revival will be something very different from what we have hitherto known under that name. It will be a spontaneous and joyful realization by the soul of its vital relations with its Creator. Ecclesiastical forms and dogmas will vanish, and nature will be recognized as a language whereby God converses with man. The interpretation of this language, based as it is upon an eternal and living symbolism containing infinite depths beyond depths of meaning, will be sufficient study and employment for mankind forever."

—JULIAN HAWTHORNE.

INDEX.

IT was night.

The world was dreaming in its troubled sleep. .

It is morning. A glad new day breaks on the weary sleepers. A little child, with sparkling eyes and refreshing vigor, comes upon the scene.

"Awake!" she cries, "It is morning. The sun is high and bright. I am glad, so glad and happy because all waking things are glad. The birds sing of the gladness, the wind breathes it, the flowers nod and speak of it, the sunshine lives it! Oh, the happy in me is all there is! Wake! Come and see!"

The morning song of the child is the jubilee of the world, for the world is awake!

CARROL'S CONVERSION.

CHAPTER I.

"Children are God's apostles, day by day sent forth to preach of love, and hope, and peace."—*Lowell*.

OH, you dear, cunning thing! Did God make you out of the rainbow?" A little girl of eight or nine years sat alone among the flowers in her mother's garden. She had spied a many-hued butterfly hovering near the taller flowers, and as the sunshine bathed his gauzy wings he seemed indeed almost like an animated rainbow.

"I won't hurt you one bit if you come and sit on my hand," coaxed the small maiden, holding out a tempting pink palm to the gay visitor; but he only sailed about with his lovely wings outspread as if to say, "Let me alone little girl, I'd rather be in God's free air than in all the pretty hands in the world. I am going to kiss this lady-finger, and then fly away with my message to the honey-bee."

She watched him settle for a moment on his chosen spot of sweetness, and then walked slowly up to the slender pink tips of the lady-finger.

"I wish you'd tell me what he said," she whispered, as if the flower were a live thing like herself. Lady-finger bowed her head, but said never a word.

11

"Are you God's messenger too, I wonder?" mused the child, stroking the graceful tassels tenderly. "That's what Aunt Lottie told me once," she continued, "and Carrol really believes it—that every pretty and lovely thing has God's voice in it somewhere—but mamma—"

What mamma thought or said she forgot to say, for just then the butterfly re-appeared and she followed him about from one place to another until she found herself in the orchard beside her own little nest in the old apple tree.

"Faith, an' bahd luk'll come to me worruk" grumbled Maggie, the new "help" an hour later, after a vain search for Mary among the currant and lilac bushes where she had found her several times before. "Jist wan more luik an' I'll away fer me kitchen."

A hasty glance through the orchard, and then she turned toward the house in such sudden haste that her hair became tangled in the branches of a tree, causing an immediate halt. Her exclamation of surprise and pain was checked by the sight that met her eyes, for there, curled up in the branches, fast asleep, her undried tears still lingering on the brown lashes and rosy cheeks, was little Mary.

"Och! but yer a swate craythur af ye did bring me most to the fate o'hangin'," thought Maggie, admiringly, as she finally tore the obstinate twig from her hair and found herself free once more.

"Sure an' it's a blissed saint yez air ef yez do chry wanst in a while," she murmured softly, intending to leave the child as she found her, but a pair of wondering blue eyes looked into hers and a childish voice asked what was the matter. Maggie explained, adding in no unkindly tone, "an' now yez must be afther tellin' yer mamma yer ristin' place, for an' how cud she think yez would be playin' intil the trees, loike a burd of the air."

Mary clapped her hands and laughed merrily.

"Why, Maggie, this is my throne and I'm a queen 'stead of a bird. Mamma knows, only I guess she don't remember 'bout the queen part all the time. Just see, Maggie, this is the way we play. You sit down there on the lowest branch. That's the place for Carrol when she's lady's maid, and I'm right here with the green crown on my head and a long green willow in my hand so. We play King Solomon and Queen of Sheba sometimes too."

"Whisht, now jist listen to the darlint talkin' o' kings an' queens an' lukin' that same herself the while," cried the delighted Maggie, forgetting her hurry.

"Oh yes, and Maggie," continued Mary, lowering her voice, " this is my dream-tree. Most every time when I'm alone out here I go to sleep like I did to-day, and God sends me such sweet dreams that I 'most wish I could stay asleep all day."

Maggie had by this time lifted her out of the sheltered crotch and they were on their way to the house, the child giving what Maggie afterwards designated as one of the "glory talks," which, by the way, was a most appropriate name for these glimpses of a child's ecstatic faith and refreshing innocence.

"Where have you been, my child?" asked Mrs. Noble, in a reproachful tone.

"In heaven, mamma—anyway I dreamed I was," seeing the startled amazement on her mother's face.

"Dreams are like fairy stories, you know, and we mustn't talk as though they were really true," said Mrs. Noble, with the helplessness of one who does not know just what to say.

"Where are Ada and Carrol?" she added, before Mary could reply.

"I don't know, mamma; but I guess they're in Bethlehem."

"Where?" exclaimed her mother.

"Why, mamma, we have a beautiful place with such pretty stones for houses and we play it's Bethlehem 'cause it's nice to think of the place where Jesus lived, and really, mamma, we play he's there now, and sometimes we meet him and he does whatever we ask him. One day Ada let a stone fall on her foot and it hurt awful, but we asked Jesus to cure it, and he did, and oh, it's the lovliest play, mamma, 'cause it's really true he's there you know."

The unbounded faith and enthusiasm expressed in voice, eye, and gesture, would have been a pleasing and impressive sight to most beholders. Not so to the mother.

"But Mary, child—" she began.

"Don't you 'member, mamma, when you read 'bout what he said, 'Lo, I am with you always', and told us to think 'bout the things he taught? So that's what we try to do," was the rather incoherent explanation.

"I tell you, Mary, you must not talk about sacred things in this irreverent way. It's wicked to play such things, too. Go call Ada and cousin Carrol now. I want to speak to them."

"Oh, mamma, I was just going to ask God to take away your crying feelings about papa, too. Mayn't I do that first, mamma, 'fore we leave our beautiful Bethlehem."

"No, no, my child."

Mary's eyes were full of unshed tears, but her mother did not see them. She was sighing and wondering what Mary would think of next. It seemed so hard for the child to understand spiritual things, for she so insisted on literal interpretations.

Maggie had gone to her work in the kitchen, and Mary proceeded on her way to "Bethlehem," as she fondly imagined.

"Ada! Carrol!" she called, as she came in sight of the little enclosure of stones. She had left them an hour or two before, to be alone awhile, she told them. As she approached, she heard voices behind the lilac bush a few rods away.

"I know it's true anyway," said Ada, with stout decision. "My foot was just as sore as it could be—wasn't it Carrol? and after that it got well just as quick," with rising inflection, "and I know that he did it," speaking the last words with much reverence.

"My! but wasn't you 'fraid?" queried a boy's awe-struck voice, that Mary recognized as Harvey Willard's.

"'Fraid? What should we be 'fraid of?" was Ada's indignant response. "Besides," she added, "we can't love anybody and be 'fraid of them at the same time, can we?"

"If you knew somebody loved you, and did great splendid things for you, you couldn't help loving back, could you?" added Carrol, although she had not the implicit faith of Mary and Ada.

"Aw, well," drawled Harvey somewhat abashed, and there he stopped, for he was not sure what his father (the minister) would think, either of the faith exhibited by Ada and Carrol, or the lack of it in himself. His opinion was never settled on anything, until he had heard his father express one, and on this theme, strange to say, he had heard nothing.

"What's the reason you don't believe it?" exclaimed Carrol, impatiently. "You're taught to believe that Jesus loves you; why shouldn't he do anything you ask him to do that is right and good?"

As is often the case with larger disputants, the spirit of the law was killed by the argument of the letter.

"I heard papa say *you* ought to learn some religion now, since you've come to your aunt's to live, for you never went to church, nor was taught anything good before," retorted Harvey, resorting to personal invective when righteous argument failed.

Carrol's brown eyes flashed and she opened her lips to speak, but with one scornful scorching look she turned toward the house, leaving Harvey apparently master of the field. At this juncture Mary appeared, looking with mild astonishment at the discomfited trio. Carrol was ashamed, Harvey frightened, and Ada quite relieved.

"Mamma wants us to go in now," said Mary, at last;

"but I would like to tell you all 'bout the lovely dream I've had ; so come on, Harvey."

With instinctive tact she ignored the schism and drew them, in her winning way, to listen to her dream.

"I went to the dear old tree," she said, taking Ada's hand in hers, as they walked along, "and I felt so kind of happy way down deep. I thought how nice it would be to sit real *still* and hear God talk, for you know I think He does, when I just listen to Him and nothing else." She turned around to look at them, "and only the leaves stirred, and the little bird on her nest over my head sat just as still as though she wanted to listen too, and—well, I felt so happy I cried a little." Mary spoke very softly, and a reverent hush fell on the group. "And then—and then," she went on, "it just seemed as though I was in heaven, for everything seemed so beautiful—oh, *so* beautiful! The light was like—well, like melted sunshine, so soft and lovely, and the air was so full of music; no, not music, but the cream of music, as though somebody had skimmed the sweetness of all the sounds and then let the wind scatter it everywhere."

Ada drew a long breath of ecstacy and clasped her sister's hand more tightly. They had paused to catch every word and look of the little narrator.

"Did you see any angels?" whispered Ada, with wide-open eyes.

"No, but I felt a whisper that sounded like, 'Suffer little children to come unto me.'"

"It must have been Jesus," murmured Ada, again ; "don't you think so, Harvey?"

"I don't know," he replied, rather doubtfully. All

this seemed very strange, but for some reason he never could disbelieve Mary, and if she said it was so, it must be so.

"But just think of the words! The very same papa used to read out of the big Bible," Mary went on; "and when I heard them, I felt so warm and taken care of, as if God was right there with me; and oh Carrol, I wish you could have felt it too, 'cause then you wouldn't miss your mamma near so much, for 'twould seem as if God's love reached down and covered you all up like a lovely, warm cloak."

Carrol choked back a little sob.

Her mother, who had always understood and sympathized with her, who had always been tender and patient, had suddenly gone out of this life six months previous, leaving Carrol to Mary's mother, her only sister. Carrol clung desperately to the memory of the only parent she had ever known, for she did not remember her father, and while she was regarded as a strange, silent child, there were depths in her nature no one suspected, much less understood. Little Mary came nearest to filling the void; but after all, things had changed painfully, as the poor girl was often reminded, especially by Harvey Willard's unkind speeches, which were all the more humiliating as they were mostly echoes of his father.

After Mary had told the dream, a silence fell upon the children as they slowly walked into the house to Mrs. Noble.

What she said to them or how she said it, no one

ever knew, but the result was they never played "Bethlehem" again. Mary said less about her "talks with God," Carrol grew cold and unbelieving, and Harvey quoted his father more than ever.

CHAPTER II.

"'Tis liberty alone that gives the flower
Of fleeting life its lustre and perfume,
And we are weeds without it."
—*Cowper.*

ONE night after Mary and Ada were sound asleep, Carrol stole out of the house and went straight to Pam's kennel.

In all her twelve years, she had never felt so desolate. Pam was the only living link that bound her to the past. A great awkward Newfoundland puppy, he had come to her one Christmas in the long ago, a gift from her mother, and since then they had been close and loving companions. Secrets that no one else dreamed of were poured into Pam's willing ears, and every wounded feeling or childish grievance had been helped or healed by Pam's loving sympathy. But it was something unusual for his little mistress to come to him at this time of night, and as he heard her steps he lifted his ears and began a sleepy growl of remonstrance.

"Don't bark, Pam," she whispered. "I've come to see you a few moments, and oh Pam," cried the child, with a breaking sob, " I am *so* lonesome and miserable."

Pam at once made himself as hospitable as he knew how and tenderly licked her hand.

"It seems as if only you and I are left, and you are

so good to me. I'd rather talk to you than to anybody else, for you understand, and you never talk back—you just love me."

She cried brokenly with her arms about the shaggy neck, while Pam looked at her with eyes full of love and wonder.

"I don't see why Harvey says such mean things. He thinks I've never been taught religion, and Pam, you know better, 'cause didn't mamma teach me to be kind to everybody, and love all God's creatures?"

Pam licked more vigorously than ever, wagging his tail as much as to say, "Of course she did, for I know all about it. Didn't she give me a lecture once when I chased a strange cat out of the yard?"

"Pam, I wouldn't tell anybody but you, but aunt Marcia isn't a bit like mamma, for she talks about God being angry with folks who don't go to church, and who don't pray and read the Bible, and she says it's wrong to talk about Him in an every-day way, like we did when we played that beautiful play Mary made up. Mamma used to say that God loves *everybody*, and only asks folks to do the very best they can. Which *do* you think is right, Pam, for I don't know any more, when aunt Marcia and Harvey's father talk so?"

She withdrew her arms and wiped her eyes on her apron. Pam put his paw into her lap, with eyes eloquent with sympathy.

"Oh, dear, sometimes I'd like to die, if it weren't for Mary and you, Pam. It just seems—as—though—I can't learn to be good, aunt Marcia's way. She even finds fault with—dear little—Mary."

A long pause ensued, during which Carrol cried as if her heart would break, and the dog looked at her with tenderest solicitude, evidently understanding the whole matter.

She ceased crying suddenly.

Her grief had hardened her to even Pam's loving caresses. She wiped her eyes with a determined air.

"I don't care; I shall not try. Mamma taught me a religion good enough for anybody, and if aunt Marcia and Mr. Willard don't like it they needn't, that's all."

Pam gazed into her face reproachfully, but she saw nothing but the clear moonlight and flickering shadows on the walk.

"I must go in now," she said presently. "Aunt Marcia'll be locking the doors, for she don't know I'm out. Good night, dear old Pam. You love me, don't you?" and she laid her cheek for a moment on the faithful head, then wiped her eyes for the last time, and went into the house.

The next day was Sunday. If there was one day more than another in which Mrs. Noble lived her religion, it was this day, and from the moment she appeared in the morning to the moment she disappeared at night, a severe solemnity pervaded her every word and attitude The children were required to read, pray, recite lessons go to church—in short, to observe the Sabbath according to the strictest letter of the law. To keep them in order was the most difficult task she had to perform, but she spared no effort to perform it well.

The girls trooped into the dining room for breakfast. Mrs. Noble looked up from her Bible. "Good morning, children," in a particularly Sunday tone. Carrol and Ada murmured a greeting under their breath. Mary ran to her mother, impetuously threw her arms about her neck, exclaiming: "Mamma, the tiniest little bird came and sat on our window before we got up this morning, and oh, he sang the sweetest song! just as if he told everybody to be happy;" and the small feet danced on the rounds of mamma's chair, utterly unconscious of Sabbath restrictions.

"'Sh—h, Mary! Be quiet. It is the Sabbath."

The sepulchral voice had its effect, and Mary reluctantly untwined her arms, and substituted for her tiptoe position a stool at her mother's side. Carrol glowered darkly in the corner, and Ada busily engaged herself in wondering how Harvey made fish-hooks out of pins.

The chapter was read in a low-voiced monotone, without comment or explanation of any kind; the customary petition for forgiveness, grace, health and strength, went up from the devout lips, after which the good lady led the little brood to the table.

Maggie came in with the breakfast.

"The top o' the mornin' to yez!" she exclaimed, brightly, as she looked at the three. "Good morning,' was the solemn rejoinder.

"Sure an' ye've not lost anythink?" inquired Maggie, anxiously.

"No, but this is Sunday you know. After you've been here a little longer, Maggie, you'll know how to act," said Carrol, with unconscious sarcasm.

Maggie involuntarily crossed herself, as she went out

of the dining room. Mrs. Noble looked severely at Carrol, but said nothing.

"I'll tell you how to be happy, Maggie," said Mary, with one of her angelic smiles, as Maggie returned looking very sober.

"Just think of the leaves laughing with gladness when they tremble in the sunshine; and think of the little birds that sing all day and work for their cunning babies in the nest. Oh, they are *so* cunning, and—"

"Mary, be more quiet; you should not talk so much."

"Och, mam, shure an' she manes the best, an' oi love to hear her tinklin' voice that has the quoitness o' brooks intil it. Faith, an' she *does* know how to mak foakes happy," said Maggie, and wiped her eyes with the back of her hand.

"That will do, Maggie. I will take some coffee, if you please;" then turning to the girls, Mrs. Noble continued: "And now children, have you studied your Sunday School lesson until you know it perfectly?"

"I think I have," said conscientious Mary.

"I can say every word," was Ada's addition.

"And you, Carrol?"—after a pause.

The clock ticked loudly, but to Carrol the silence seemed louder. At last she spoke:

"I couldn't understand it and didn't try to learn."

There! it was said, and she was careless of consequences.

"Why did you not bring the lesson to me for help?" in an I-must-see-to-this tone.

"Because, one day I asked you something, and you

told me God did not intend we should understand every-thing, and that I must not wonder any more about it," was the startling answer.

A martyred look of resignation settled down on her aunt's face, but she said nothing until they were ready to leave the table; then, with a glance peculiar to her-self, she requested Carrol to go into the sitting-room and await her coming. Left alone with Mary and Ada, after Carrol's departure, she heard them rehearse their verses, read the questions from the lesson leaf and patiently waited until every one was answered satis-factorily, then left the girls to strengthen the weak places in their memory while she looked after Carrol. An arduous duty, but since it was the Lord's will she would do her best to accomplish the right result.

She was not an unkindly woman, only a conscien-tious one.

She took the lesson leaf with her. She was pre-pared for wilfulness and perhaps obstinacy, but scarcely in the way they met her that morning.

"Now Carrol," she began, in a soothing tone, "what is it you could not understand?"

"Why Uzzah was struck dead for putting his hand on the ark."

"Because God had said no one should touch it, and he was disobeying—"

"But wasn't he doing the best he knew how to carry the ark safe, and wasn't that working for God?" inter-rupted Carrol, with all a child's ardor for justice burning within her.

"Carrol Evans! how dare you?" cried her aunt, aghast

at this startling irreverence. "This is the result of Lottie's liberal religion," she added. "A nice field she left for me to harvest."

"Aunt Marcia, I *believe* my mother's religion. It is good enough and I want to be like her."

A new soil had been turned in Carrol's nature. What it might yield if cultivated was an important question.

"Hush, child," commanded her aunt; "you don't know what you are talking about. I would not have you go the way your mother did for anything in the world. She was an *infidel*."

Carrol looked as if turned to stone.

"Do you know what that means?" questioned Mrs. Noble, with rising emphasis.

"Yes, but I don't believe it."

That moment the soil was yielding flint.

Carrol burst into tears. So quickly had bitterness turned to despair.

"It just seems as though you want me to forget all that mamma ever taught me," the child went on, passionately, vehemently, before her aunt had sufficiently recovered to administer a rebuke; "and to even think she was bad because she didn't believe the Bible like you do! It's real mean of you and I wish I was dead, so there!"

She ended with an explosive little shriek that should have convinced Mrs. Noble of the intensity of the undercurrents, but she was no person to look for signs or to interpret them when found.

"Hush! You are a wicked child to talk so. Get right down on your knees and ask God's forgiveness for this—" she paused for lack of language. Presently, in no less severe, though somewhat calmer tones, she said, "I wish you to remain here, Carrol, until you are in a proper mood."

"I don't care for God's forgiveness, if He is like you say He is, and I'll *never* feel in the proper mood," was the rebellious answer, in the midst of a terrific sobbing.

A little scratch at the door and it opened to admit Pam, who came bounding up to his mistress with the warmest demonstrations of love. "Go out, sir!" commanded Mrs. Noble. "Go out!" she repeated, in a terrible voice. Poor Pam slunk away as though he had been whipped.

"You have brought all this on yourself, Carrol," said her aunt at last, as she rose to go. "It is my duty to teach you the right way, whether you like it or not. As for your mother, I loved her and promised to do what I could for her child. Learn your lesson now, and then it will be time for church."

The tone was more kindly, but the wound was too deep to be healed with a few surface words. Carrol was left alone with the shadow of a great darkness— alone, with no mother, no friend, no Pam even. Oh, the loneliness that comes to a misunderstood, motherless child, whether the child be small or of larger growth, for the Godless mortal is always motherless!

The lesson leaf lay on the floor, likewise the family Bible, but Carrol heeded not. She was fighting the first real battle between her own conscience and the conscience of somebody else.

Poor girl! She knew not the beginning nor the end.

For some moments she sat disconsolate and miserable. Then she remembered her aunt's parting words. She must learn those verses then—understand or not, as she might—that was the decree. It was hard to bring herself to the obeying of such a command, but she did, though not without an inner contempt for the task and herself too. "I can't help hating God for killing Uzzah, anyway," she thought, as she threw down the lesson paper at last.

When Mrs. Noble returned an hour later, she found the verses learned and every sign of storm gone from the horizon.

Carrol had learned more than one lesson that day.

CHAPTER III.

"The verdict of all ages has pronounced that the exclusively scientific man, he in whom the scientific side is everything and the spiritual side goes for nothing, is but half a man, developed only on one side of his nature, and that not the highest side. If God is to be apprehended at all in a vital way, and not merely as an intellectual abstraction, it must be first from the spiritual side of our being—by the conscience, the spirit, the reverence, that is in man—that he is to be approached."—*J. C. Shairp.*

O sir, it can't be done. Such a life is impossible."

The professor puffed a long wreath of smoke from his cigar and musingly watched it circle about his head separating into little blue rings as it rose.

"I tell you, Fernlow," he continued, "there is nothing practicable or possible in this Christian religion. It is an utter failure."

He took his cigar between his fingers, and looked at his friend for an instant, as though he half expected to be contradicted.

"On what grounds, Prof. Thornbush, do you consider it a failure?" asked the younger man, whose keen blue eyes scintillated with argumentative light.

"There are two reasons in the main," replied the Professor. "First, it is unphilosophical, and consequently illogical; and second, it cannot be lived. Find me a Christian who lives up to its central precept, 'Love your neighbor as yourself?'"

He smiled triumphantly as he leaned back and sent forth another challenging puff.

"I admit that there may be few who follow that principle of life, but that is not saying they *cannot.* Furthermore, I object to judging a principle wholly by the persons representing it. I—"

"Aha, my friend! you're getting around the question just like all the rest of them. I never knew a religious fanatic yet who could answer a straightforward question; faugh!" As he said this the Professor wrathfully knocked the ashes off his treasured weed, and leaned forward, with one hand on his knee, while he deliberately surveyed the "fanatic."

Mr. Fernlow smiled good-naturedly as he said: "That doesn't hurt me in the least, Professor. I can bear such names as fanatic and crank. In fact, I am getting quite used to them."

The Professor seemed discomfited. "I—I beg your pardon, Fernlow," he stammered. "You're always taking up the cudgels in defence of religion, and you— well, you'll have to bear the consequences." He finished with an uneasy laugh.

"You don't mean to tell us, Professor," resumed the other, "that you disbelieve in the possibility of a moral life?"

"Oh no, not exactly that, but—" The Professor had not quite recovered his composure. His cigar had gone out and he gazed at it disconcertedly. "But," he continued, "I hate cant, and it seems to me everybody not agnostically inclined, uses it *ad libitum.*"

"Cant!" Mr. Fernlow paused thoughtfully after

the word. "Cant is a much abused term, and I think it is the word as much as what it implies that disgusts such people as you. But there is cant in everything, even in materialism," with a sly look at his friend, who flushed a little, but stoutly maintained his critical attitude, while he said in a rising voice: "Materialism is the only rational ism of the whole calendar, and Herbert Spencer its greatest philosopher."

He threw aside his cigar, drew a long breath that exhaled itself in a slowly uttered po-oh of possible defiance, and looked absently out of the window.

Neither spoke for some moments.

"Where are you going to spend vacation this summer, Professor?" asked Fernlow, at last.

"As far out of the bubbling, buzzing world of argument as I can get. Think I'll stop in the backwoods, where I can be free from this confounded church business the whole three months if I like," was the irate answer. "It's a bore, and I tell you, Fernlow, you're too sensible a fellow to waste your time thinking of such nonsense. It's too much like—"

He ceased abruptly, and began talking of other things.

"Hold on, Fernlow, you needn't hurry off," as the young man rose to depart some time later. "Hold on; you mustn't mind the brusqueness of an old fellow like myself."

But Mr. Fernlow excused himself, saying he must keep an appointment.

The Professor looked about for his cigar, forgetting he had consigned it to the grate.

"Strange that a young man of Fernlow's intellect and abilities should be so wrapped up in these threadbare problems, but then, he is young yet. The dew of morning still lingers on his landscape. Wait till he finds the lack in his philosophy, till he finds the glowing fire of hope turn into ashes of despair, heaven a mere child's dream, and the story of Jesus Christ an interesting myth that is no more reliable than yesterday's cobweb."

A bitter smile played over his features. His ruminations were evidently not pleasing. "Religion! Conversion!" he muttered again. "What did it do but ruin Lucy! Humph! the biggest humbug that ever deluded humanity!"

He sat musing thus till late in the night, as he always did after such a talk. Once turned to this subject, he dwelt on it with a grim persistence that amounted almost to fascination. It mattered not to him whether Mr. Fernlow called himself a Christian or not. Practically he was one to the Professor, because he was lenient in his judgment of Christian principles; hence this conversation with Mr. Fernlow had the same effect as a hot conflict with Rev. Brown, or any other doughty theologian. Why such talk should so thoroughly disturb him, and arouse such a feeling of evident bitterness, no one of the few who knew the fact that it did, could tell.

Prof. Thornbush, as a teacher in the Bardville academy, was looked upon with great respect by most people, not unmixed with awe and hatred by others. Put to the open question, some might have said, that if it were not for his excellence as a teacher of mathematics, and the difficulty of filling his place, he should long ago have been discharged; but, fortunately for the Professor, this latter class rarely heard him talk of anything but his legitimate labors, and mathematics prevailed. He was a man of keen intellect and deep thought, strongly opinioned and brusque mannered.

His loneliness of life, his peculiar moods and morose terseness had caused an atmosphere of mystery to spring up about him that no one in Bardville had ever penetrated. His only close companion known was a bird. Whether he had ever married, or whether he had a wife pining away somewhere for the love he could not be imagined as giving, no one knew. The fact was, his mind was so continually in the line of geometrical calculations, that he measured himself and everybody else with his cold mathematical plummet; so instead of the soft, curving outlines of Love's carving, his face exhibited the square corners and rugged furrows cut by cold reason. If there were a fault in his own or his friend's methods, he was immediately ready with square and compass to right it.

In this manner he had gone to work with his friend, Richard Fernlow, who was a favorite with him, but one whom, notwithstanding his intention to study for the ministry, he could not help rubbing out and writing over. This habit made him more and more crusty, and it was almost like bearding the proverbial lion in his den to make a successful call on Prof. Thornbush. His landlady had learned a few signs by which she knew he was approachable by even a moderately brave person like herself. One was the state of his hair. If the short, stubborn, iron-grey locks bristled fiercely around his face, it boded ill to whomsoever dared to address him; but if they lay smoothly in the proper place and order, the visitor might venture to make known his errand.

"No visitors admitted," said Mrs. Cobb to a young man who stood on the front steps, waiting for an answer to his ring. It was ten o'clock on the Sunday morning following Mr. Fernlow's visit. The caller left a note and departed.

Good Mrs. Cobb had developed both wisdom and tact in all the six years Prof. Thornbush had boarded under her roof, and that morning she knew by the ominous silence in the Professor's room that he was not going to church, and would therefore be invisible till after luncheon. It was one of his whims to do as he pleased on Sunday, notwithstanding the fact that he, as well as the rest of the faculty, was expected to set an example before the students.

After the one o'clock luncheon, when the Professor had settled himself back in his chair for a comfortable smoke, the note was handed to him.

"What's this?" hastily adjusting his eye-glasses, as he took the small piece of paper. Hurriedly he scanned the writing and glanced at the signature. "Oh, its only Fernlow. I wonder what calls him away." He read the note again. Something about the writing struck the same chord that had vibrated so earnestly the night before.

He had begun to feel a peculiar interest in Mr. Fernlow, and went on musing to himself about him. Sometimes his thoughts became audible, as in the present instance, but there was no one to hear him except Bob, the canary, who alone, of all the Professor's acquaintances in Bardville, had the privilege of hearing confidences, though perhaps he was the only one who could be trusted. At any rate, he never told secrets, many as he knew.

For some reason, the Professor was troubled. He tried to read an essay from his favorite philosopher, but it was stale and uninteresting. He walked excitedly back and forth, while he threaded his fingers through his hair, or glared through his glasses at the scene in front of his window.

Bob sang his sweetest, but he was not noticed. The strides became longer, the hair more bristling. Mrs. Cobb would have said no to any caller now, had she but glimpsed her boarder's face. He was evidently under a strong stress of excitement. Some long-buried care or sorrow seemed resurrected in the hard drawn lines around the mouth and brow.

In the evening he walked under the trees in the park. A something, there he always found that soothed and calmed him. It was that in Nature which was all the God he knew,—a hidden force, like life itself, invisible, exhaustless; a tender, brooding love, that gave richly of its healing potency.

This vein of appreciative sensibility was occasionally so manifestly touched, that he seemed like a different man.

Different ! Who has not prismatic sides as well as hues that distort and deceive, or flash and dazzle with ever shifting variableness ?

In the softened mood that came over him, his thoughts turned again to the far-away spot he called home. He had not seen it nor any of his family for many years. One by one, the familiar faces had dropped out of the circle, until only one except his own remained; but the impulse was strong upon him to go back, and he finally decided to obey.

That night, before he slept, a letter was posted to his sister, telling her when to expect his arrival.

CHAPTER IV.

"And judge none lost but wait and see,
With hopeful pity, not disdain;
The depth of the abyss may be
The measure of the height of pain,
And love and glory, that raise
This soul to God in after-days."
—*Adelaid A. Proctor.*

IT was a bright June morning in Tintuckett. The air fairly quivered with its summer odors and delicate beauty of leaf and tree and flower. Over Mrs. Noble's windows the morning glories ran riot, and their white, pink and purple cups held glistening drops of refreshment for the earliest honey-rover that might call.

Gay sweet-peas, with their jaunty capes, and velvet-clad pansies vied in joy-giving brightness. Birds held high carnival in the maple and cherry trees about the house, and yellow sunshine, with its magic shadow-fringes, flooded everything.

A long drawn "O-o-oh!" of ecstacy from a sunny-faced child in the door way revealed little Mary. She had come forth to meet the new day and all the joys it promised.

Pam lounged lazily forward, with a speaking tail and careless tongue.

"Oh, Pam!" cried Mary, "isn't it lovely? Let's have a play!" Whereat Pam giving hearty assent, away they ran as only a child and a dog can run. Up and down the narrow path, around the house, out to the lilac bush, they raced, each in a perfect gale of delight, and each expressing it in his own peculiar fashion.

"Oh, what fun, Pam!" panted Mary, as she breathlessly threw herself on the back steps and pulled the black silken ears.

Pam's vocabulary was not voluminous, but he made the most of what he had, and they managed to carry on quite an animated conversation.

"I know something you don't," said Mary, in a tantalizing tone, as if the dog understood every word.

Pam gave a little bark of inquiry

"Uncle Mayn—, run and find Carrol, so I can tell her, too. Quick, now. I don't believe she knows."

At the first word, Pam bounded into the house and went pattering about until a quick, sharp bark indicated his success. He came back, leading her captive.

"Here we are; what is it?"

"Why Carrol, do you know that uncle Maynard is coming to see mamma and all of us, next week? We've never seen him a single once."

"When did you find it out?"

"Just now. Mamma told me when she tied my apron. Aren't you glad?"

"Oh I guess so, but then I don't know him."

"Mamma says he went away ever so long ago," resumed Mary, "and she hasn't seen him since. Do you know why he's staid away so long, Carrol?"

"Maybe he's been shipwrecked on some wild island," suggested Carrol, in a mischievous tone. She did not know how much truth there was in her analogy.

"Yes, we'll find out, 'cause I'm real sorry," mused little Mary.

"What are you sorry for?"

"Oh, because he's had to go without love so long."

"What a funny girl you are Mary! How can you love him when you never saw him?"

"Oh, I don't know. Only by thinking love thoughts 'bout him, I guess. But then, mamma has done that."

"Well, we can make up for lost time when he comes." And Carrol turned to Pam who had been patiently waiting for his share of attention.

"Pam, do you want a romp?"

An eloquent wag of the tail and the dancing brown eyes gave an emphatic "yes."

"Get the ball then."

To his own secret haunts he sped, soon returning with a ball, which Carrol threw high in the air. In the descent the dog dexterously caught it and roguishly scampered away out of reach of the pursuing girls.

"Pamlico Pound, you're a fraud!" cried Carrol at last, pouncing upon him and holding his ears with pretended fierceness. "No, no, Pam," relentingly; "you're just the bestest old doggie; I take it all back," putting her arms about the shaggy neck. "Come, shake hands."

One massive paw was lifted solemnly. Pam could be dignified as well as playful.

"Me too, Pam, give me a shake," said Mary, going close and holding out her hand. He turned reproachful eyes upon her as he lifted the paw again. The next instant a surprised, half-uttered bark, uplifted ears, eyes eagerly alert, quite metamorphosed Pam's appearance and caused the girls to look toward the gate.

A carriage containing a lady had stopped there.

"Good morning, little girls," she called in a cheery voice. "Is your mother at home?"

Mary bashfully affirmed that she was, slowly approaching the vehicle as she spoke.

"Please run and tell her that Miss Allbright would like to see her a moment."

Mary flew to give the message. In a few moments Mrs. Noble appeared, adjusting her hat as she walked.

"Good morning!" she said.

The visitor nodded and smiled brightly, "Good morning! isn't it beautiful this morning? Beg pardon for this early call, but I was so sure you would favor me." She lowered her voice and leaned confidentially over the wheel.

Mrs. Noble glanced back at the girls, but they had resumed their play with the dog.

"The fact is," continued Miss Allbright with suggestive sympathy, "we want to help that poor Mr Crampton who has just returned from the penitentiary—forgery you know," in a pitying whisper—"to a position at Eastman's. His friends think he can get it, with a little lift to begin with, and a few of the ladies are taking hold to see what they can accomplish." She continued bravely, though the outlook was not promising. "I, as a representative of The Voluntary Helpers, am collecting a little sum for clothing for the family. It's a special case and we haven't quite enough on hand."

"U-m, well," began Mrs. Noble.

Miss Allbright took a small box from her reticule. "You see" she interrupted, "everything is voluntary (I don't believe in subscriptions), and it may be anything the donor chooses to give, from a penny to a pound. Then we propose having an afternoon appointed, when those who desire may help with the sewing."

She paused at last.

"Very laudable purpose, I'm sure," began Mrs. Noble again, with a peculiar straightness of the lips; "but aren't you really afraid to put the man in the way of temptation again?"

"Oh I don't know; it seems too bad to let the poor man's family starve *for fear he should fall.*"

"Yes, yes, that is true, but 'the way of the transgressor is hard'—always must be, you know."

"What about the prodigal son, then?" queried Miss Allbright, with a smile.

"Well, of course if he *is* the prodigal, it is well enough to receive him, although we must not judge."

With her long whip Miss Allbright flicked the encroaching flies off her horse a little impatiently.

"But we must take it for granted that he is sincere in his repentance, mustn't we?" she asked, inquiringly.

"To a certain extent, yes, but what are the signs?"

"Signs! Are we not told to judge not according to appearances, and to forgive seventy times seven?"

"Certainly, but—"

"Well, Mrs. Noble, this man has suffered for, and I believe wholly expiated his sin. He returns to his family almost heartbroken, willing to begin at the lowest round of the social ladder, if he can only get the consent of society *to* begin, and as you say, society has no right to judge. *I* believe 'love is the fulfilling of the law.' If we are filled with love we can do nothing more than give it, and nothing less than withhold it. To withhold it means to withhold everything worth having in this world. There, Mrs. Noble, I've given you my reasons for helping poor Crampton." She looked frankly into her neighbor's face and waited for an answer.

"They ought to be everybody's reasons, if everybody could only see them in your light. I believe just as you do about love, but the question is, when to withhold and when to give?"

"*Always* give, I say," interrupted Miss Allbright, with such emphasis the horse thought she meant to go. She pulled up the lines. "Wait a moment, Queen. So you will assist us in this project, Mrs. Noble?" handing out the little box, with a frankly expectant air.

"I—I certainly wish to give the cup of cold water where it is necessary, but—"

"Well well, sister; anything, even a bunch of flowers will be a cup of water in this case."

"Flowers, mamma? Does the lady want flowers?" questioned Mary eagerly, overhearing the last few words. "I'll give you some from *my* bed, they are so pretty;" and without waiting for her mother's reply

she bounded away, soon returning with a handful of
dew-bathed blossoms. Beaming with pleasure, her face
almost outshining the flowers, she went straight to the
carriage with her gift and timidly held it up to the lady,
who took it with unconcealed pleasure.

"Oh thank you, little cup-bearer. This is love
indeed," and she buried her face in the fragrant mass.
"I wish you might go with me to deliver it. Mayn't
she ride awhile, Mrs. Noble? I will bring her back
safe."

"Oh let me, mamma, do," supplemented Mary.

"Very well," replied her mother, not without some
doubt as to the propriety of the step, considering Miss
Allbright's liberal views; but she returned the box, after
adding a trifle to its contents, and said nothing further.

Miss Allbright had accomplished her object, and
Mary went on "mercy's errand swift," like the sweet
little sister of charity she was.

Would you like to become acquainted with Miss
Allbright?

She is well worth your friendship, although (I must
confess it) what the world calls an "old maid!"

Not one of the sour-faced, eccentric type, with no
affection but for a shaggy-faced poodle or shrill-voiced
parrot (though she has a favorite cat, I believe). Oh,
no; she is fair, plump, sparkling-eyed, sweet-voiced,
great-hearted, rich in love for the universe and all it
contains. She has plenty of money too, but she does
not let it lie in the toe of a stocking, or tie it up in real
estate. She keeps it where she can put her hands upon
it at any time, and where others may feel its beneficent

ministry in time of sore need.   She is a veritable Providence to the poor of her own town and State, yet few recipients know their donor by name.

If she has ever been disappointed in love no one knows it, but why she has never married is a source of unceasing wonder to that peculiar individual known as "Mrs. Grundy."

Of friends, she has scores; lovers, none.   Why, I cannot tell, unless because of that air of disarming candor she carries into her relations with everybody. She never pines for a sphere, but fills the one she is in.

CHAPTER V.

"How poor and helpless, how mere a pilgrim and a stranger in the world, over which he has no rule, must he be who has not God *at one* with him! not otherwise can his life be free, save as moving in loveliest harmony with the will and life of the only freedom—that which wills and we are!"—*George MacDonald.*

IN due time Professor Thornbush appeared at his sister's, who, as you have perhaps already guessed, is Mrs Noble. He had not been in Tintuckett since he was a young man, years and years before, and his arrival created no small commotion. Many of the towns-people remembered him and his history. The rest curiously wondered at the difference between him and his sister. Tintuckett, like many places of its size, was but a small wheel rolling over the common highway of human experience, crushing much of the richness, carrying and adding a great deal of the sordidness, and never neglecting to creak loudest over the misfortunes and sorrows that came in its way.

Of course, wheels that go into ruts get muddy. Tintuckett was no exception to the rule.

"And so he's come back! Poor fellow; I never thought he could stand the sight of this place again," commented one good neighbor.

"The Lord deals wisely with the froward, and brings him even through sorrow and tribulation to know his Maker," sighed Deacon Rice to his patient wife, when speaking of the new arrival.

"What a dreadfully wicked man! They say he doesn't even believe there is a God!" whispered one awe-struck voice to another; and so the wheel went on in its ceaseless round.

And now a word of explanation: In the first years of a bright, hopeful manhood, Maynard Thornbush had lost his wife. Becoming unsettled on religious matters, she had ended her days in an insane asylum, since which the unhappy husband had railed unceasingly against aught that claimed to be Christianity

Here in Tintuckett there was one thing he absolutely refused to do, and that was to go to church. His sister's entreaties, expostulations or prayers were of no avail. He would not see the inside of the sacred place he had in earlier years so faithfully visited every Sabbath.

"Why, Maynard, why can't you at least try to get the consolation that only the Lord can give you?" pleaded Mrs. Noble in final despair, the second Sunday after his arrival.

He turned upon her almost fiercely. "Marcia," he said hoarsely, "I shall leave your house this hour, if you dare to suggest such a thing again. Go, if you choose, and get all the consolation you can in the church, but allow me to get mine, if I am to have any, where no mouthing hypocrite can offer it second hand."

He strode out of the house, leaving her to regain her composure as best she might. Was there no place in the civilized world where one might escape this jargon of religion? he thought, savagely.

He walked forth into the fields, woods—anywhere, he cared not where, angrily resolving as he went, to leave town the next day.

He turned into an obscure, deeply shaded road, leading farther into the woods. Here at least, was a semblance of the solitude he craved.

Bitter, was he, do you say?

Yes, but think of his reasons; such reasons as come from the volcanic depths of experience. Is it not such blinding crater smoke that hides the real self of God's child? that veils the natural greenness, the smiling beauty, and the transcendent peace, belonging to him?

On and on walked the unhappy man, not heeding time nor space. A terrific energy possessed him and he went, as it were, challenging the world to do battle with him.

It was several hours before he realized his surroundings, and then he paused but a moment ere hastening on again. The road grew broader and the way more open, hinting the near approach to human haunts. Before he was aware of the whither towards which he traveled, he suddenly found himself listening to a swelling volume of human voices. A moment later, and one glance told him he was on the outskirts of a thriving camp-meeting.

Hastily turning to retrace his steps, his foot caught in the meshes of a tangled vine, throwing him violently forward. A fierce pain in his right ankle was the herald of unconsciousness, that lasted he knew not how long. After coming to himself, repeated attempts to regain his feet proved fruitless, and he was compelled to sink weakly back upon the ground and wait.

So intent were the worshipers on their service of song that no one noticed his downfall; and as he happened to be in the rear of the audience, it would very likely be some time before he could expect assistance.

At first he tried to shut his eyes and ears to everything; but he might as well have tried to stop the tide of the sea. He had suffered too much to be indifferent. At first he was angry, wildly, rebelliously angry. The pent up memories of years rushed through his mind like a foaming torrent. How well he remembered the dear face of his long-lost wife, and how it had turned from smiling youth to piteous, fear-filled age after a six weeks' revival that awful winter.

And here he was, a helpless victim of accident, doomed to hear the whole despised lingo over again, so he thought, as he lay writhing in pain, and anticipating at least an hour's torture before the meeting broke up, for, bitter as he was, and suffering, he would not call to them for help. All the obstinacy and fierce determination in his nature helped him in his foolish heroism.

Hark! what words were these? Was it the old message? This surely was not the preaching he had heard so long ago! Involuntarily he listened. A woman's voice, sweet, penetrating, yet soft, and, oh! so soothing, was saying:

"Do you know, friends, the Spirit is Love itself? It is not a different love than yours for your child or your mother. And it is with you *always*. It is like a living Presence, and if you talk to it it will answer you. If you are lonely it will comfort you, *I* know, for only last night it spoke to me for the first time. Oh, brothers, sisters, if we *only* become as little children we can hear, can feel, can *know* the Holy Spirit that God sends as His Comforter.

"I never knew before last night what it meant to be as a little child. I have been hard and angry and bitter against God ever since my darling boy was taken away from me. I could not believe there was a Comforter. I did not want to pray to a cruel God, and I was wicked and rebellious. But last night in my anguish and despair I cried out, '*O God, my Father,*' and my heart seemed melted. And suddenly a light brighter than anything I ever saw, and glorious with a wonderful whiteness, was round about me, and a Voice within myself, yet out of the light, spoke to me. It said: '*Thy son liveth.*' There was much more, but, oh, brothers, oh, sisters, *it is true!* The Holy Spirit *is* the Comforter. It comforted *me.* It taught me. It quickened me into a new life, for I *know* now that I was dead. Listen! It was my selfish, ignorant hardness against God that kept me in suffering and wicked rebellion. The moment I gave up, even though not knowing I *was* giving up, my Comforter came. . . . I see it all now. For that moment I was as a little child; I could do nothing; the weight of a thousand mountains seemed crushing me, but I turned to the Father. Then in an instant the glory came. And then the meaning of life, death and immortality was revealed. I saw myself as a child to be taught, and the bitterness of my sorrow was taken away, because in that moment I knew life as something eternal. It cannot be taken away. My precious boy was only loaned to me for a while in order that I might learn to *love* and *serve*. How could I know anything about our Father's love, if I had not loved? The taking away seemed cruel and awful because I did not know that life is deathless, but *now* I know. *Now*, oh, my dear brothers, my dear sisters, the same law of the spirit of life in Christ Jesus hath set me free from the law of sin and death. I know now that this is Love, the Love which lays down life in order to find it. Don't you *see* what life means to us, to each and every one of us? It means an opportunity to *love* and *give* and *serve*. All this seemed put into my heart in that one blessed instant, and such a peace, oh, *such* a peace, fell upon me and has been with me every moment since. . . ." Deep and full was this joyous voice, and more than any words were the subtle sweetness, the indescribable tenderness which in the quality of its tones conveyed the soulful message.

Silence held the great audience as in a spell, broken at last by sobs and groans in the audience. Maynard Thornbush fainted. . . .

When he came to himself the sweet voice was saying: "Oh, the joy of it all! This nearness to God is wonderful! I feel every moment as if I were in heaven and the former things have passed away. This moment hath God made His tabernacle with men. *This moment* the Comforter will whisper to *you*, yes, to *each* one of you, as you listen. Only be empty of self. Give up oh, give up the arrogance of judgment and conceit. *Be*

like a child, sweet, trustful dependent on your Father
to do all." Shouts of "Amen," "Hallelujah." Then a
hymn was started. The organ's full tones thrilled and
trembled through the volume of earnest voices, and out
upon the air, besides the sound, went forth a wave of
something too subtle for words, but powerful, uplifting,
comforting, *wonderful* to all who felt its nameless
influence.

And Maynard Thornbush? What strange thing had
happened? He, the strong, the untouchable, the man
of adamant, wept! Yes, during all the singing and the
after prayers he had been like a rock heaved from its
mountain fastness and hurled into the rushing torrent
of an angry stream. . . . And then a peace indescribable and rare had dropped over him as a mantle.

Was this death? he thought, and waited for the end;
but no, instead it must be life, the very life that voice
had talked about, the very life that came, they said,
like a new birth. And the old memories, the bitterness,
the fierceness—all seemed fading, fading into a dim,
passing mist. . . . And his foot? Ah, the pain
was gone completely, though he could not rise, but he
was content. Let the next rise of the curtain reveal
what it would. This was only a dream, but too sweet
to dispel. . . . So, thinking he was dreaming a
pleasant dream, he let his mind entertain unhindered
these new and entrancing fancies. He even imagined
himself a guileless, trusting child, and reveled in the
sense of rest it gave. No past, no future, no care,
nothing but rest and joy and a happy expectancy of
what might come.

In his dream, as he thought, he remembered an incident of his childhood, an occasion when he was almost killed by a fall from a tree. He recalled the pain, the awful sense of danger, and then the return to consciousness and the joy of being in his mother's arms.

What a restful security, a surpassing peace, he had felt when he heard his mother joyfully sobbing out her prayer of thanksgiving! She was a rare believer in God and her prayers of faith were noted, so much so that he remembered the frequent calls made upon her to go and pray for the sick and dying. He seemed to hear her dear voice again in his dream and live again in the happiness of her presence. Even when he awoke it never occurred to him that these people about him, singing, praying, exclaiming as they were, had for years represented what had been to him the most distasteful, hypocritical, despicable type of human beings. No, they seemed earnest, noble, tender-hearted brothers and sisters. Not that he analyzed this to himself in words, but part of his restful joy was due to the sense of kinship, of real sympathy, which, without naming it, he felt in his heart, not alone for them, but for all things.

This warmth and nearness for everything in or on the earth was surely the most wonderful phase of his dream, he thought. Pity it could not last, but he would enjoy it as long as he could, and thus half-conscious, yet unknowingly awake, his thoughts drifted, and his heart beat in rythmic fellowship with the music and the spirit of the worshipers.

"Thou art a perfect harmony,
   The universe doth sing;
 Creation beats its journey out
   Upon a happy wing.

"O fashion me, such tuneless reed,
   Unto Thy blowing breath;
 Then play on me Thy spirit airs,
   Enchanting even death."

CHAPTER VI.

"The child like faith that asks not sight,
  Waits not for wonder or for sign,
Believes because it loves aright,
  Shall see things greater, things divine.
Heaven to that gaze shall open wide,
  And brightest angels to and fro
On messages of love shall glide
  Twixt God above and Christ below."
                                    —*John Keble.*

When Maynard Thornbush came to himself a familiar face was bending over him. He stared vacantly a moment and then feebly asked: "Is it—can it be—"

"Fernlow?" interrupted the other. "Yes, and now, my friend, you must tell me how best to get you home, for I expect you are stopping somewhere hereabouts, though I did not expect," he added, smiling, "to find you at camp-meeting."

The injured man flushed. In an instant he remembered his old self—and his new. He pointed to his ankle.

"Well, well, see here, we must find out the difficulty with this foot. I wonder if there is any doctor here. Wait a moment while I investigate," said Fernlow.

He ran here and there among the breaking throng,

and finally re-appeared with one Dr. Robine, who volunteered assistance.

The ankle was badly twisted, muscles strained—possibly a broken bone—but with careful nursing and cheerful thinking three or four weeks at most, would, the doctor thought, set the patient all right again.

"Dismal outlook, but necessity is no chooser of circumstances," concluded the medical adviser, after various pokes, twists, turns and a final application of bandages.

The next thing was to get home. The Professor told them he was stopping in Tintuckett.

"'Whew!" whistled the doctor. "Pretty long ride for you—eight miles, but I guess we'll find somebody going that way. I live there myself, but there's no room in my carriage for you, in your condition." He meditated a moment. "Hold on," as he caught sight of a man whom he knew. "There's deacon Rice. I'll speak to him; he can take you."

The deacon's light open wagon was filled with straw, and this, with a blanket shawl thrown over it, promised a fairly comfortable bed for the ride to Tintuckett, whither the good deacon and his little family were just starting, when the doctor called for help.

"We've been down since Thursday, and jest had to tear ourselves away," said the deacon, apologetically, as they were ready to start.

"You can console yourselves by playing ' the good Samaritan,' any way," were the doctor's parting words.

"Good-bye Professor, I'll surely be down to see

you _n a day or so," and Mr. Fernlow grasped his friend's hand heartily as the little wagon started on.

And so the journey began. A strange though peaceful oue it was. The deacon and his thin-faced wife tried a few words of condolence at first, but soon desisted for lack of response. So they sat patiently on the seat with the two boys in front, and the guest behind, with his hat over his face. The Sabbath stillness was broken only by the sound of the horses' feet, the creaking of the wheels, and the varied, low-toned chorus of the woods through which they passed.

Thought, the untiring arm of the Almighty, toiled on in its silent workshop, while the slow hours passed into eternity, leaving . joyous experience to mark their transit.

"Oh, mamma, uncle's hurt *awful* and they're carrying him in as if—" gasped little Ada, as she rushed into the house to tell what was coming.

"What is it, child? Don't be so frightened," said the mother, and hurriedly cast her book aside to look out of the window to see, she scarce knew what.

"A judgment! O Lord, a judgment!" she murmured, under her breath, "and so soon! God have mercy on you, my poor brother," hastening to meet them.

He gave himself up to a war of doubts, trying to explain the condition of mind which he thought belonged to his dream at the camp-meeting—for dream he still called it. In the days that followed Maynard Thornbush found himself indeed a new creature. A fierce fever seized him, but the tender ministrations of a woman, and, more than all, the timid sympathy and strong faith of a little child, were the ropes that drew him safe to land. Only once did Mary falter in her trust, and then it was after she had said to her mother one evening, while the fever was at its height: "I know uncle will be better soon, mamma, 'cause I've asked God, oh, so hard, to make him well."

Her mother glanced at the child in a puzzled way, and said, in a deprecatory tone: "Of course dear, you must pray, but you cannot change the Lord's will. It may be one thing and it may be another that He desires, and we can only submit to whatever that is."

"But, *mamma,* if we ask Him as Jesus did, when he cured people, won't He answer the way we want Him to?"

Such a depth of earnestness appeared in the child's voice. Fernlow, who sat out on the porch in the twilight, waited almost impatiently for the mother's reply.

"We cannot have the faith that Jesus had."

"Oh, but *mamma,*" a wave of disappointment quivered through the words, "*mamma,* didn't Jesus say we might ask for anything we wanted, and if we asked right we would get it?"

"Sometime Mary, you will understand these things. We will not talk any more about them now, as I must go to poor uncle."

Richard Fernlow was painfully conscious of something happening, he could not tell what, but he felt as though the petals of a fragrant blossom had been rudely torn asunder.

For a few days Mary's sun was veiled, and then it beamed more brightly than before. Peace sat once more enthroned, for the fruit of the spirit is peace, and the teaching of the spirit is truth.

Again Fernlow overheard a dialogue; this time between two children. Ada sat under the cherry-tree, crying softly to herself.

"What is it, Ada? Tell me quick," commanded Mary, hastening up to her sister.

"I'm so sorry for Uncle Maynard, 'nd I'm 'fraid he'll die," sobbed the little one.

"Why Ada, you don't b'lieve God will let him die, if we pray to have him live, do you?"

"N—o; but I haven't prayed."

"Well, I have, and I *know* he'll live, 'cause I felt that same something that always tells me when I've prayed hard enough."

And the days went on. The sister ministered with prayers and sighs and hopeless tears; the friend with bated breath and sickening hope; while the child watched and thought and smiled and prayed all by herself. She and God were working silently but surely.

The crisis came and went. Convalescence proved marvelously rapid. Dr. Robine's praises were sounded on every side. Such an acute case! Such dangerous complications! Such a quick victory!

Wonderful!

In a fortnight or so he was up and about, ready to go forth into the world again, renewed and cleansed as from a bath, and who can tell if such a bath is not the most cleansing—this that takes us down into the depths of an unknown sea? The cleansing had done wonders. Was this the same man of a few weeks before?

One bright morning the children and their uncle started out for a walk. Harvey joined them, as a matter of course, as he had always done since his mother died.

It was a fair summer morning, redolent of a thousand delicate odors, the very essence of luxuriant flower and foliage. That inspiring something in nature which brings out the brightest and best in the human mind was felt especially by the restored invalid. Mary was a very sun in herself. Carrol alone felt a gloom of sadness steal over her mood—a gloom that was like to come of late, she knew not why. The nucleus of a great bitterness was forming in her young life, but there was none to see or pity or enlighten. As yet it was only in her solitary moments, in her sad outbursts of despair, that a suggestion of shadow was visible. Had it not been for her naturally vivacious disposition, and the unconscious influence of her cousin Mary, she would by this time have been a strange, morbidly sensitive mystery to everybody. As it was, her aunt grew more and more discouraged in proportion to her efforts to teach the child. Time and circumstance would tell how this invisible nucleus would develop.

They walked briskly down the hill-side path.

"Uncle Maynard," said Mary suddenly, looking up with a child's easy confidence; "do you teach school like God does?"

Carrol hastened a step nearer. Professor Thornbush looked confused. What could he say of God? Were his feelings to be trusted?

"Well, I don't know, Mary," he answered slowly; "I am afraid not."

"Why uncle Maynard!" She waited a moment, then asked again, but with less confidence: "Don't you b'lieve God lets us see all these beautiful places and things," sweeping her hand towards the fair landscape, "and hear all these lovely sounds a purpose to teach us something?"

"Oh, if that is what you mean, perhaps I do teach something after that fashion, for I show by things we can see what other things mean that we cannot see."

Mary was delighted. "Yes, just like we learn in the first reader that the picture of a horse only means there is a *real* horse somewhere," she explained.

The learned man started. He had received a new idea. What wonderful child wisdom!

"I'll tell you Mary, you can teach me about these things in nature and I'll teach you about things in books."

"Ho, Mary'd teach you anyway; she's always saying reg'lar Sunday lessons; 'nd I tell you what, she can do it prime too," interposed Harvey, with a smack of appreciation.

"Oh Harvey," pleaded Mary, reproachfully, "you know I can only say what God makes me think, and every day I ask Him for beautiful thoughts."

"And does He always answer your prayers?" asked her uncle, with a curious desire to hear her answer.

It came speedily and forcibly.

"'*Course* He does, if I only *b'lieve* He will."

Her face clouded at the mere asking of such a question.

"Don't you always b'lieve when you pray, uncle?"

Harvey came to the rescue. "Pooh! Mary, you don't s'pose *everybody* b'lieves as much as you do?" he exclaimed, with a shrill laugh. "Why, once when papa prayed for a man that was going to die, I asked him if he really thought that prayer would make him well, 'nd he said he didn't know as 'twould, 'cause if 'twas the Lord's will he'd die anyway. So you see even preachers don't *always* b'lieve," concluded the boy, triumphantly.

An instant Mary's face clouded, and then the sweetest smile broke over it, as she said: "Well, Harvey, I am not learning to be good of anyone but Jesus, and he *never* prayed without b'lieving God would answer him."

Maynard Thornbush started. The light was coming.

Carrol had been kicking a little stone in front of her, seemingly so absorbed that she thought of nothing else; now she looked at Mary with a sudden resolve in her face, a resolve to say something in spite of the effort it cost her.

"I asked God to let mamma live, Mary, and I believed He would, but He didn't."

Her uncle looked at her with a new interest.

"Did you really and truly b'lieve He would let her live, without the teentiest little fear that He wouldn't?" asked Mary, turning back to look at her cousin.

"Yes, and I've prayed for things lots o' times, and they didn't come."

"Then I'm just sure you didn't b'lieve hard enough. Sometimes its awful hard to do, but if you keep on trying, it gets easier 'n easier, 'n then all at once it just comes, like a breath of love straight from God."

"Mary's a really true Christian, she is," remarked Ada, "'cause she knows how to 'love one another' and that's all you have to do, aunt Lottie used to say."

Uncle Maynard grew tired after this, and they returned to the house. The next day he was not as well, and instead of walking, lounged about on the lawn, under the trees. Mary and Pam were playing near by.

With coming health came touches of his old enemies—bitter thoughts—and this day he seemed particularly beset. His book lay unopened in his lap, and in absent-minded mood his eyes rested on the scene before him. For the moment he felt like his old self.

Mary came running up to where he sat, with outspread arms, her face fairly shining with happiness.

"Oh uncle, I feel like a bird, only my wings haven't any feathers! Wouldn't you like to be a bird, and fly away up to heaven?"

"Confound it all! Am I to be forever pursued by such words as 'God' and 'heaven,' and such foolery?" he thought, but he only said· "Flying would be an accomplishment, but I'm afraid I'd never reach heaven, Mary. I'd be apt to land lower down."

His face wore a grim smile. With confident assurance she came closer to his side, saying: "But, uncle

Maynard, if you *did* fly somewhere else, you couldn't get away from God, and heaven is—"

"Child," he interrupted, almost fiercely, "what do you know about God, or heaven either?" His old anger against "cant" began to rise and show itself like a visible crest on his head.

She gazed at him in wide-eyed wonder.

"I *know* He loves me."

"But *how* do you know it?" he persisted.

With the old habit upon him, he combed his rebellious locks, until each particular hair seemed drawn up in battle-array against its neighbor.

Ah Mary, if Mrs. Cobb were there, she would warn you against even a whisper now. But Mary knows neither Mrs. Cobb nor her wisdom. She knows nothing but love and its dauntless ministry.

Two soft arms steal about his neck, two loving eyes look into his, two sweet child lips say: "I love *you*, uncle Maynard, and that's why I know God loves *me*."

O, rare philosophy of childhood, that so surely reads the secret of the universe! No reason but the simple one that furnishes its own premise and its own conclusion.

He let the limpid stream of her faith flow from her heart stream as freely and as sweetly as it would. In spite of himself he was sprayed and washed by its pure waters.

CHAPTER VII.

"When we believe that God is the common Father, and that all men and all things which He has made are dear to Him; when we think that He is near to every one of us, and that in Him we live and move and have our being, then we can not call any man or any thing unclean. We believe that there is a divine element in each man and each object, and our constant effort must be to draw out this divine element." — *W. H. Freemantle.*

THE Voluntary Helpers was the name of a club founded, sustained and presided over by Miss Allbright. She did it, as she did everything—well, and she made people feel the importance of the work accomplished, as well as the necessity of its accomplishment. Once a month the Voluntary Helpers held an open meeting at the home of their president, at the beginning or close of which, anyone was privileged to contribute to the charity cash-box, or clothes-basket both of which stood behind a screen in the spacious reception-hall. No allusion being made in any way whatever to this part of the programme (except the occasional announcement in the paper, as to the purposes, methods, etc., of the society,) there was no constraint in giving nor in withholding, and consequently nothing but voluntary giving. With the money and clothing thus received, the various committees of the club were kept busy the following month in distributing to, in providing and arranging for their respective communities or individuals, as the case might be

"Not that we are to give to any and all who come along," said the president in her frank, fearless way, on the occasion of the organization of the society, "but that we are to have something *to* give in case of worthy necessity, that worthiness being proven by a willingness on the part of the recipient to make some return for the 'value received.'"

She carried her point, and before two years of the "Helpers" existence ended, its plans of work had been so manifestly successful that one of the churches thought seriously of venturing to adopt them.

It may be mentioned in passing, that Miss Allbright sailed under the banner of no church, although she spoke respectfully of all, and that she quietly proclaimed herself non-sectarian in her deeds as well as her beliefs; in consequence of which she had at first been shunned, feared, anathematized, praised or blamed, according to the religious or non-religious convictions of the critic. Notwithstanding all this, there were now members from nearly all the churches who attended her monthly "Help meetings," thus secretly aiding and abetting the "work of Satan," as one devout shepherd had put it to his flock.

It had been the custom established from the beginning, and based on a belief in humanity's intrinsic goodness of heart and a common interest in all things good, to have discussion of all social and ethical questions, and free expression of opinion concerning them. Any one was also privileged and invited to bring an epitomized result of his soul experiences for the month, providing there was a moral or spiritual benefit to be derived from them. Inspiring short poems, or thought gems from any noble mind of past or present were read and freely commented upon by one or all, and thus a heart-to-heart communion was gradually established, which promoted a wide charity, good fellowship and the carrying out of that law supreme for all mankind—the law of love.

A large placard, printed in gold letters, hung from the hall chandelier on the evening of these meetings, and acquainted every newcomer with the motto of the society, and the basis upon which he was expected to co-operate, or at least concur, with its members for the evening.

The following were the words that confronted Professor Thornbush and Richard Fernlow the evening they attended:

"Believe the good only,
  Think the good only,
    Speak the good only,

and thus bring courage, hope, and comfort to all who need the cheering word. Enter with us into a contemplation of the universal Good."

"And so you see, Professor, here, at least, we must be optimists," said Fernlow, in a playful undertone, as he deposited his hat upon the hall tree.

" So I understand from this accommodating legend here," responded the Professor, taking out his handkerchief and going nearer for a closer inspection.

" If you please, gentlemen, it is time to begin. Walk this way, please," and a trim little maid, who acted as usher, led the way into a large library, where were grouped a goodly number of persons of all classes, of whom the majority bore upon their faces the stamp of honest effort and noble aspiration.

"On this evening, friends," said the president, a she rose to address them, "it is our privilege to celebrate the second anniversary of our society. We do so, in part at least, by a recapitulation of its purposes and some of its benefits. Started as it was, for the relief and uplifting of a few, its circle of usefulness has ever widened, and we have found indeed the blessedness of both giving and receiving. Inasmuch as the only way to give true help is to effect a mutual exchange of benefits, we have found it right to recognize all humanity as endowed with equal rights and gifts, and belonging to one common family. The results of such recognition, such co-operation are most gratifying most inspiring.

"We have found the keynote of reform to be, *belief in and acknowledgment of the good* of a man's character, instead of *belief in and condemnation of the bad.*

"We have discovered that to trust humanity, to believe in the honor instead of the dishonor of man or woman, is to so prove the dominance of the higher nature, that the radiance of a faithful conscience shines out and illumines the righteous pathway of future action. We have discovered, and do most earnestly believe, that the Principle of Good takes care of its own, and that whosoever trusts and believes in the good, will see the legitimate fruit of such seed; it has, therefore, become a part of our creed—if creed it can be called—to keep our attention fixed upon the positive instead of the negative side of life, and thereby cause the flowers of hope to spring up in the deserts of despair.

"Finding such blessedness in the co-operation of work, we concluded to establish the interchange and co-operation of thought; hence these meetings, open to all lovers and speakers of goodness. Voluntary speaking, voluntary giving, voluntary doing, are the spontaneous results of the law of love, which this work implies indeed declares."

She paused a moment. The kindling eyes and faces responded warmly to her own.

"On the threshold of another year of helpfulness," she resumed, "we pause to welcome all who come within our gates. The weary, the disconsolate, the poverty stricken, will always find here some word or thought dropping from the height of an undimmed outlook of the good that will bless and comfort and uplift.

"Our circle is but typical of the Divine family circle, our home and meeting place typical of the light and love and sheltering care of the Omnipotent.

> O, strong is the armor of Love,
> And warm is the breastplate of Faith
> To strengthen and lift us above
> The darkness of misery and hate.
>
> O, wide are the portals of Good,
> And clear are the windows of Hope,
> O'ershadowed by white wings that brood
> Like prayers little children invoke.

O, enter, ye poor of the earth,
And ye that are lowly of heart,
And learn the true blessings and worth
Of Good, that Itself doth impart."

There ensued a long pause, one of those heartful pauses that mean the mingling of souls and the wearing of thought's whitest garments.

At last an old lady, with white and wrinkled face, arose, saying in trembling accents: "Little children, I'm over seventy years old, and I'm just learning what it means to become as a little child. I want to tell you how I came to know. I have a little grandchild only two years old, but she has been my teacher." . . . The old lady stopped to brush away some quiet tears, and then continued : " She can say only a few words, but they contain the secret. When she first came to us, we could think of doing but one thing, and that was loving her. Bye and bye, we found that, though she could do nothing else, she was loving back again.

"When she was a few months old, I began to attend these meetings and thought I would see only the good everywhere, at home as well as here." She again broke down and there was a hint of a sob in the quavering voice, as she continued : "Friends, I've been a bit of a fault-finder, and my daughter and son-in-law would often wish I didn't have such critical eyes. I knew they did, for I could see it in their faces, though they never said much. But after I began to look for the good, I declare it was surprising how much I found, and baby Maude kept showing me more all the time. I noticed how her little face was always fairly shining with love every time she looked at me, or any of us, and how she always expected an answering look of love in return, and how disappointed she was if it was not given.

"The last month, somehow, I've had a kind of review, and have been summing it all up. Our dear little blossom is truly one of God's apostles, and she, like other children, is expressing the nature and power of love. She is sweet and beautiful and happy because in all her little life she has received and given nothing but love. She expects nothing but love, and therefore it is the fulfilling of the whole law to her. She has helped me . . . and I trust she will help you . . to become as a little child. This is one of the benefits of these blessed meetings."

After a few moments a tall, slender man, with an intellectual face and sensitive mouth, began to speak. He seemed very much embarrassed for a few moments, but had evidently braced himself to take a stand.

"I—expect you all know me. I'm Crampton. To say that means to say a good deal. A–hem—ahem— well, I'm bound to tell you that if it hadn't been for the principles and acts of this society I should have gone as straight to the devil—beg your pardon, but that is what I mean—as ever a man went. But thanks to the Good, as Miss Albright would say, I'm on my right feet and seeing with my right eyes. The Good is God to me, and I thank God for salvation from—"

"That will do, brother; don't look on the other side. I want to tell you of this way of speaking in the school-room," interrupted a bright-eyed school-teacher, noted

for her success with incorrigibles. " It's really remarkable
how the children respond to an expression of confidence
and a little wholesome praise. I have learned to take
it for granted that they are always doing the best they
know, though sometimes it takes considerable patience
before I see it. One boy, when he first came, seemed
proud of his reputation as the worst boy in school. By
telling him of all the wonderful possibilities and powers wrapped up in his nature, I soon got him to looking for them, and now he is quite turned in the other
direction. I believe we are getting practical hold of
how to do good. I wouldn't exchange the understanding and principles of the Voluntary Helpers for all
the 'gold of Ophir.'"

Another silence, and then Miss Allbright called for
questions.

"Since the privilege is given, Madam President, I
would like to ask on what grounds you require the
speaking of the good only? Is it because you wish to
ignore evil, or is it simply your method of dealing with
it?" questioned Professor Thornbush, respectfully.

"Very proper question, sir, which I shall be most
happy to answer. It is our method of dealing with
it. We believe in the Divine creation; that is, the
spiritual creation, perfect, whole and beautiful in every
respect. This conclusion coincides with that of every
great religious thinker the world has ever known. To
some people, the simple Bible statement that the
omnipotent God created all things good and man
in His image and likeness, is authority quite sufficient, while others are never satisfied until this

grand truth flashes upon the individual consciousness, as it surely will to everyone who becomes as a little child. This, then, is a statement of truth, and what we believe to be universal truth.

"What follows a statement? A conclusion, of course. Very well. Truth is positive or absolute. Then, if it is absolute truth that we have a perfect spiritual nature, it becomes our duty to recognize and speak of that, instead of the negative or imperfect nature, which *seems* to belong to us. For two reasons we make this rule concerning right speaking: because we believe in always speaking of the true man and his possibilities; because we have noticed the effect of thinking and talking.

"To condole with a poor woman over her trials and poverty only makes it harder for her to bear them, because we talk of the untrue or negative side, and there is no real help in such talk. To talk to a man of his failures and weaknesses is to make them more apparent, and thus induce discouragement and remorse, thereby unfitting him for even an attempt at betterment. To think despondently over the evils and disagreeable conditions of our environments is to kill hope, and hope is the sunshine of our mental world. Without sunshine, nothing grows. Leaf and fruitage die, and we are like the dead stalk of a plant whose living time is over. Evil is the untrue, the not-side of existence, and since by a recognition and continual acknowledgment of its opposite—the good and the true—we gain power; so, by recognition and acknowledgment of evil, we lose power; hence we believe in this method of overcoming the evil with the good."

"We are to understand then, that this is the philosophy underlying your work?"

"It is, sir; and I believe, the only true philosophy."

"How will it apply to all the great labor organizations that are so full of the recognition of evil they are willing to risk their lives in its destruction by force?"

"They can never destroy evil with evil. When they learn this law of love they will be content to wait until their own faithfulness shall advance them to higher positions."

Miss Allbright paused and looked over the audience. Addressing herself to a sturdy young working man, she said: "Martin Shane, can you tell us in a few words, something of your experience in the shoe factory?"

Martin rose with a flush on his rugged face, but spoke in a clear voice: "It's only this, Missis President, there's been so many strikes everywhere, that when Gleason's machine shops was shut down our boys wanted to cut, too; an' one night they threatened to duck everybody who wouldn't go with 'em, an' they was that riled they didn't know what they was doin'. Jim Mitchell, him that comes here with me sometimes, though he ain't here to-night, him an' me thought we'd jest talk to 'em a little like you'uns do here. So Jim, he's quiet an' deep-like, an' can speak powerful good when he feels like it, he jest asked the boys to wait an' give him a chance to speak, for they was after *us* more'n anybody else, bein's they knowed we wasn't in for strikin'. Wal, Jim he tole 'em how as he didn't feel zif we orto be rash with the boss, 'cause, when you come down to the pint, he ain't a bad man, only he was jest doin' what everybody else in his shoes does; an' Jim talked to 'em as how they was better 'n a balky horse, an' could prove theirselves better by usin' their own best thinkin' an' workin' powers, an' bringin' theirselves to a higher stand by quietly *bein'* suthin' 'stid o' blusterin' round tryin' to force other folks to be suthin'. 'You can shet a bird up in a cage, but ye can't make it sing,' says he; 'so you can force people to do some things, but ye can't force 'em to *do* their best or *be* their best; so the only way is to grow in your own ground, an' see that ye raise a good crop; fer there be always a market fer what's good.' By the time he got through a tellin' 'bout the good in theirselves, they was ready to listen to the good in the boss. Then he tole 'em to remember how Sam Brown's wages was paid while he laid sick of a fever, an' how the boss always give 'em kind words an' sich like. At last they agreed to wait awhile longer. They waited, an' the strike never struck. Last week the boss said they was to have half Saturdays an' the same wages through the hot weather. That's all."

"That is practical application, I'm sure," said Miss Allbright. "Are there any further questions?" turning to the Professor.

"I would like to know if you believe in any corrective measures, or if, in your experience in this work, you have found them necessary?" he questioned.

"The need of correction is recognized by each individual as soon as the consciousness is awakened to its own power and responsibility. Our effort is to awaken it to this fact. The invisible something that brings out the beauty of a flower brings out the beauty of character. We do not aim in any way to govern individuals, but merely to recognize and develop their power to govern themselves."

She looked at her interlocutor questioningly, but he shook his head, saying: "Nothing more at present."

"And now, friends," she resumed, "if there is nothing further, we will have our music, the one indispensable harmonizer of the Voluntary Helpers."

"If you please," said a weak voice in the rear, "I would like to thank you for the privilege of coming here to these meetings. We are too poor to go to church and—but here I get such blessings that I cannot even name them, and—life is not so dark as—it might be."

It was poor Mrs. Farney, whose husband was a drunkard who spoke, but it was not the only time she had testified to the help and benefit that had come to her home through the society.

"Dear hearts," said the president again, "let us not forget, in all our ways, to give thanks for all the blessings that surround us, to continually remember the gracious Presence all about us, the ever-loving God who is our health, our strength, our intelligence, our ability in every way. Let us strive to make the marvelous Word manifest in the flesh, even as our Elder Brother who bade us 'be perfect as the Father in heaven is perfect.'

> ' The noblest prayer is when one evermore
>   Grows inly liker Him he kneels before.' "

A silence long and thoughtful, and then she made a signal for the singing, in which all joined. A time for social converse followed, and the good-byes were said. The monthly Help Meeting was at an end.

This was the foreshadowing of a mighty work to be done for the establishment of true human Brotherhood.

CHAPTER VIII.

"Let a man believe in God, and not in names and places and persons." —Emerson.

WEEKS slipped by and summer was nearing its close. The hills and woods were already touched with spots of autumn brightness. Professor Thornbush had gone back to his post at Bardville; Richard Fernlow was to remain in Tintuckett, having secured a lucrative position as principal of one of the best school wards in the city. He continued to make his home with Mrs. Noble, much to Mary's delight and his own satisfaction, for he was greatly interested in the children.

"O—oh, goody, goody! There's Aunt Creesh," cried Mary, one Saturday morning, as she stood by the window, talking to Pam. This was her father's sister, and an aunt of whom Mary was very fond. Aunt Creesh always came unexpectedly, but seldom staid very long, although no one knew just what she would do or when she would do it, since she followed her own private plans without publicly expressing them. Her coming was an event of varying importance in the family.

"Aunt Creesh! dear me, no warning, of course," echoed Mrs. Noble, as Mary ran out to meet her aunt. "And there's the missionary meeting to attend this afternoon too," she continued. "Well, I'll—"

"Here again, Marcia," was the matter-of-fact greeting, as the guest entered, extending her hand.

"Of course; how do you do?" kissing her. "We expected you soon, as it is getting close to your usual time, but I am surprised that you could get here so early. On what train did you arrive?" and Mrs. Noble busied herself in helping to remove her visitor's wraps.

"Started at midnight; got in at seven. Thought I wouldn't bother you any earlier than I had to," with a grim smile.

She sat down in the rocker and leisurely took off her mits.

"How Mary does grow!" surveying the little maid, affectionately. "Quite a nice child, I declare," as she put on her glasses and drew Mary close to her with one hand.

"Yes, I think she *is* growing in grace."

"Oh 'grace,' fiddlesticks! that comes of itself." Then, turning to Mary: "You run out and play with the dog, and gather flowers and have good times, I suppose?"

"Course we do, Aunt Creesh; and we play outdoors is God's parlor. Ada and Carrol—"

"Bless me, I'd most forgotten—where are they? Go tell 'em to come and see Aunt Creesh."

Mary ran out, delighted.

"I see you wear mourning yet, Marcia? Was in hopes 'twould be off by this time. What's the use going round like a walking coal heap? I don't think James thinks a bit better of you, though he's been gone nearly two years, and I'm sure the rest of us don't."

Aunt Creesh sniffed contemptuously, as she tucked her mits into the black hand-bag.

"Oh well, Lucretia, I think it is best to keep it on awhile, at least. It is customary, and I feel that there would be a lack of respect to James if I didn't."

"Lack of respect! Oh! I thought you could have respect for people without wearing a regalia to remind you of it. Well Marcia, go on. If you'd rather be midnight than morning, you can, I s'pose."

Mrs. Noble made no reply, but asked some question about a certain business difficulty in which the lawyers of Aunt Creesh had been engaged for several months, and which furnished a convenient by-path.

Aunt Creesh was something like a kaleidoscope; she was always turning a different side to view. In reply to Mrs. Noble's question she said, carelessly: "Oh, they've been trying to settle for six months now. I just let 'em go on. I know it'll all come out right some way. It's no use to think of the might-be's. Of course, if the case should go against me, I'd have to work for my living a good deal harder than I do now; but then the Lord'll take care of me if I only do my part, which isn't to grumble or whine, or be curious about what He is going to do."

She smiled cheerily as she looked for her handkerchief. She had carefully folded her veil and shawl into compact little squares of neatness and laid them by to put away when she should go up-stairs, and had taken out of her small satchel several small packages which now lay expectantly on her lap.

A pattering of feet on the porch, a buzzing of shrill

voices, and the door opened to admit Pam and the girls, for Pam had succeeded in getting into Mrs. Noble's graces far enough to be admitted into the house when his feet were clean, which meant in fair weather.

"Oh, here you all are, my dears, and the dog, too. Well, well, Ada, you are the same little chub, and loving as ever. I see it bubbling all over your face. Give me a good kiss now and run away with your booty," giving her one of the packages.

"And Carrol's come since I was here last year? Yes, dear, give me a kiss too. The good Lord has a work for you, child; be faithful and you'll know what it is some day."

Carrol choked back a little sob as she took her gift and walked slowly away to stand by Ada's side.

"Here, Mary, I've brought you something you wished for long ago. Hang it up where you can see it, and grow like it, for that's what you wanted it for."

Aunt Creesh had talked so fast, as she always did, that no one else could say a word. The children opened their papers. Ada's contained a doll, with materials for an outfit of clothing, cut and basted, ready for sewing.

"Oh," she cried, in delight, and ran to the table to display and admire her prize.

Carrol's was a gilt-edged Testament; Mary's gift a small but fine engraving of Correggio's infant Christ.

Aunt Creesh, on a previous visit, had overheard her pray for a picture of Jesus when he was a little babe. She had, with infinite pains, finally secured this for the child. Mary gazed at her treasure in rapture. Her face was radiant with a sweet surprise. "Oh God, I can never thank you enough," she whispered under her breath, clasping the picture close to her heart. In her complete abstraction she seemed unconscious of what her mother considered her first duty.

"Mary, why don't you thank Aunt Lucretia for the beautiful gift?"

"Oh, but mamma, I must thank God first, and then Aunt Creesh for bringing what God sent. She is His messenger, and oh Aunt Creesh, I *do* thank you, for its lovelier 'n I ever asked for, and I'm *so* glad."

She burst into tears. Aunt Creesh's eyes were wet, too, and so were the mother's. Carrol and Ada had slipped out of the room.

"There now Auntie, the rainbow's come," suddenly exclaimed Mary, looking up and smiling through her tears. It was a veritable April shower, and the sun shone all the more brightly after the cloud passed. "Oh, but won't I keep it nice though; and mamma, will you have it hanging where I can see it as soon as I wake in the morning, 'cause it will teach me so much?"

"Law! How do you expect a picture to teach you?" asked Aunt Creesh, wishing to hear Mary's answer. "It can't talk."

"Oh, but I can see how sweet it is! The goodness shines right through, and I want my face to look that way." She laid it on the table, while she threw her arms about her aunt's neck, kissed her and went out, taking the picture to show to Maggie.

"Bless the child, she's a regular little preacher,"

muttered Aunt Creesh to herself. She thought she was alone, but presently discovered Mrs. Noble standing in the doorway, seeing which she blew her nose violently, and said she would go up stairs and wash off the dust.

"Come right down then, and we'll have some breakfast for you."

"No, Marcia, I've had breakfast. Ate lunch on the train. If you've a cup of coffee handy—but then, I don't need it," with which she disappeared up the stairway.

Mrs. Noble braced herself to bear the cross. Her greatest cross was duty, and sometimes it seemed heavier than usual. It did to-day. Conscience insisted on some earnest words being given, where in all probability they would not be received. Never mind; she would not flinch from a religious necessity. After dinner she appeared before Aunt Creesh in full mourning garb for the street, and said, in the most inviting tones she could command: "Would you like to go to the missionary meeting with me, this afternoon?"

"Me go to a missionary meeting?" cried Aunt Creesh, with a smile of astonishment. "When I don't see any more heathen to be taught in our own country, I'll consider the matter of sending missionaries to foreign ones. God's just as able to look after 'em as I am, and a great deal more so. Come Marcia, what's the use of wasting your time? Don't you know God is everywhere revealing Himself, and that even the God worshiped in ignorance must be the right one if there is but one?"

Mrs. Noble paled visibly. She felt that the time had come. "Lucretia," she began in a severe tone, "it seems to me you are more heathenish in your notions every time you come here. The way you talk is perfectly dreadful, and I should think you ought to be disciplined. A Christian in good standing in the Methodist church to make no account of a Christian's duties! Are you really backsliding?"

"No Marcia, I think not," was the calm reply; "just growing."

"Well, it's an awful way to grow. I don't see what this world's coming to; but I suppose it's the last days when people are to be 'heady and high-minded' and believe in the anti-Christ," she sighed, hopelessly.

"Well, go on to your meeting, Marcia; never mind me. I guess the Lord won't desert me even if the Church should, so I can stand it."

"Yes indeed, I shall go. You must not expect me to forsake my duties because you forsake yours. I speak this way, Lucretia, because I have seen your tendency to grow away from the Church for two or three years, now, and I feel it my solemn duty, as a Christian and a sister, to warn you before it is too late."

She looked very much distressed, but Aunt Creesh remained placid.

"I'll be all right, Marcia. Still, you may pray for me, if it will relieve your feelings."

"I have, many a time, Creesh, but the Lord hasn't seen fit to answer yet, and I'm not satisfied."

"Then you can only wait, I suppose."

" Well, I must go now. I see Mrs. Doall's carriage at the gate.   She has stopped for me."

She turned back for a moment as she reached the door.   "Good-bye, Lucretia," with a last prayerful look.

"Good-bye! I'll try not to grow any worse while you're gone."

Mrs. Noble fortunately did not hear the latter part of the speech.

"Poor Marcia! what a hard time she always has bringing other people into the kingdom; but then, Lord forgive her, she does the best she knows;" with which kind thought Aunt Creesh composed herself to take a nap on the sofa.   The children were out playing somewhere on the lawn or in the garden, and she was left alone.

CHAPTER IX.

"'But,' Mrs. Bowles, is a word that cools many a warm impulse, and stifles many a kindly thought, puts a dead stop to many a brotherly deed. Nobody would ever love his neighbor as himself if he listened to all the Buts that could be said on the other side of the question." —*E. Bulwer-Lytton.*

RICHARD often found himself wondering about Carrol. There were times when he fancied he caught a fleeting glimpse of the woman back of the child. Once he had found her great brown eyes fixed upon him as though she would read his very soul. She seemed to be weighing him in an invisible balance and waiting for some nameless service at his hands. What was it, or was it anything but his absurd imagination? he asked himself.

One evening—one of those rare mild nights that occasionally bless us in September or October, when we have taken leave of summer and are growing used to the cooler breath of autumn, he sat in his room writing his reports for the month. The table stood near an open window, leaving the air to blow in unobstructed, save for the thin white curtain. He heard a noise below on the gravel walk. Pushing the curtain aside, he looked out. Bright moonlight flooded everything, the still air brought no sound for a moment, but as he was about to return to his work, he fancied he saw a dark object disappearing round the corner of the large square box known as the dog's house. Presently he heard a low sound as of some one talking or sobbing in a smothered tone. He looked out again and listened intently.

"Pam, I've had a dreadful dream and I wish I could just sleep with you, for you are so good and loving, I could never be afraid where you are." Richard heard this much and surmised that it was Carrol. The sound of sobs came up to him. . . . "Oh Pam, what can I do? Won't something ever happen to make—" he lost the rest of the sentence, and felt ashamed to listen longer. . . "I thought maybe the new teacher would—" involuntarily Richard leaned forward again, but the words died away, and he only heard heart-broken sobs.

"Poor little thing, I wonder if I ought not to go out and comfort her;" but he quickly resolved that that would not be practicable. Then he fell to wondering what made her sorrowful and what she had expected of the "new teacher." The matter grew more and more puzzling as Carrol continued to cry and talk to Pam as though there were no one else in the wide world.

Some minutes elapsed and he felt that something must be done—perhaps he ought to call Mrs. Noble; but then he knew instinctively that the child would rather be left alone than have anyone pry into her little secrets; for of course, Richard reasoned, it must be some childish affair that troubled her. He remembered how he had felt, when a boy of eleven. His father sold a favorite horse that Richard called his. A heartbreaking grief it was, and now he concluded this must be a similar trial that had overtaken Carrol, and yet,—

he thought again of that look of the woman, and was troubled.

Presently he heard steps on the gravel, then a muffled tread on the stairs. The room door at the end of the hall opened and closed. . . .

The mystery around Carrol continued. She had her times of romping and merry-making, but they were getting less frequent. She was friendly and even confiding with Richard at rare intervals, but the longer he knew her the more perplexed he grew; she kept so much of her real nature in reserve. Mrs. Noble was far from feeling at ease about her, and strove harder than ever to do her religious duty. She felt that something must be done, or soon it would be beyond her power to reclaim the child.

"You know how hard it is for me to see you go on this way, Carrol, and how anxious I have been that you be a follower of the Lamb," she began, one afternoon some weeks later, when Carrol chanced to be alone with her, (which seldom happened, for Carrol avoided private interviews whenever it was possible). "Haven't you any desire to be converted?" she continued, solemnly.

"I want to be good, aunt Marcia, but—"

"But what?" hopefully.

"I don't know what you mean; but if it is what I think it is, I don't want to be converted."

"Oh, to be converted means to give your heart to Jesus, to believe in him as your Savior, and join the church." Mrs. Noble tried to be explicit enough, and congratulated herself on having spoken when Carrol

was in such a teachable mood.   Carrol's reply somewhat disconcerted her.

"I don't know *how* to give my heart to Jesus.   I
don't know what you mean by believing in him."

Mrs. Noble put down the stocking she had been
mending, and looked earnestly at her niece as she said:
"Is it possible you don't know yet what it means to
give your heart to Jesus ?   Why, Carrol, I am surprised.
Haven't you heard the minister preach about it, and
Miss Joyce talk about it in Sunday School, and haven't
I gone over it time and time again ?"

"Yes ma'am, but how *can* you give your heart to
anybody and keep it yourself too ?" cried Carrol, desperately.

"To give your heart to Jesus means to serve him
with all your mind and strength, to believe that he
died for you that you might have eternal life."

But all her explanations seemed in vain.   The more
Mrs. Noble labored, the more Carrol misunderstood.
She wished Mary or Ada, or even Harvey Willard would
come and interrupt this tedious catechism.

"Well, Carrol, I never would have believed you
were so stupid, and I can't believe it yet," said her
aunt finally, after a vain argument.

"Truly, Aunt Marcia, I do try, but how can I give
my heart away to Jesus and then have him dwell in
my heart too ?   And how can I understand what you
mean by eating the body and drinking the blood of
Jesus ?   Oh dear, I *want* to be good, but this seems such
a hard way," and she sobbed disconsolately.

If Mrs. Noble could only have known the quality of

mind she was trying to feed, and could have ministered to it aright, she would soon have gained her wish; but ignorance leads into more blunders and sadder ones than anything else in this world. She only saw the darkness and despair, not the tender rootlets of high aims and aspirations that reached out so frantically for air and sunlight. So she grew hard and stern in her earnestness, laying out, as she supposed, the clearest outline of the plan of salvation, showing the inevitable punishment that came to those who heard but would not receive the gospel.

Carrol listened respectfully enough, but she was no wiser than before, and much less satisfied. She had been gradually forming an idea of the inadequacy of the language of Christianity in explaining the meanings of Christianity, and now she was quite convinced she knew nothing of either. By her silence, Mrs. Noble concluded she had finally received what was given, and when she rose to go, patted Carrol's shoulder with an affection she had not manifested for months. She felt that at last the child was on the right road, and one of her greatest burdens lifted.

As for Carrol, she had learned that silence kept peace and speech made war, so she smothered or stifled all questions that rose out of the depths of her unsatisfied longings. After her aunt left her, she communed with her own bitter thoughts, for they were not only dark, but bitter. She had thought much of late, no one knew *how* much. She was alternately filled with fear lest her aunt were right, and her mother wrong, or she had a rebellious desire to get away where she might never hear

religion or the Bible mentioned. Then she wondered
if God cared anything for such a wayward child as Aunt
Marcia said she was. From Aunt Marcia's view, He
did not; in fact, she might look any time for the coming
of His wrath as a punishment for her sinfulness and
obstinacy. She remembered her mother's God, who
was kind and forbearing, tender and loving, even to the
most erring one of His flock; but then again that awful
fear—what if Aunt Marcia were right? . . She would
give up trying, and forget everything pertaining to God
or religion; she would become a splendid scholar and a
famous teacher, and ——

It was not in any set forms of speech that Carrol
thought over her problems. Vague and shadowy would
have been her expressions had she attempted to put her
reverie into words, but that she would not and could
not do. Close within her own breast were locked alike
the darkness of doubt and the bitterness of despair.

She sat there in the gathering dusk, watching the
firelight in the open grate. Long fingers of flame
pointed upward or stretched into corners and crevices as
if pursuing imps of darkness. It seemed suddenly
as though a small man, with a very bright but tiny
sword, approached a towering form of darkness. The
dark form stooped and the valiant soldier of light disappeared. Carrol looked again and held her breath, for
here and there, like lightning gleams, could be seen the
flashing of the tiny sword. Then the black monster
leaned down once more; a shower of sparks, a thunder-
ing noise and all was still. The crackling and the flashing ceased. A dull red glow in the centre with encir-

cling darkness was all she could see. She looked in vain for the small soldier. Was that the end, after all? And then the red spot seemed to grow larger and larger, until it became as the mouth of a cavern. Far down in its depths she once more saw the form of light, but only for an instant.

The whole scene changed. She felt an awful darkness wrapping its folds about her. Not the darkness of night, nor of cloud, but a fearful pall-like darkness that made her tremble. She looked up, and in the gloomy vault of heaven beheld a mighty serpent advancing in writhing menace toward a single brilliant star. They met, as it seemed, in deadly combat. The earth was stilled in awe and terror. Not a breath to break the stillness. Not a sound but the hissing of the serpent. Birds poised on wings powerless to move. Leaf nor insect stirred, while that awful war went on. Thrust after thrust made the serpent, but with undimmed majesty the star beamed on its deadly foe, nor wavered, nor withdrew for a single instant its golden glory. Brighter and brighter it became, until heaven and earth were bathed in its transcendent light; until the serpent trailed its defenseless length along the sky, in token of defeat; until each darkly glowing scale became a glittering ray of light, and the whole body of darkness was swallowed up in the light that knows no darkness.

A startling peal, like thunder, rent the air. White and luminous clouds appeared, in one of which was the form of a man. Stars fell from heaven like rain. The sun stood still. People gathered from every corner of the earth, to throw themselves before the great white throne that came forth with indescribable majesty. Ah now—now was the time for a hiding-place: where could that be found ?... " Oh God, let me try once more! " cried Carrol, in an agony of fear. Then she awoke. Mary sat by her side and they were alone in the darkening twilight. Carrol wiped the perspiration from her forehead and drew a shivering sigh. Little Mary nestled close, as she said, in a soft voice:

" God always lets us try once more, Carrol. Did you have a bad dream?"

" Yes, Mary, and I was afraid.   O-h it—"

" Tell me about it," said Mary.

" Not yet, oh, no; let us talk of something else."

" I used to be afraid, too," interposed Mary, "but not any more now, since I found out what God's love means.   I can't be afraid—no, not of anything, though sometimes I have to think a long time before I feel the love; but it always comes, after a while."

"Mary, do you think people get good by going to church and praying?" asked Carrol, suddenly.

Mary was silent a moment. "Not always," she said at last. "When we went to church at the time they had meeting so often last winter, it didn't make me feel right.   They made too much noise, and that wasn't the way Jesus did, and he did right.   He never prayed or talked so loud.   He was real still, and when people got so noisy he went away from them, and I believe he goes away now, too," she added.

"Do you?" asked Carrol, dreamily. She was thinking of what Mary had said about being afraid.

" 'Cause, do you know," Mary went on, not heeding the question "when everybody makes such a noise, groaning and saying *amen* so hard, the happy goes right out of me, and I feel like crying for the sinners. Then it seems as if God has gone away off and left me and the sinners too."

"Mary, is God with us when we are happy and away from us when we are not?"

Mary grew thoughtful again. "He is with us always. It's when we get full of something else, that He seems far away. When we think of Him and feel real well acquainted, He is with us, and Carrol, don't you know that Jesus always talked as if God was with him all the time? Her eyes sparkled like two bright stars, and she held Carrol's hand close in her own.

"Yes; and do you know, Mary, I haven't been hardly a bit happy since that time we played Bethlehem?" said Carrol.

"Then you must be full of something else, if God seems away from you, was Mary's reply."

"But then," pursued Carrol in a low voice, "I've tried and tried what you've told me about reading the Bible, and I've been to church and prayed, and everything, and Mary, He's farther off now than ever. I think and think, and then they all talk about so much which I can't understand, that I just don't know what to do. Then the dreadful dreams—oh !" She put her hand over her face with a shudder at remembrance of what she never could forget.

"Tell me about it, cousin Carrol."

"Maybe I can sometime, but not now. I want *you* to know just how wicked I've been about wanting to for-

get God, but I wouldn't tell anybody else.   They make
me worse, but you make me better."

"Oh no, Carrol, that's wrong.   It isn't I at all.
It's God's goodness that runs over when I'm full of it."

"Then I wish everybody could run over," was the
gloomy reply.

Mary leaned over, resting her head on her hand, as
she gazed into the fire with a far-away look.

"Once, when I was out in the dream-tree," she
began, suddenly, "I was having a hard think 'bout you,
Carrol, and your mamma, and thinking how you
couldn't ever have her again; and it seemed after 'while
as if God's goodness reached right down to you, and
me, too, and—as I sat there, feeling so glad and happy,
something warm and soft touched me, and one of
the stars stooped down so low I could see everything by its light, and—and—then I knew God was
teaching me that His love is for everybody, 'cause the
stars shine for everybody in the world."

Carrol wiped away a tear.   "How could you tell
what it meant, Mary?" she queried, softly.

"I don't know," she replied, simply.   "Only it
seems as though God whispers in my heart, and tells me
'bout everything, if I only wait, and listen, and think."
Her face was full of a sweet peace.

"Oh dear, why can't I be good enough to see such
things?" cried Carrol, with a great longing.

"Oh, but you mustn't talk that way.   God's your
father, too, and He's good to everybody, only you must
always be *expecting* something lovely and then you will
soon know it is with you."

"I don't know how, Mary; do tell me. Am I not always wanting something?"

"Yes, but we must *expect* it every day, and keep on thinking of God and all He made being good; that means to *always* think of something good. Then He is always with us, and does lovely things for us."

"Isn't He always doing that?"

"Yes, but if we are thinking 'bout something else we don't know 'bout God. But oh, Carrol, I want you to know how good He is and how He loves you, and what a chance He gives you to get acquainted with Him."

The door opened and Mrs. Noble entered. She saw the girls sitting there, and bustled about to find a light.

"Come, children, it is Saturday night. Get the Bible and your Sunday Sschool lesson papers and go to work."

CHAPTER X.

"Trust hearsay less : seek more to prove
And know if things be what they seem:
Not sink supinely in some groove,
And hope and hope and dream and dream."
—*Alice Cary.*

THANKSGIVING'S most here ! Oh, ain't we glad ?" cried Ada, clapping her hands and dancing about the floor, one evening, after hearing Mr. Fernlow read and explain the President's proclamation.

They were all in the family sitting-room, enjoying the pleasant fire and light within doors, while a cold bleak wind blew outside. Carrol sat by the study table, trying to get her history lesson. Mary and Pam lay on the rug before the grate, and Mrs. Noble was sewing on a plain little apron to be sold at the next church fair. Aunt Creesh, with her knitting, sat on the sofa. She was making her visit unusually long this time.

"Ada, why are you more glad about Thanksgiving than other days?" said Richard, laying the paper aside. "Come, sit on this stool while you tell us."

She sat down on the footstool and, clasping her hands about one uplifted knee, she looked up in his face as she said, in a ringing, childish voice: "Well, I like it 'cause it's the day you have plum pudding and turkey, and can eat too much if you want to." Catching a reproachful glance from her mother, and thinking she had not given the right idea of the day, she added, "'nd then, it's the day there was only six grains of corn on Mayflower rock, and they all took some."

Everybody smiled. "Ada, you've quite distinguished yourself," laughed Richard. "Now let us hear from somebody else. What's your opinion, Mary?"

" I think Thanksgiving is nice because it's the day when everybody goes to church and thanks God before everybody else for all the lovely things He's given us."

" But do you think we have to go to church in order to be thankful ?"

Mrs. Noble dropped her sewing to listen. She looked at Mr. Fernlow, as if questioning his motive, but said nothing.

" No," replied Mary, after a moment's pause ; " 'cause we can feel little whispers of thanks going all over us inside, and only showing through our eyes and in our smiles ; but when we go to church, it has to be talked and sung right out loud."

" Good," said the teacher. " Next."

Carrol was next. "I like to have the day come, when I can see something to be thankful about, but this year mamma's—"

" Tut, tut," interrupted Aunt Creesh, straightening up so suddenly as to send her ball rolling away to be captured by Pam's paws ; "you can see something anytime, if you only look in the right direction. Don't talk that way, child ; learn to look for the blue, instead of the black, in your sky. Every day ought to be a thanks-

giving day, and everything ought to be thanked for.
Thanksgiving's all very well as a public day, but people
mustn't forget to keep the private ones. Be thankful
for even the miseries, I say, for then you'll turn them
into blessings." Aunt Creesh knitted away as if her
very life depended upon it.

"St. Paul says, 'Rejoice always, in everything give
thanks,'" quoted Mrs. Noble, solemnly.

"But Ada's glad we have more than six kernels of
corn at our Thanksgiving feasts," said Richard, with
a smile, "and so are we all. That is one of the great
things to be thankful for."

At this moment a loud knocking was heard at the
door.

"A telegram for Mrs. Lucretia Briggs," said the
messenger, as the door was opened. She calmly let it lie
on her lap while she signed her name in the receipt
book, and then as calmly opened it.

"Thank the Lord, it might be worse, but it isn't,"
she ejaculated, at last.

"Any bad news?" inquired her sister-in-law.

"No, nothing's bad unless you think so; but I
don't think so. Jenks says the case has gone against
me. That's all."

Mrs. Noble threw up her hands in dismay. "Why,
Lucretia, what will you do?" she asked.

"Do? Give thanks first. Go to work next."

"But what can you do?"

"Don't know yet. 'Sufficient unto the day is the
evil thereof', and the blessed part of it is, that day

never comes unless you look for it, which I don't propose to do."

"But, but, Lucre—"

"None of your 'buts,' Marcia. If you have any
'all rights,' they will be thankfully received. Bring
me the ball, Pam! Thank you. That's a smart dog of
yours, Carrol." She folded up her knitting and started
upstairs.

"What are you going to do?" Mrs. Noble ventured
to enquire.

"Pack up," was the laconic reply. "Good night."

"Well, I never! What in the world she will do with
no home to go to and winter coming, is more than I
know," exclaimed Mrs. Noble.

"Why, is it so bad as that?" asked Richard, sym-
pathetically.

"Yes, indeed. You see, Mrs. Briggs was left, a
few years ago, with her farm heavily mortgaged. She
worked along as hard as she could, and expected to
clear it all last fall. When the time came for settle-
ment, she found that the agent had not endorsed some
of the payments, and, as she had neglected to demand
receipt whenever a payment was made, she was unable
to prove that they had been made at all; so the bank
foreclosed. The case came to trial this present term of
court, and this is the end of it."

"What a shame! She seems very cheerful over
the matter."

"Yes; and that's what seems so strange—won't even
plan about what she's going to do. I can't understand
it."

"But, mamma, didn't you read the other day that we must take no thought for the morrow?"

"Yes, Mary, but a great many things in the Bible are only for the benefit of our souls after we die, and are not to be understood literally at all."

Mary looked puzzled, but said nothing further.

"I don't see what good it does to read the Bible, and not understand it or get any good out of it," Carrol could not help saying, a little sharply.

Mrs. Noble gave her one look. "All that long talk for nothing then," she thought, and began planning what to do next. The burden had returned and was heavier than ever.

The next morning Aunt Creesh took her departure, cheerful to the last. "All I ask of you, Marcia, don't send any of your worries after me," she said, as she put on her bonnet. "If there's anything that tempts me to be unhappy, it is to feel people's dark thoughts flying into my face like a bag of feathers turned loose in the wind."

"Well, I'm off," waving the black bag as a signal, after the good-byes were said, and she was on the path to the gate. Carrol saw the last flutter of the shawl as it turned the corner, and a gray sky of loneliness once more closed around her horizon.

After much thinking and praying, Mrs. Noble had at last hit upon a plan that she thought would be of the utmost benefit, not only to Carrol, but to her own children, for she had begun to seriously fear Carrol's influence upon Mary, especially. She decided to make arrangements with Deacon Rice to receive Carrol into

his family for a few weeks. A good man's influence
would undoubtedly assist in breaking the colt to wear
the religious harness, (these are not Mrs. Noble's
words, however). So the plan was duly acted upon, and
a week later found Carrol installed at the worthy
deacon's, who lived on a farm a mile from town, with
the understanding that she was to be company for his
wife.

Mrs. Rice was a spare little woman, with great
mournful, faded blue eyes and thin gray hair. Carrol
had seen this much when she was led up to be introduced to her that day after Sunday School. Mrs. Rice
had looked at her kindly and murmured something
about being glad to see her, and then went on winding
the white nubia about her head, preparatory to the
journey home. They seated themelves on the bottom
of the big sleigh—she and Mrs. Rice and the boys—with
robes and quilts tucked all around them, while Deacon
Rice sat on the seat in front, with the minister, whom
he had invited to spend the night with them. The
protracted meeting had opened propitiously, and as
usual, Deacon Rice was a prompt attendant. He was
one of the stand-bys of the church, as a deacon should
be of course. He could always be depended upon
to pray, to exhort, or in any way assist the minister.
His house was always open to visitors, especially the
preachers during revivals, and a very pleasant home it
was, as far as comfort was concerned.

Carrol followed her hostess to the broad porch
and into the clean, warm kitchen. The nubia was
quickly removed and then, with her shawl still unpinned,

Mrs. Rice turned to help Carrol undo her hood and cloak. She said little, but there was an atmosphere of kindliness about her that quite won Carrol's heart.

"We will try to make you feel at home, my dear, but I don't know what we have to offer you, except a welcome."

She evidently expected no reply, and certainly Carrol had none to give just then. In another moment the rest came in. The minister, Mr. Slocum by name, and the boys, then Deacon Rice, bringing robes and blankets.

"This is a right cold night and I'm afraid my ear's nipped; wife, ain't it white?" The deacon turned to his wife with an expectant air, while she examined the suffering member.

I don't see anything, Joshua; I guess it's all right."

"Glad to hear it. Draw up to the fire, Brother Slocum, and have a seat," was the deacon's hospitable invitation.

After a few moments conversation the deacon turned to Mrs. Rice and suggested that she put the coffee on. "Brother Slocum must be hungry after his hard day at church." The preacher demurred in a faint voice, but the coffee went on and the kitchen table was drawn out and dressed up with an array of cold eatables. After a long grace from Brother Slocum, he was invited to "reach to" and be filled with the temporal blessings of the Lord. The boys watched hungrily from a respectful distance, but knew too well that they were not allowed to eat lunch with the preacher, as no one ever did except their father.

Carrol was not hungry, but sat quietly in the corner, content to study the company and surroundings. Mrs. Rice stood meekly near the table, waiting for further orders, or listening to the talk between the two functionaries of the church.

"There's one young man I have my eye on for the mourners' bench. We nearly got him last winter, if you remember," said the deacon, taking a huge bite of bread and butter; "but some way he backed out. It's that Bill Watson, who most breaks his mother's heart by drinkin' all the time. You know him, don't you?"

"Why yes, I think so," said the minister slowly. "Didn't we offer special prayers for his soul last winter?"

"Yes we did, and I have been prayin' off an' on ever sense, but it does rile me to think a young man like him ain't got better sense, an' I've told him so, too, but it don't appear to do no good. Howsoever, I've set my heart on gettin' him into the fold this time, and I hope you preachers will fire the best shot you've got into satan's stronghold."

"The Lord grant that we may gather many souls for His harvest," replied the preacher, fervently.

They rose from the table, and after some moments further conjecture as to who would come forward, the deacon brought the Bible for family worship. A chapter was read and a prayer offered by Brother Slocum, during which every one knelt beside his or her chair. The preacher had a tender heart and left no stone unturned in his instructions to the Lord, by which every poor soul might be blessed or saved, or at least brought to a conviction of sin. He lifted up his voice in supplication that the labors of the servants in this vineyard might be abundantly blessed, and then he asked a special blessing on the good deacon and each member. of his loved family. While he was thus earnestly engaged the deacon was emphasizing every statement by a fervent and long-drawn amen. Mrs. Rice knelt motionless, save for a slight sigh; now and then the boys looked askance at Carrol, or cast longing looks towards the table, or pinched each other by way of variety. Carrol tried to be unconscious of all these diversions, but curiosity would prompt the occasional lifting of an eyelid, and in one of these occasionals she saw Ned slowly and slyly reaching out for a doughnut that had been dropped upon the floor, during the hurry of getting lunch: This time the eyelid remained lifted, and the eye peered through the fingers so devoutly covering the forehead and face: Brother Slocum had just reached the younger members of the deacon's family, and was ardently pleading that these young sons of the household might be fed with the bread of life, nourished and strengthened with the hidden manna. "Amen," said the deacon's deep bass voice, just as Ned, in his frantic efforts to get the prize, overreached himself, and in spite of his efforts to gather himself together, his feet went in opposite directions, making a loud noise on the bare pine boards. Brother Slocum had presence of mind and continued without interruption: The deacon looked around and glared at his son for a moment; then resumed his "amen" at precisely the right time. Carrol coughed once, Ralph snickered, but Mrs. Rice never moved. The devotions were ended at last.

Brother Slocum was shown to his room; Ned was sent to bed in disgrace, and then the deacon retired, with a good conscience. After he had gone, Mrs. Rice talked more freely. She cleared away the table, washed the things, and then went with Carrol to a neat little room upstairs, " where Lina used to sleep," she said, wiping away a quiet tear. Lina was the little girl they had lost some years before.

Carrol had a long reverie after her hostess had gone down. She was not at all sure she would like to stay here, but would stand it for Mrs. Rice's sake awhile at least.

Mrs. Rice kept no help. The deacon could not afford it, and there was no need of it, he said. They only kept five cows now, and it wasn't much to take care of the milk and do the housework. He had a hired man, to be sure. It was not possible to get along with all his outdoor work and running about without somebody. During these protracted meetings, it was his duty as a deacon to help entertain the ministers, so it was sometimes one, sometimes more, that he brought home to dine, sup or lodge; oftener all these.

Of course the deacon's wife was expected to attend every session, especially the evening ones, and also to pray in public as well as private, although the former she rarely did.

" Come, come, Lizy, we'll surely be late; you must try to get through with your work earlier. It will never do to keep the preacher waitin'," sputtered the deacon, the next evening, as they were about to start to church, for the third time that day.

"Yes, Joshua, I'm nearly ready," was the patient answer.

"Ain't the boys ready? You know they'll have to get their lessons some other time now, besides the evenin'."

"They are coming. Come Ralph! Don't stop for that now," called their mother, as she finished pinning the shawl and flung the nubia round her head. The boys were bringing in some kindling to save their mother a few steps, but there was no more time now, so it must be left for her to finish in the morning.

Carrol had been ready and waiting some time. All that was said during the ride was the discussion between the deacon and Brother Slocum, as to the better methods of helping the heathen.

CHAPTER XI.

"Wherefore keep saying, I am saved by the blood of the Lamb and the Cross of Christ, stained with His precious blood? . . . Of what avail are all these sayings when our lives do not demonstrate the fruits of the Spirit—love, joy, long-suffering, gentleness, goodness, faith, meekness, temperance—against such there is no law?"—*Mrs. Eldredge Smith.*

MOTHER, I don't want to go to the meeting again to-night. I ought to get my grammar lesson. Missed it to-day just on account of being out last night," protested Ralph, petulantly, as the children came home from school a few days later.

"Well, my son, your father wants you to go, and I will not ask you to help me to-night; so you can sit down and study right after supper," answered Mrs. Rice, quietly.

She said not a word of how much she had to do, in order to go at all, but she would never hint of staying at home when her husband desired her to go.

"Can't I help you, Mrs. Rice?" asked Carrol, feeling strangely drawn to this meek, patient woman, who was a Christian and yet unlike Aunt Marcia.

"Thank you, dear; I'd rather you'd help Ned with his arithmetic. He was complaining of being behind this morning, too. Wouldn't you like to have Carrol help you?" she asked, appealing to Ned, who had just entered the room in time to hear his mother's reply.

"Bet your life, I'll take help from anybody. 'Rith- metic's a reg'lar bore, 'nd a feller's got to have help er git bounced," and Ned threw himself lazily into a chair with a mischievous twitch at Carrol's hair.

"There, that will do, Ned. Please remember mother doesn't like such language."

"Oh, I forgot. Bet, yer—now mother, I really didn't mean it," and the frank young scamp calmly seized his mother's nose, by which he pulled her face down to his and kissed it. She smiled with a loving mother's smile. Suddenly they heard the deacon's footsteps. The smile faded. "Come, boys, help your father with the chores, and we'll soon have supper."

The deacon entered with two ministers, and after ushering them into the sitting-room, he returned—with not his Sunday, but his week-day countenance—and, clapping his gloved hands briskly together, exclaimed, a little impatiently: "Come, come, boys, don't be settin' around here. We've no time for foolin'. Boys of your age must depend on their own thinkin', not their father's. You ought to a had the cows up and the calves fed by this time."

"They came from school only a few minutes ago, Joshua."

"Wal, I can't help it, Lizy; school 'll have to let out earlier then. I'm gittin' old, and Jake can't do every- thing alone. Seems as if the boys git home later every night." He turned to the boys, who by this time were ready to accompany him. They made no reply, nor did their mother. There was nothing to say.

Half an hour later the deacon and his guests sat

down to the table spread as for a king and his court, such unlimited pains had the faithful wife taken to have just the dishes the deacon liked best. Nothing had been omitted. Snowy bread, delicious jellies, cold ham, roast chicken, were all there to pamper and satisfy the appetite. Of course no one thought of the hours of labor spent in the preparation of it all; no one noticed, except Carrol, that one of the patient hands was bound up in a white cloth; no one noticed that the wife and hostess must wait to serve instead of waiting to be served; so the minister, with bowed head, and solemn voice, thanked God for so bountifully providing for the wants of his creatures, and asked a blessing upon the food for their use, for Christ's sake.

The deacon waited upon his guests with anxious solicitude, heaping an abundance of the good things on each plate. He even had his wife bring some of his currant wine from the cellar for their special delectation.

The theme of conversation was the revival and how best to make it a success. Brother Slocum recounted several experiences they had had in other places, and told, with justifiable pride, of the number of souls brought to Christ, through a six weeks' course of meetings. "We want to convert the children, too," he asserted, with a fervent look at the young faces around the table.

"And have you given your heart to Jesus, my little girl?" he suddenly asked of Carrol.

She blushed and trembled with nervous terror.

"N-o-o, sir," she faltered at last, in a scarcely audible voice.

Brother Slocum fixed his restless, sharp eyes upon her.

"Do you not want the crown that fades not away?"

Silence of several moments ensued. She grew more terrified under that searching gaze.

"I want to be good," she stammered at last.

"Yes? Well, my dear child, that will not redeem you. You are still black and slimy with sin. But there is a way to be clean. You can be cleansed by the blood of Jesus, by just saying a few words, by just believing on him as your Saviour. Then everything is done for you, and you are washed white as snow."

Carrol kept her eyes fixed on her plate.

"Speak up, Carrol, the preacher wants to help ye," interposed the deacon.

She looked up, but still said nothing.

"Do you pray every day?"

"I—I don't know."

"What! You don't know such an important thing as that?" exclaimed the minister, in a horrified tone.

"She hasn't seemed to take to religion since her mother died," explained the deacon.

"Poor lamb; we must bring you into the fold, then. You will soon learn to pray."

"But I want to know how to *live*," rejoined the child, with bright eyes and glowing cheeks.

"Of course. But everything in its proper time. You are quite right in wishing to know how to live, child."

They rose from the table and, as it would be nearly an hour before the time to start for church, the minister proposed a season of worship. Carrol wondered if they did not intend to wait until Mrs. Rice had eaten her supper, but no one thought of it evidently; so, pushing the chairs back a little from the table, each knelt down beside his own. The children being the special objects of concern, they were taken in hand separately. After each petition, and during its utterance, there was a plentiful sprinkling of amens, which made the whole room resound with dolefulness.

When it was over, all was hurry and confusion, in the necessary haste of starting. There was no time for Mrs. Rice to sit at the table, so she quietly took a sandwich in the one hand, and, with a cup of coffee on the pantry shelf, began her meal. Before the coffee was half gone, the deacon came in to have her remove a splinter from his hand, which, as he expressed it, was "mighty painful." Quickly removing the cloth from her own smarting member, to avoid all question concerning it, she turned to minister to her husband.

Then it was time to go.

It was late, dark and cold. Everyone scrambled into the sleigh, without waiting for the others. Ned came last and hung on at the end, boy fashion. No one noticed that, as they neared the church, he quietly dropped down and disappeared in the darkness.

He had resolved to find other entertainment than being preached to and prayed with, that evening. A certain set of chums were just then being fascinated with card playing, and he had been especially invited to meet with them in Jack Loden's barn, where there would be no danger of discovery and every opportunity to enjoy the treat.

Ned knew well that his mother would be grieved if she found it out; but then, he argued, she was always feeling bad about such things anyway, and if he waited for her or his father to consent, he would never have any fun in the world. So he beguiled himself into believing that it was all right, especially as he knew the game was harmless.

They missed him when they reached the church, and the deacon concluded that the boy had been left behind, on account of his slowness, and said as much, but no one else had even that theory to offer. The mother's heart was heavy with apprehension. Twice before had something like this occurred, with what result, she even yet trembled to recall. Carrol wondered, but said nothing, and Ralph remembered Ned's half-muttered protest that he wanted something better than preachers to amuse him.

The two boys were very different in disposition. Ralph, the eldest, was studious and quiet, like his mother. Ned was a bright, rollicking boy of fourteen. He was bubbling over with life and strength, but owing to the severe repression of his nature at home, he had been growing rebellious.

What wonder? Do not even the great forces of nature burst their bounds when their outlet is obstructed? Oh ye parents, that have within your homes unseen, and possibly unsuspected, channels of the Great Force, let liberty have her perfect sway—liberty of the good. Direct the glorious strength and the springing joy of youth into beautiful outlets. Turn destructive force into constructive power. Turn mischievous idleness into aspiring application, by making application as interesting as idleness. Let individuality assert itself. Let each flower bloom with its own beauty. Then wait; not in fear and trembling of a volcanic outburst, but with a sublime patience, for the overflow of a Nile that will bring to your vision and enjoyment great harvests of use and beauty.

The meeting was over at last; Ned was still nowhere to be seen. They rode home silently. The mother's first glance, as she entered the house, was directed toward the place where usually hung Ned's hat and coat. They were not there ! She opened the stair door and called in a shrill, quavering voice, but no answer came. "The Lord help him !" was all she said, as she turned back with a deep sigh. She staggered to a chair and tried to unfasten her shawl. Carrol assisted, and, by the time Ralph and his father came in, Mrs. Rice appeared like herself, except for an extreme paleness.

"Where's Ned ?" inquired the deacon, looking around, as his wife had done.

"I don't know where he can be, Joshua; but perhaps he's just stepped out."

She tried to be calm and even cheerful, and for a few moments nothing more was said.

"If that boy has sneaked off to play cards again, I'll give him such a thrashing he'll remember it as long as he lives," exclaimed the father, suddenly rising to pace back and forth across the room, and casting wrathful glances at his wife, as though she had something to do with the misdemeanor.

Poor thing, she was suffering enough already. It neared eleven o'clock and she was wondering how she could get the rest off to bed, when a great noise and clanging of bells startled them all. Looking out, they beheld a fire that appeared to be, as Ralph said, "Mr. Loden's barn." "Can't I go father?" cried Ralph, eagerly, putting on his coat.

"No!" thundered the deacon. "One boy out is enough. I expect that confounded young rascal is there now, maybe did the mischief."

"Oh, Joshua," burst from the mother's lips. But the deacon had forgotten his fervent prayer for the sinner, uttered scarce more than an hour before; he had forgotten everything but that he had a disobedient son, who was a shame and a disgrace, and as he stalked back and forth across the room, his rage was terrible to see. No thought of the frail little woman who sat there, with hardly breath enough to keep conscious, no thought of anything but the awful wrench to his own pride. That was great. He cared more to have the good opinion of the world than he would like to say, but now this son would bring ruin and disgrace upon him. Wrath and prejudice always find plenty to feed upon, so the deacon raged.

A few minutes before twelve, they heard the latch of the shed door softly lifted, and Ned's footsteps on the loose board floor. All waited in breathless silence. As he opened the door of the kitchen the deacon glared at him savagely, scarcely refraining from clutching the boy by the collar.

"Where have you been, you miserable son of—satan? Tell me the exact truth," demanded the angry father.

Surprise and terror quickly gave way to resentment. "I expect to tell the truth, and nothing but truth, but not now," doggedly.

Here was defiance added to disobedience. The deacon's fury knew no bounds. "I'll show you how to answer me that way, you rascal," and he shook the boy till his boots flew out of his hand.

"Don't, father, don't do that," pleaded the mother.

"Come, Carrol, let us get out of the room," whispered Ralph, who, though his blood fairly boiled, dared say nothing, knowing too well it would only rebound on his mother. Such a scene as this had been burned into his memory once.

After Carrol went to bed, she heard groans, loud talking and crying, mingled with shrill exclamations and heavy thuds, that told of the terrible punishment poor Ned received. She lay awake a long time, thinking about it, but could come to but one conclusion, which was, that Christians, with all their prayers, were the worst people she ever knew—but then, there was little Mary.

The next morning Ned was not at the breakfast table. Mrs. Rice was red-eyed and pale, and Ralph looked years older than he did yesterday, but the deacon was severely rigid, and said not a word.

"What makes you so quiet, Carrol?" asked Ralph,

as they walked home from school together, the following evening.

"I was only thinking."

"Thinking of Ned's disgraceful actions, I suppose," answered Ralph, rather bitterly, for he felt angry at his brother, as well as sorry for him.

"Oh, I was just wishing cousin Mary could be at your house to comfort your mother and make Ned better."

"I'm afraid he'll not get better the way he's treated now. Father didn't gain anything by whipping him. I don't believe such punishment ever makes us better," he continued, after a moment's silence.

Carrol wiped her eyes with the back of her mitten.

"I know one thing," Ralph went on, "Ned won't stand it. He said this morning he'd run away if he had to be treated in this fashion, and I don't blame him. Somehow, father's always picking at us, especially Ned, and Ned wouldn't be so bad if he could do as other boys do, but you see we're never allowed any fun at home, never have company, never can do anything we want to on Sunday—can't even read what we like—and I tell you it's pretty tough on a fellow." In his excitement Ralph did not realize how much he was revealing of family life.

"But then, Ralph, think of your mother, and—and I haven't any," said Carrol, with a break in her voice.

Tears sprang to Ralph's eyes, but he wiped them away hastily. He would not for anything Carrol should see him cry.

"That's so," he said at last. "Mother's a regular

angel, if there ever was one; but, when I think of how she suffers and how much she thinks of Ned, I feel mad enough to flog him myself."

He kicked viciously at a board lying across the path. "But then, that would make her unhappy, too, and besides, it would not be right."

They walked through the gate thoughtfully; past the woodpile and into the shed. A great, black dog rose from his bed on the mat and gave a deep, bass growl.

"Why, Pam!" was all Carrol could say, as she put her arms round his neck.

CHAPTER XII.

"Love! blessed love! if we could hang our walls with
  The splendors of a thousand rosy Mays,
Surely they would not shine so well as thou dost,
  Lighting our dusty days."

—*Alice Cary.*

IN THE house they found Mr. Fernlow, Mary and
Ada.

"Oh, Carrol, Carrol, I've just brought a bushel of
love for you. I wish you'd come home again," cried
Mary, impetuously, throwing her arms about her cousin's neck.

"Yes, we just wanted you lots. I cried for you an'
Pam howled last night, awful," added Ada, in an
aggrieved voice.

"You see, Carrol, how indispensable you are, and
how your friends love you," said Richard, with a warm
smile.

"Well, I am glad to see you all. Don't eat me up,
Pam. Come and see the puppies, girls, they are so
cunning. Mr. Fernlow can talk to the big folks." Carrol thought he might want to ask why Ned had not been
to school, and, with an intuitive delicacy, left Mrs.
Rice to talk with him privately, as the deacon was not
at home.

So they all trooped to the barn to inspect the "royal
babies," as Ralph laughingly called them.

It was such a relief to talk freely and joyfully once more. Somehow, with Mary, she always felt so free. Carrol did not know, then, that it was the outblossoming of Mary's love nature that gave such charm to her life and presence.

Ada was busy with the puppies. Ralph made them show off their pudgy little bodies and cunning little ways to the best advantage.

Carrol suddenly seized Mary's hand and drew her aside, whispering, with suppressed ecstasy: "You love me, Mary, as well as I love you, don't you?"

"I know it," replied Mary, composedly; "I just wanted to see you so bad to-day, I 'most cried in school, and all at once I felt your thinking. It seemed like: 'Mary loves me, Mary loves me,' and I said: 'Yes, I do, Carrol, I do love you.'"

"I believe I felt it, Mary, for something brought those words right to me."

"P'raps it was the angels that carry love talks from God, 'cause really, Carrol, I know angels do such things. Once in the tree," she went on, lowering her voice, "it seemed as if I went to sleep and all at once I felt a warm wind on my cheek, and an angel flew by—oh, I saw it just as plain—and out of its white wings such sweet thoughts floated like real snowflakes; they were so white and beautiful."

"How did you know they were thoughts?" asked Carrol, with carefully veiled doubt.

"I can't tell exactly, only it was God's way of letting me know, without words. He often does that, you know."

"Yes, yes, that is what you say, but He never teaches me when I ask Him."

" Haven't you got a single answer? "

Carrol shook her head sadly.

"Well then, Carrol, there's something you've left out. It's never God's fault that you can't get it, 'cause He is always the same—a dear, kind Father, that is Love itself. P'raps you keep wondering and thinking too much 'bout what you'll see or know.   Now, I just sit down in my tree's lap, and first of all, hush my thinking—keep ever so still, and then I shut my eyes, waiting for God to give me some sign.   I can't begin to wonder what the sign'll be, 'cause if I do it doesn't come, but I just keep waiting and waiting all the time so happy, that it seems as if I'm listening to a birdie's dream-song.   But after awhile, when I've most forgot everything but God, then He sends things for me to see or think of.   'Course I know they're only pictures out of God's beautiful picture book that He teaches us with, but they are so beautiful and I love to learn that way.   Maybe if you'd try real hard, when you're alone, just all alone with God, 'cause He's everywhere, you can learn that way too. I'm sure you can, Carrol, if you try real hard and ever so many times."

" But Mary, if God is everywhere and loves me, why does He let me get frightened in my dreams, and why don't He send somebody to love me as mamma did, and why does He let good people like Mrs. Rice be so unhappy? " was Carrol's almost bitter outburst.

" It's 'cause you're afraid and don't know of His love, that you shut it out.   He never stops loving you, but if you don't take His love, how can it keep you from being afraid? And Carrol, you mustn't say you haven't anybody to love you like your mamma, 'cause God *is* love.

"Yes, but Mary, He's so far away and I can't see Him, and He's not at all like mamma, and it don't help me to read about him."

"Don't it, Carrol? Then I guess you'll just have to open your thinker to God, and He'll fill it for you. But I know one thing, Carrol, somebody you *can* see loves you. Can you guess who?" bending over and looking roguishly into Carrol's eyes.

"Of course I can, my sweet little cousin. Now tell me what you and Ada have been doing while I have been away."

Carrol would not be caught in tears. She had too much reserve, and would never show her inner self if she could help it. In these questions, therefore, she shut herself away from even little Mary.

"Oh, Ada is happy most of the time," replied Mary, "but once in a while she thinks of you, then she wants to come down to see you. Mamma won't let us go away after school often, 'cause we have to learn some verses out of the Bible."

The time passed all too quickly, and when they were ready to go, Mr. Fernlow asked Carrol if she were not going with them.

"No, I'm going to stay another week," she announced, suddenly deciding that she could not leave Mrs. Rice just yet. So the rift in the cloud of her own thoughts closed again as suddenly as it had appeared.

"Mamma," said Mary that night, as they were

cosily seated around the fire, ''mamma, why isn't every Christian happy?''

"I think every Christian is happy, my child," replied her mother, looking up and wondering what the shadow on Mary's face betokened this time.

"Why, Mrs. Rice isn't, Carrol said, and neither is Deacon Rice, an 'most all the folks that go to church, 'cause they cry and talk to God as if they were wickeder than ever."

"What makes Mrs. Rice unhappy?" asked Mrs. Noble, preferring to deal with a particular rather than a general problem.

"I don't know; but mamma, didn't Jesus promise everything to the folks that believed in him, and aren't the church members the ones?" Mary was in no mood for evasions.

Mrs. Noble was busily threading a needle, and when she had finished she replied slowly, "The people who belong to the church are expecting sometime to receive every blessing, but they are not yet good enough to deserve everything."

"Oh," was Mary's only answer.

She relapsed into silence and seemed to be thinking deeply. Finally, she looked up at her mother with a sigh of relief.

"Jesus said, 'everybody that loves God, is born of God,' and when we are full of love there isn't room for any fear, and then of course we can ask for anything we want, because we believe. Isn't that so mamma?"

"Yes."

"Then, why don't all these folks get full of love, and they can have what they want right now?"

"Well Mary, everybody hasn't Christ in their heart, and so the devil tempts them to say and do things that are not right, and they feel badly, because they have sinned."

The shadow came again on Mary's face.

"Can they do wrong after they have been born of God, mamma?"

This was a hard question, but Mrs. Noble did the best she could to answer it.

"Can they, mamma?" persisted Mary, still unsatisfied with the reply.

"Yes, because they do not keep the whole armor of God about them all the time."

"What is the armor of God?"

"It is the faith that Jesus is our Saviour."

"But if they have been baptized, haven't they been baptized into the new life the Christians are always talking about?"

Mary had not been carefully trained in Bible lore and church customs and expressions for nothing. Neither had her own conversion and baptism an idle meaning for her.

"They ought to be able to walk in the newness of life that you speak of, Mary," answered her mother; "but they cannot all at once."

Another silence. "Then, mamma, there's no use to be a Christian, because it isn't true that we can be perfect, even after we've been baptized."

Such a doleful tone as there was in Mary's voice

would have told, if her words did not, that she had come into unusual darkness, which she frequently did after one of these talks with her mother.

Mrs. Noble hastened to assure her that she must not judge in that way, but try all the harder to be a true little Christian.

"But, mamma, I've *never* tried. I've just 'Cast the burden on the Lord,' and He's taken it. I didn't know before that we had to bear any burdens. I thought we had only to love each other, and trust God and He would do all the rest."

Mrs. Noble secretly wondered what poisonous influences had been at work with Mary. It did not take long to settle her suspicions on Carrol, and she wished within herself that some way might be found that would remove Carrol from the family during the whole winter.

She prayed over it, and before a week was over, she felt that her prayer was answered.

Ned Rice had run away from home. One night he did not return from school, and after hours of weary waiting and suffering on his mother's part, and strong denunciations from his father, a little note was found tucked away in his mother's spectacle case. She discovered it when she had given up in despair.

With trembling hands, and streaming eyes, she read what was written :

"DEAR MOTHER: Don't worry about me. I've gone away to live, for I couldn't stand it any longer at home. I will try to be good whenever I think of my mother, for that was the only thing that ever made me good, anyway. Sometime, maybe, I'll come back and see you, or write, but it will do no good to look for me now. Tell Ralph to be good to the mother who has known only sorrow on account of   NED.

"P. S.—I had nothing to do with the burning of Mr. Loden's barn."

That was all, and the tender mother heart cried out in exceeding great sorrow for her youngest son, her baby, who only this morning had kissed her good-bye, but she dared not give vent to her feelings before her husband. He read the note and tore it into bits before her eyes. Then he peremptorily ordered Ralph to bed, and giving Carrol the candle, bade her go also. What he further said to his wife they never knew, but in the morning she looked like an old, old woman, instead of the matron of forty. That day she bore up bravely, but by night she was raving with brain fever. The deacon would allow no steps to be taken for the finding of his son. "He has made his bed and he must lie on it," he had quoted, severely. Moreover, he would come back soon enough when he found himself hungry and friendless. This was all he ever was heard to say on the subject. In the meantime Carrol staid, and Mrs. Noble had her wish.

The deacon was very glad to have Carrol remain, and when Mrs. Rice recovered, no one thought of sending her away. She was there all that winter and the following summer, doing what she could to make the pain less hard to bear for the patient, long-suffering little woman she had learned to love next the dear lost mother.

Sometimes, as the weeks grew into months, the longing to see her boy would be almost intolerable; but as no word came, Mrs. Rice settled back into a condition of chronic melancholy.   The deacon still maintained his place in the church and prayed louder than ever for hopeless sinners.

The next few years we shall pass by, noting only that Richard Fernlow taught another term as principal of the Tintuckett schools, and then returned to college, but not as a theological student.   He had decided not to be a preacher.   Carrol was sent away to school where Mary finally joined her, and both in due time, graduated with honor to themselves and teachers.

CHAPTER XIII.

"There are times when the troubles of life are still;
  The bees wandered lost in the depths of June,
  And I passed where the chime of a silver rill
    Sung the linnet and lark to their rest at noon."
                              —*E. Bulwer-Lytton.*

IT WAS toward the end of a warm day. The sun was already beginning to dip his golden disc below the western hills, and long grotesque shadows fell athwart the green lawn in front of Mrs. Noble's cottage.

The odor of lilacs and roses filled the air. In the house, these flowers and many others were scattered about in rich profusion, smiling from vases, peeping from all sorts of odd corners, while a large pan of exquisite roses seemed waiting for dainty hands to arrange them. An air of festive expectancy pervaded everything.

Suddenly the door opened to admit two young girls, who might fittingly be called blossoms of a rarer kind. One was tall and dark, the other slender and fair. One had eyes dark and questioning; the other, blue and trustful. One had a forehead low and broad; the other, broad and high.

"How shall we arrange these roses, Carrol?" said the fair one, whom the reader will recognize as little Mary grown to maidenhood.

"Let me see," replied Carrol, pondering, as she

daintily stirred and lifted the roses. "Here are red and cream, why not make a bank of them, and put them in that old silver cake basket?"

"Do you think there will be enough?"

"Oh yes, surely, for this is a solid panful."

A few moments later they were busily sorting and arranging the golden-hearted beauties, while they chatted on the home-coming and the reception that was to celebrate the event.

As soon as it was noised abroad that Mary and Carrol were to return from school, (Ada had not yet finished,) the friends expressed such warm interest and desire to see them that Mrs. Noble decided to give the opportunity at once, and so appointed the evening after their return as most convenient and appropriate.

To Mary it was a real delight. Carrol enjoyed the prospect fairly, but she had not forgotten the shadows of her child life. In thinking of this, she said suddenly: "I wonder if Harvey Willard is here now?"

"I think he is. Mamma said he was to spend his vacation in Tintuckett. You know he is studying for the ministry."

Mary looked up artlessly, as she selected a more perfect rose to take the place of a defective one. Carrol burst out laughing.

"Studying for the ministry!" she echoed. "No, I didn't know it, but I am not surprised very much. He began early enough. Don't you remember how he used to quote his father, on every occasion?"

"Yes, but I suppose he is learning from higher authority now."

"I dare say he will lecture me just as he used to."

"You won't mind it now as you did then," said Mary, quietly, as she laid aside some lovely buds.

"I'm not so sure, Mary. I think I can bear less now than then, for then I was half afraid Harvey was right; now I've outgrown those superstitious fears, and can judge for myself."

"What times you did have, trying to do what was right, and believe what was true," replied Mary, thoughtfully.

"Yes, and if it hadn't been for you I would have been a regular heathen. Perhaps some folks would call me that now, for I don't pretend to be a Christian." The expression about her mouth was a trifle more grave, but the frank voice and eyes redeemed the severity.

"You need never be afraid I will think you a heathen, for I know too well your honest purpose to live up to the highest you know, and that in itself will lead you into Christianity. Growth can never be forced."

Mary leaned over, ostensibly to let Carrol smell a half-blown rose, but really to give one of the loving heart-glances that sometimes came through the windows of her soul.

"If all Christians were like you, Mary, I can see how I could believe, and—well, you know how it is. I can't bear the bigotry and uncharitableness. There! now we mustn't talk any more, or we shall get too sober for to-night."

Mary smiled re-assuringly. Nothing could disturb her peace centre.

"Well, these roses are done; now what next?" said Carrol. She put the pan with its stems and waste leaves on the table, while she held the basket in her hand a moment. "Oh," she exclaimed impetuously, with a caressing touch, "what is more beautiful than flowers? To me they are heaven's own messengers. I only wish I were wise enough to know what they say."

"They speak of love and beauty and noble contentment; at least we can read that much," responded Mary, rising.

She linked her arm in Carrol's, and together they stood there, looking at the flowers—themselves a lovely picture of peace and beauty.

"Come, girls, it is time you were dressing," said Mrs. Noble, bustling in to inspect the adornments for the last time. "You have succeeded wonderfully well," she added, stopping to admire the basket of roses.

"Yes, isn't it fragrant?" said Carrol, holding it up for her aunt to smell.

"Fragrance and beauty go together, or ought to. Now put it away and run; you havn't much time." With that she playfully pushed them through the door, and remained to give the last touch here and there.

Mrs. Noble has changed somewhat since we saw her last. She has grown more charitable and less critical of other people's beliefs. Mary's sweet child nature and Christ-like life have softened more than one hard spot in her character. She finally recognized the straightforward simplicity of Mary's religious life, and from that time put no hindrance to her unfolding, and thus she was herself unconsciously led into broader avenues of thought and a higher plane of action. She loved Carrol, though still disapproved of her religious attitude, but she gladly welcomed her home for the usual summer vacation, being no longer afraid of her skeptical influence.

Carrol was now twenty-one and Mary eighteen, and Mrs. Noble was proud of the opportunity the evening would afford of showing to the friends and neighbors young ladies any town might well feel honored to know.

An hour or so later, the rooms were filled with many familiar faces, old and young. Mary was the centre of attraction for the elders who had watched her progress from babyhood to maidenhood, and who had been equally awed or delighted with her wise sayings and winning ways. The purity and innocence of her countenance were not lost, but rather enhanced by the charm of fresh young girlhood that gave everyone in her presence a nobler idea of life and a stronger aspiration to attain their ideals.

Carrol had made or attracted fewer friends, but those few were sufficient in her world. To be known for what she really was, always meant friends of the truest character, but among certain classes the frankest person is not always the best understood.

As she came into the room, a murmur of surprise was audible from a group in the corner.

" Why, is that Carrol Evans? Who would ever recognize in her the little, dark, silent child we used to know?" one lady exclaimed, who had been a great friend of Mrs. Noble's during Carrol's first summer with her aunt.

"She has grown handsomer," whispered an answering neighbor; "but there's something in her face, you don't see in Mary's—an unrest, an eagerness that gives one the fidgets. Dear me, who's that speaking to her? Ralph Rice, did you say? Oh, yes, he's the young lawyer that's just set up on D—— street. And who's that pale, slim-faced woman that seems so glad to see her?"

"Deacon Rice's wife, Ralph's mother, who never gets over grieving for the son that ran away. That's what makes her so pale, I guess."

"Oh here comes Mary. Doesn't she look sweet in that simple white dress, with the roses at her belt? Do you know, I think white the most appropriate of anything for young girls."

"They always look well in it, especially—"

"Who is that handsome dark gentleman, that just came in? Surely he can't have known the girls, for he is a stranger here?"

"Who, that one with the high forehead and keen, black eyes? Oh, I suppose he is a friend of one of the guests. You know the people here are not formal, and at any rate this is a sort of a general reception."

"There! he's been introduced to Mary. I wonder who he is?" and Miss Billings peered over her fan, apparently unconscious of any exhibition of curiosity.

People kept coming and going, as they always do at

receptions; chatted a few moments, sat down to be social, or partook of refreshments and departed.

It was but a few moments the gentleman lingered, and then he passed out into the next room, so Miss Billings quite lost sight of him; but she wondered, nevertheless.

"And here, Carrol, is another of your old friends, " said Mrs. Noble, smiling, and bringing forward a solemn looking young man, who wore his hair *a la pompadour*.

"Oh, yes, Harvey Willard. How do you do, Harvey?" holding out her hand frankly.

He bowed low, smiled slightly, and laid a thin nervous hand in hers for a moment. "I am glad to see you back, Miss Carrol, " he began.

"That is right, call me Carrol," she interrupted; "we want to begin our acquaintance where we left off. "

This put him quite at ease. He entered into conversation naturally and easily, spoke of the changes that had taken place, in the people of the community, as well as in themselves.

"Oh, I don't know, " she responded, "the people here to-night are much the same as they were years ago, except of course the young folks; they are changed, as you say Mary and I are, but perhaps after we've learned to see back of the years that have come to us, we shall find ourselves the very same children we used to be, ready to play or pout, laugh or cry. "

"Ah, Carrol, I see you have not forgotten the sad times we had; I trust there will be no inclination or occasion to bring the tears now." He rubbed his hands together in an embarrassed manner, but straightened himself up with conscientious dignity.

Her face flushed with the old annoyance, and she abruptly turned away for a moment, then regained her composure, and said with a mischievous smile: "Of course, our opinions won't clash as they used to."

"'When we were children we spake as children, but when we are grown, we put away childish things,'" a little stiffly. He had not lost his *penchant* for quoting.

"Yes, some of them," was the roguish reply, as she went forward to meet Miss Allbright.

"Oh, here you are," said that lady with her old sweet smile; "I've been looking for you everywhere. Come sit down here and tell me all about yourself and Mary. We are so glad to have you back again."

Carrol excused herself, inwardly rejoiced to get away from Harvey. There had always been a deep admiration in her heart for Miss Allbright, and she hoped not a little from a closer acquaintance, for no one could know Miss Allbright and not be wonderfully enriched thereby.

They went apart and sat down in the recess of the bay window. Miss Allbright looked exactly the same as when Carrol had first seen her, that summer morning, so long ago. Carrol spoke of it wonderingly.

"Do you think there is really no change? Well, my dear, I have discovered the fountain of perpetual youth which poor Ponce de Leon searched so long to find." She smiled quietly, and Carrol asked:

"Can you impart the secret to another, or is it only to be found by individual seeking?"

Miss Allbright looked startled, for an instant. "I never thought of it in that way, my dear, but it is true. it cannot be imparted. I will tell you what it is. The finding and the living of the Universal Good. No one can do that for another. Each individual must live his own life, according to his highest light, and he must search till he finds that which will make life a rounded whole. To me it is the recognition and consciousness of supreme good. That means loving ministry to all humanity. It is that which takes away the lines and wrinkles, and leaves smoothness and beauty instead. Do you know what wrinkles mean?" she asked, suddenly.

"No," was Carrol's wondering reply.

"They mean the withdrawal of perfect trust, perfect love, perfect satisfaction."

"But tell me," pursued Miss Allbright, suddenly, "what are you going to do, now that school-days are over?"

"I expect to teach in some capacity; I hardly know in what, yet."

"Have you a position in view?"

"Not yet."

Don't think me inquisitive. Perhaps I can help you. Come and see me soon. I want to know you better. Ah, there comes Mary," and she rose to meet her, as Carrol stepped forward to be presented to the dark stranger who had caused Miss Billings so much perturbation.

"Mr. Temple, of Lynn Heights," said the mutual friend who introduced him. Mr. Temple made a few courteous remarks, bowed politely, and then retired to give place to older friends.

Carrol gave him a casual glance as he turned to go, but in the brief instant she could not have defined what distinguished him from others around her. There was something that impressed her both pleasantly and the contrary. This was no time or place for an analysis, and ere many moments she had quite forgotten the circumstance.

Later in the evening she found herself beside Mrs. Rice, who was overjoyed at the privilege of a few words with her.

"I'm glad to find you again, auntie; your presence is like a haven of rest," sighed Carrol, as she sat down beside her old friend.

"I want you to find us at home, Carrol, for I've longed for you so much, and *you* were a haven of rest to me—once—that—that winter and summer when—"

"Haven't you heard, yet?" whispered Carrol tenderly, knowing well what the poor mother wanted.

"Not a word."

"Never mind. It will come, for he promised, and I have faith in him;" and she was away again, but the balm had been given—the balm that no one knew better than Carrol how to give. . . .

"Well, what of the evening?" asked Carrol, as she and Mary ascended to their chamber, after the guests had disappeared.

"Yes; what of it? We have stepped back into the old places and taken up the threads of life as we left them. It was a pleasant evening on the whole, but rather tiresome."

They had reached the top of the stairs, and with arms entwined about each other they entered the same room they had occupied as children. There were two beds in it still, and Carrol was to have the one in the alcove, as when a little girl. It was a pleasant chamber, with a large closet or smaller apartment at one end, which was used for a dressing-room, or for writing.

"It is always tiresome talking to so many people and feeling the responsibility of hostess. For my part, I shall be glad when we can lay aside the formalities of society, and talk to people as we really feel. It is making such an effort to say nothing, that tires us," was Carrol's emphatic remark, as she put the roses she had worn into fresh water.

" An effort to say nothing and *be* something," added Mary, "but after all, Carrol, it would not do to be ungracious to society, simply because we might see a better method of entertainment."

" Oh, I didn't mean that; I was only wishing the best in people would impel them to speak face to face, as it were, instead of spending so much time in mere common-places. I had a very nice visit with Miss Allbright. *She* never talks common-places.

Carrol was beginning to yawn, and for a moment nothing more was said, as each prepared to retire for the night.

" I wish you could have seen Harvey Willard's face when I was talking to him," exclaimed Carrol, reviving at the memory.

"He is evidently in his old *rôle*," she continued, "and now my turn has come. See if I don't tease him a wee bit, to make up for all his past triumphs."

Mary seemed so absorbed in thought that she scarcely answered, except by a slight smile. Presently the light was extinguished and only the moonlight came in through the window.

"Oh," said Carrol suddenly, but rather sleepily from her bed, "were you introduced to Mr. Temple, Mary?"

"Yes, I believe so." Mary was glad Carrol could not see her face, for she felt herself blushing, although there was no earthly reason for it.

"Something striking about him, I thought."

"I spoke with him but a moment," was all Mary said, and it was said in such a quiet tone, Carrol held her peace and went to sleep. But Mary lay awake till long after; then she dreamed fitful, uneasy dreams that made her awake with an unconscious start.

CHAPTER XIV.

"He is the half part of a blessed man,
Left to be finished by such a she."
—Shakespeare.

HAVE you ever noticed how we invariably desire the fairest flower that we see along the roadside or in our woodland walk? Although there may be loveliness in the greatest profusion all about us, it is the best and sweetest we pluck for our own enjoyment. And we choose all things in life from our standpoint of the best, be they flowers, jewels, clothes, or companions.

A carriage wound slowly along the timber road leading from Tintuckett to Lynn Heights. The only occupant of the vehicle was a man, apparently between thirty and thirty-five years of age. He was thinking deeply, and as the carriage passed under some overhanging branches by the wayside, he idly switched the leaves with his whip. Sometimes a startled bird flew from its lonely covert, and sought securer refuge elsewhere; sometimes a rabbit sprang out of the bushes, or sat motionless with ears erect, waiting to examine the nature of the intrusion, or, perchance a squirrel paused in his hurried ascent to the tree-top and listened; but the gentleman had no eyes or ears for the inhabitants of woodland, and as the horse moved lazily along, his master grew more and more absorbed until his meditations became audible.

"I *will* have that girl for my wife; but she is too fair a blossom to remain long unplucked, and I must not wait. How shall I manage to pursue the acquaintance? Let me see: I can have business in Tintuckett. Possibly I can board there a few weeks while I am working up this Scott case. Capital! and when the district court convenes in September, I shall have to be there anyway."

His face cleared up and he began to notice more of the surroundings, as he started his horse into a brisk trot. A ride of ten miles brought him to his home in Lynn, and hastily throwing the reins over the dashboard, he sprang out and called a half-grown boy that stood near the gate, to put up the horse.

Harry Temple (for it is almost needless to say that the gentleman we have so carefully noted is no other than Mr. Temple, whose acquaintance we made at the reception,) came forward and took charge of the horse and carriage, while his brother went into the house.

"How do you do, mother? Can you get me a cup of tea in a hurry? I have some business to see to down at Watson's."

Mr. Temple threw himself into an easy-chair and drew out some documents for examination, while his mother went into the kitchen and herself assisted the girl to prepare a lunch for her son. It was easily seen that he was the very apple of her eye, and every word was law, requiring implicit obedience. Nevertheless, she exerted a strong influence over him, although he was as unconscious of it as herself. They were people of excellent social standing, comfortable means, and, as Mr. Temple was ambitious and capable in his profession as a lawyer, there was every reason to suppose that he would some day be a wealthy man. He and his mother and his brother Harry, who was preparing for college, composed the family that Judge Temple had left at his death some years before.

Felix, the elder son, after his graduation had spent a year in Europe, before settling down in his native place as a successor of his father in the firm of "Temple & Hawley," and he had now been well established for nearly two years. Had his own wish been consulted, he would have preferred to begin in a new place, but the especially fine business opening afforded him as his father's son, and the desire of his mother to pass her days in the old homestead, induced him to remain at Lynn Heights. He was a fine-looking man, with a splendid physique and strong features, the latter slightly marred for the close observer however, by a cynical expression, that seemed to be habitual, and which his heavy dark mustache did not modify. He was a man who could easily adapt himself to any society, and in whatever *rôle* he appeared he gave the impression of great reserve force. His will from a child had been imperious, and the fostering indulgence given by his mother had not curbed nor weakened, but rather developed and strengthened it. If he determined upon a certain course, heaven and earth, so to speak, were moved till it was accomplished.

His life, so far as anyone knew, was temperate and

uneventful, his amusements being confined to an occasional visit to a good play, and the reading of what he would be pleased to term good literature. Since his return from Europe, he had not been what would be styled a society man, and though thrifty mammas and charming lassies had cast longing thoughts towards so good a "catch," they had given up in despair and retired from the field, contenting themselves with calling him an inveterate old bachelor. It had at one time been whispered that he had left a sweetheart on the other side of the water, and again, that he had been dreadfully jilted by a fair-haired Gretchen, or a blooming English blonde; but nothing transpired to prove either of these theories, so even rumors had ceased to float on the tide of public opinion, and Felix Temple was left to the tender mercies of an unknown fate.

Whether Mr. Temple had ever indulged in the tender passion or not, we are not prepared to say, but that he had an eye to comeliness and beauty, innocence and purity, is evidenced by the fact that he had discovered, and chose to pluck, the fairest flower in all the "rosebud garden of girls" from which he might have selected.

Our sweet-voiced Mary, the beautiful, was the one of whom he spoke, when he announced to the listening squirrel and the flying bird that he would have her for his wife. How he was to succeed, is yet to be learned. Certain it is, that he never closed his eyes that night, until he had planned all his business affairs, so that he might leave for a fortnight or longer if necessary. The next morning he made known to his mother the necessity(?) of his presence in Tintuckett or one better to conduct an important case. He was not sure how things would turn out there, but with the usual faith in his ability to make circumstances subservient to his will, he started in the afternoon, with his handsomest lap-robe in the carriage, and a new dress suit in his valise. He smiled a little as he thought how unsuspecting his mother was of his real business, and it never occurred to him for a moment that Mary might already be appropriated.

If such a thought had presented itself, it would not have altered his plans in the least, for to him there was no such thing as a negative when he determined upon an affirmative. He did not pause to ask himself whether he was in love, or whether he would be. That he had found a jewel of which any man might be proud, he was satisfied. The next thing was to possess and wear it.

This day he was not inclined to loiter by the wayside, so he kept on at a good pace, till he came within a mile or so of his destination. Then he let the reins hang loosely over his horse's back, while he leaned against the luxurious cushions and indulged in a rose-colored dream.

It was somewhere near six o'clock, and the evening shadows had begun to fall in the woods through which he passed. In Mr. Temple's absorption, the horse had wandered at his own sweet will for the last half hour, and as his master then discovered, had left the main road for a less frequented one, which now seemed to be lost in the hazel brush.

"Whoa !" The animal halted obedient to that familiar command. Mr. Temple looked about him. "Where in the dickens are you going, Flanders ?" he queried at last. Flanders pricked up his ears and looked wise, but said nothing. Perhaps he might with equal propriety have asked his master the same question. Persisting in his search for some way out of the difficulty, Mr. Temple finally noticed an old weather-beaten house a little back of the hazel bushes to his right, and alighting, he left Flanders for a few minutes, to go and inquire the way back to the road. He was soon driving in the right direction, and had not gone far when he espied two young ladies a short distance in front of him. He gave them a casual glance at first, but presently it changed to a keen scrutiny. The very Fates were helping him. Was not that the very form and face he had been dreaming and planning about ? It must be ; yes, now as she turned to look at the approaching stranger, he was sure of it.

Flanders was suddenly aroused out of his torpid mood by a slight tap of the whip. He started on more briskly, but was slackened in his pace while passing the young ladies. They scarcely looked up until the carriage was almost by, and then they bowed slightly and the gentleman touched his hat with the utmost politeness. Flanders was given loose rein again.

Mary's face flushed with the faintest tinge of rosiness, as the carriage went out of sight, but she merely remarked in an ordinary tone, that that was the gentleman from Lynn Heights, who had come with the Grants to the reception.

"Yes, I recognized him. I wonder what sort of a person he is. I must say he is a character one would notice anywhere, because of his strong personality," answered Carrol, not noticing the flush on Mary's cheeks.

They walked on a few steps, Mary stopping to gather some wild honey-suckles that grew by the path." Isn't Miss Rogers a queer woman ? " she said at last, changing the subject abruptly.

"Decidedly so," was Carrol's answer; "but, after all, she has a kind heart and good intentions towards everybody. We cannot always judge from appearances what a person really is. Apparently, she is curt and morose, but she doesn't mean to be. If we could know her real feelings, I have no doubt we should see a lovely character. She must have had some great sorrow in life, that has caused such eccentricity."

They were both thoughtful. "Everything depends on how people bear their crosses," said Mary, "whether they can give or receive good out of seeming evil. I believe everything can be turned into good by truly believing in God. When sorrow comes, with the grace of God we can overcome it, and so keep our lives sweet and free from all warped conditions, for of course, it is more or less a warped condition to be eccentric or odd."

She glanced at the red blossoms and then, with a yearning look on her face, she exclaimed: "Oh, I sometimes long to tell people, if they would only learn more lessons from the flowers, they would be more like them—sweet and natural and pure, with no hidden nature that would not bear revealing, but faces open and frank for all to read."

"Sometimes I wish folks were less like brambles and thorny plum-trees," said Carrol, suddenly thinking of Harvey Willard and what he had said that very morning, for he was fuller than ever of his "pig theology," as she expressed it, and he had evidently made up his mind to give her a good dose whenever the opportunity presented itself.

"But then, Carrol, as you said yourself a moment ago, we can't always judge from appearances," replied Mary, with a smile, the dreamy look giving place to one of amusement.

"Sometimes you *feel* when you do not *see* the thorns," was the reply.

"That may be, but you must not forget that there are many things besides the thorns to be conscious of."

"Oh, I know it," sighed Carrol; adding, "now there's that good old Grandma Rogers; she is so kind and tender, I can overlook the rough places and thorns (for it is a thorn in the flesh to hear such bad grammar as she uses), just because a great love shines through all her actions and makes every feature beautiful; but— well, I must say, Mary, Harvey is himself a thorn I always persist in seeing."

"Why Carrol, I think he is very conscientious, and that in itself ought to be sufficient excuse for his zeal. Why not make that the seed from which will come forth many fine plums?"

Carrol laughed. "Well, my dear, when you see the plums growing on that tree let me know."

Mary's love found many excuses and much palliation for Carrol's skepticism, and she had faith to believe that Carrol's love of justice would yet redeem and purify all uncharitableness and bitterness, and that she would one day be baptized with the Christ-love, which is the fulfilling of the law. It was not her way, however, to say much. She won people more by reaching down and lifting them gently to her plane than by rudely telling them how much they would have to climb before t he reached it. " You will find them yourself if you only wait long enough," she said finally, referring to the plums again.

" The idea of that young snip telling me. this morning that I must study theology if I were not satisfied with what the preachers give," cried Carrol, wrathfully.

"As if there would be no appeal from their old, creed-bound opinions," she continued. "For one thing I would like to study theology, and that would be to bring reason out of it, or expose its wretched weakness. I'd like to be a preacher myself, then —— "

Her voice was filled with a forcefulness that made Mary look at her in astonishment. "Well, I would, Mary," she went on, rather apologetically; "I would delight in nothing better than breaking the chains of superstition and the false assumption of popular theology. Why can't a woman preach as well as a man ? "

She walked on a few steps, switching the grasses as she went with a small twig she held in her hand. Her cheeks were flushed, and her eyes sparkled with a hidden force.

" She can preach publicly when she has proved her fitness privately and I believe the world will listen too, said Mary, calmly ; "but as yet women are so aggressive and vindictive when they speak in public that it is considered unwomanly, but it is right for them to speak if they do it in the right way. You know I don't agree with Paul about woman keeping silence in the churches, for I realize that he was merely speaking of what was customary and proper for a woman of those times. Jesus never repelled or silenced women. He paid much respect to them, and recognized their work and motives, and even Paul was glad to get their help whenever he found one who was capable of giving it."

"Mary, when *you* talk of Jesus, you make me love him and all his teachings, but when most people talk, and especially Harvey, I can't bear the subject. There is such cant about the expressions of the church people !"

She was evidently strongly stirred, and although Mary had not seen her in this state for a long time, she wisely said nothing to oppose.

"I see a great future before you Carrol, if you can only be patient and trustful."

The sun was gone, and the dewy coolness of a summer evening seemed like a cup of refreshing water to the parched earth and thirsty flowers. Arm-in-arm, the two girls walked up the lilac-scented path and disappeared in the doorway of Mary's home.

CHAPTER XV.

"Ah, silly man, who dreamst thy honor stands in ruling others, not thyself !"—*P. Fletcher*.

THE days sped by on swift-winged hours. It seemed that the blessed summer would soon be over, and Carrol had planned so much to be done. Since the reception, both she and Mary were beseiged with invitations, first here, then there, in the social round.

"Once more," said Carrol to herself, as she stood before the glass putting the last touches to her toilet. It was to be a drive to Crystal Lake, with a picnic at the last. On this occasion she was thinking of Mary and how much she had been monopolized by young and old. Mary the maiden, was as charming as Mary the child.

Two gentlemen, in particular, were evidently seeking her society with "serious intentions," as a noted gossip had suggested in Carrol's hearing, which perhaps was the cause of the reverie. One of these was Charlie Fairfax, a school-boy admirer who, nevertheless, aspired to be as mature in judgment and ability as any sage of forty. The other was Mr. Temple of Lynn Heights.

At school, Mary had been a general favorite with boys and girls alike, in the innocence of her own pure heart, treating each with a charming courtesy and con sideration which made him feel that he was especially

149

favored. It was really her faculty of reciprocity that attracted her admirers. But after all, what is it we seek in human companionship, if not the sympathy and appreciation a reciprocal and generous nature alone can give?

Carrol went on with her musing as calmly as though she had half a day instead of half an hour, in which to complete her preparations.

Mr. Temple—why did his name come to her so persistently? Oh yes, she was thinking of these two gentlemen who had serious intentions. She and Mary had met him nearly everywhere. He was brilliant and fascinating, and yet there was a subtle something about him that struck her unpleasantly. She never could have told what it was. In his attentions to Mary he had not been obtrusive or insistent, although perhaps he was growing more so. His regard was shown in the most delicate ways, and with the most winning thoughtfulness. True he was gallant and polite to all, but his glance never rested on anyone in quite the same way it did on Mary. He stopped with one of the first families, and she knew all about him as far as his social and business standing were concerned; still, she was not satisfied. But then—

"Come, Carrol, aren't you most ready?" called Mary from the foot of the stairs.

"Yes, yes, I'll be there in a twinkling," she answered, hurrying into her dress and rushing about for a button-hook. "Serves me right," she muttered; "I've been thinking about other folks instead of attend-

ing to my work, so I'm late, but I do wonder how
Charlie and Mr. Temple will get on to-day."

She hastily tied a fresh ribbon around her neck,
lingered one moment to see that her dress was straight,
and tripped down-stairs where Mary had been occupy-
ing her spare time in making button-hole bouquets for
the party.

"There come two carriages," announced Carrol,
from the door where she stood to take a survey of the
expected arrivals.

"Whose are they?"

"I do believe, Mary, they belong to Charlie Fairfax
and Mr. Temple, and of course they will both want
you."

"Well, I can't go with both; and you know I promised Mr. Temple before Charlie returned from his trip
to Clayton. I don't see why Charlie always has to take
it for granted that I will go with him!" exclaimed
Mary, a little impatiently.

"Probably he isn't in favor of monopolies," laughed
Carrol, teasingly.

"Now, Carrol, please don't; I can't help it this time;
and really, cousin, you must help me out. Can't you
get Belle Barnes to ride with him? She has no way
provided, and I told her to be ready and somebody
would have room."

Carrol had never seen Mary so perplexed. "You're
getting to be a regular coquette, Mary; I'm surprised,"
said she, in mock severity.

"Nonsense, Carrol; don't be foolish. It will only
be till we get there; then we shall not be exclusive at

all. I will help entertain Charlie and all the rest. Besides, I can probably arrange to ride home with him."

With this sensible view of the case, Mary was quite satisfied, but Carrol burst out laughing, as she said, with a most provoking gesture of disbelief: "Don't deceive yourself, my fair cousin. Mr. Temple will not relinquish his place, out of even his inexhaustible fund of politeness, for one who is so evidently his ri—but there! they are all here; now who shall manage Charlie?"

It was fixed up in some fashion, and the procession started. A merry one it was, with the exception of one face in it, which looked like a miniature thunder cloud. Carrol noticed it and was relieved when they arrived at their destination.

It was a beautiful spot in nature's lap which they had chosen for their play-ground. Croquet balls, mallets and arches were soon brought out, tennis courts marked, and those of the party disposed to play were soon busily engaged, while others sauntered away for a walk or quietly betook themselves to the little row-boat somebody had found moored to the shore.

The day passed quickly to the happy-hearted ones. Carrol was vaguely uneasy, and in the afternoon she withdrew from the rest of the party for a brief respite from all the gaiety. She looked out over the glassy waters, and saw the trees and clouds mirrored to the life. All about was calm and beautiful, and yet Carrol pondered cloudily.

She had seen strange signs to-day. Mary was not at all like herself; she had not succeeded in entertaining Charlie, indeed had scarcely spoken to him. Carrol suspected it was owing to Mr. Temple's influence. She had watched him narrowly, hoping to find some cause of complaint before speaking to Mary, but she could discover nothing but the most delicate courtesy in his attentions—no visible effort to monopolize, and yet it was evident Mary was monopolized.

Long ere this, Ralph Rice had decided the question in his own mind, but was content to remain a mere spectator as long as Carrol remained unmolested. That would have been a hard blow to him, for she had been enshrined in his heart ever since that summer in the long ago. And yet, even from Ralph's impartial standpoint, this Mr. Temple did not seem the proper one for Mary. What subtle something it was of which he disapproved he could not have told.

These thoughts flashed rapidly through his mind as he glanced up from the croquet ground to the little boat skimming over the glassy mirror. There were only two people in it; one a tall, dark, handsome man, the other a fair, clear-eyed girl.

"Where is Miss Evans?" queried Ralph, missing her for the first time, and leaning on his mallet, as he looked about the grounds.

"I declare! Missed that arch again! Miss Evans? I don't know," returned his partner, willing at last to think of something besides the ball she had been pursuing, with faint success the last ten minutes.

"I congratulate you on your patience, Miss Belle," said an onlooker. "That ball has been wandering long enough to go to Europe and back."

"Patience is one of my virtues," with a pouting smile; and this time a carefully poised mallet sent the delinquent straight to the mark.

"That counts us out. You came in at last with flying colors; guess I'll choose you for partner next time," said Ralph.

"Thank you, but I'm already engaged."

"My compliments to the successor, then," and Ralph sighed with a vain hope that she might not think him glad to go.

He sauntered carelessly towards the large tree where he had last seen Carrol. She was not there, and he threw himself upon the green grass under the broad spreading branches, and gave himself up to musing, occasionally glancing at the little bark as it floated, or loitered, in some leafy covert overhanging the water's edge. He was so intent upon an analysis of his own feelings concerning a certain person, that it was very little he thought or cared for the couple in the boat. He had idly noticed Mary leaning over for the water lilies, and then his thoughts wandered, until suddenly he heard a smothered little scream, and saw her caught around the waist by the handsome Temple, just in time to save her an unwelcome plunge into the clear waters below. The boat narrowly escaped capsizing, but after a motionless silence, and a few strong strokes with the oars, it was righted again, and soon disappeared in the friendly refuge of a clump of willows.

"The black-browed villain! He deserves a thrashing for his carelessness," muttered a voice from some invisible retreat near by, which Ralph tried in vain to discover.

"That must be Charlie Fairfax," he thought, after a moment's pause, during which he could no longer hear the muttering. "Jealous! Well, this is interesting. Who would ever have thought of little Mary in this *rôle?*"

It could never be that she would trifle or even encourage a man she did not love. Did she really love Charlie? If not, why was he here? This perplexing question remained unanswered, yet Ralph was satisfied as to Mary's integrity. Could he have heard the conversation at this moment taking place in the boat, he would have pitied as well as excused her.

"Mary, darling, were you much frightened?" said Mr. Temple, tenderly embracing her with his free arm, and thus bringing his dark, glowing eyes close to hers.

"Not much," was the faint reply, as she gently tried to free herself, blushing meanwhile like a delicate rose.

"Not much," he echoed, "but enough to be glad you had a protector," as he held her closer, and looked into her eyes, putting all the intensity of his deep nature into that burning glance.

"Mr. Temple—" she began, but she returned his gaze in spite of her desire to withdraw herself. "Mr. Temple, I—*please* let me go."

"Certainly, my sweet one, but tell me I may soon have the privilege of holding you always thus," and his voice was very low and tender.

A startled look came into her eyes, and she trembled like a frightened fawn. She had admired him from the first, and there was a subtle attraction always in his glance. At this critical moment it was dangerously fascinating. She turned away, and put her hand into the water where the wavering shadows played.

"Tell me, my pearl, my precious jewel," he pleaded, bending near but not touching her.

"Not now. I cannot!" she faltered at last.

"Cannot—has some one else a previous claim?"

He was no weak wooer. He had entered the lists victorious, and certainly had no intention of withdrawing vanquished. He met her imploring glance with one equally imploring but more forceful.

"No," she said slowly and reluctantly.

It seemed as if she were impelled by some curious fascination to look at him and answer his question. For an instant, a gleam of triumph came into his dark orbs, but she did not notice it.

"Then you are mine, sweetheart, are you not?" He was jubilant, but tender as a lover could be. He was content now to look at her and touch her hand with his lips. She felt his tenderness, and the magic charm of the moment was upon her.

With the sublime assumption of egotism, he claimed her then and there, as he repeated, for a second time, that she was his very own—his fair, sweet bride to be. But the moment was gone. She looked into his face, and in a dazed but decided way, begged him to say no more but take her back to the rest of the party.

Mr. Temple could afford to wait. He knew that he had at least sealed her lips to any other suitor, and, though she might demur with a maidenly modesty, there was no doubt as to her final yes. He could even afford to be magnanimous enough to let Charlie Fairfax ride home with her, if she wished it so, and with every stroke of his oar, he could have proclaimed his victory to the world; but one of the strong traits in Felix Temple's character was his ability to think one thing and act another. His deepest feelings were his own private property, and no one else had as yet been given the key to his secret chamber. So now, while inwardly absorbed in his own plans and the execution of his victory, he was outwardly the same tenderly thoughtful, delicately attentive gentleman he had ever been since Mary first knew him. She was grateful, more than she could have expressed, for his unobtrusive silence, and this was a strong point in his favor of which he was well aware.

They met Carrol at the landing, waiting for them. She was quick to notice Mary's perturbed manner and flushed face, as they all wended their way back to the picnic grounds.

Charlie did not ride home with Mary. On second thought, Mr. Temple had considered it imprudent; hence, he occupied the place of honor by her side himself, but not once during the homeward ride did he allude, by word, look or gesture, to the momentous question he had asked in the boat. Charley withdrew from the field from that time, not from choice, but from necessity.

CHAPTER XVI.

*"Provided only you love him. Ah, child, be sure of that.
Do not mistake fancy for love."—E. Bulwer-Lytton.*

CARROL, how could you ?"

"How couldn't I, you mean," replied Carrol,
with a careless laugh and a spiteful toss of her head.
"He's forever flinging some ancient dogma or dried-up
theological ism at me, and I tell you, Mary, I will not
stand it without retaliating. Thank heaven I am able
to defend myself now, if I wasn't when I was a child."

"Oh but Carrol, you might do so much for him if
you would be more patient," and Mary's reproachful
eyes rested for a moment on her cousin's face. They
were sitting in the alcove up-stairs, looking over their
freshly laundried muslins.

"How ?" was Carrol's terse reply.

"By letting him argue it all out in his own way, and
then waiting for the right time to sow your own seed."

"Pooh ! as if I could teach the conceited bigot anything. Why, Mary, you don't know how intolerant he
is, and if he keeps on, I shall regain my old opinion of
all who call themselves Christians. I've been trying to
keep a respectful state of mind toward them, but I shall
speedily have to give it up if Harvey Willard continues
to advocate their cause."

The pained look on Mary's face brought her to a

sense of the wound she was inflicting so mercilessly. "Forgive me, little cousin. You are always excepted;" and she leaned over to Mary caressingly.

"Never mind me. There are no exceptions. But tell me, Carrol, why do you talk religion so much to Harvey ?"

"For the simple reason that he will not talk on anything else, and seems possessed with the idea of converting me. "

"All the more to his credit I should say," was Mary's quiet reply.

"But he can find somebody else to practice on. *I* don't care for the honor. "

Carrol spitefully threw her dress on the bed, and with a gloomy face looked out through the window. It was another word-battle, just such as Carrol had been describing to Mary, which caused her exclamation at the beginning of this chapter. Carrol had said something particularly aggressive, at which Harvey went home— "to pray, I suppose, " she added a little maliciously.

"Never mind; let Harvey rest for awhile. I want you to drive over to Owl Creek with me this afternoon. Aunt Creesh is there, and I would like to see her; wouldn't you ?"

"Yes, indeed. It will be delightful. What a refreshing memory I have of Aunt Creesh, and that can't be said of everybody. "

"No, because all have not the sweet faith and charming good nature that she has. She is really a marvelous woman. Just think how she went out into the world, single-handed, as it were, after that dreadful lawsuit and the loss of her home. "

" I know it. She never wasted a day in fretting or mourning, but went right to work—went out as a nurse, didn't she ?"

" Yes, that is her occupation now, and she is very successful. Mamma had a letter from her a few weeks ago saying she is in Owl Creek, and would like to see some of us while she is there. "

The afternoon found them early started for the six mile drive. Mrs. Noble had always kept a horse and carriage, and Mary was perfectly familiar with the art of driving, so it was renewing one of the pleasures of past years to take the reins again. The day was cloudless, yet comfortably cool, for it had rained the night before, and nature wore one of her brightest smiles. Their way lay over a winding woodland road, and the wild charm of wandering on with no one to guide or help, even should help be necessary, was subtly felt by both. There was a shade of reserve in the thoughts of each concerning the other. It had come at the night of the reception, when Mary first came under the influence of Mr. Temple, as Carrol thought,—sometimes jealously, for Carrol would persist in secretly calling it an influence. Ralph had hinted it too, but she would not listen to his opinion on the matter. She could not bear such judgment of Mary, and strictly avoided the mention of Mr. Temple's name. As for Mary, she intuitively felt Carrol's anxiety for her, but seemed powerless to break the barrier of reserve. She could not even bring herself to tell what she knew must be told very soon now. It was with an infant hope that the way would be opened in some fashion that she had planned this journey, but the mile-stones were passed one by one, with nothing but common-place remarks to fill the gaps of silence.

Aunt Creesh received them with open arms. "Why, it's good for sore eyes to see you," she said in the first moments of greeting; "and you are"—standing back to take a survey—"yes, you are both pretty, young sproutlets. I thought you'd be—but there's one thing you must learn, girls : be yourselves, and walk in your own strength—that is, the strength that God gives you—there's nothing else like it. If there's one thing I'm thankful for, it's the being turned loose to find *myself* and the strength God gave me. Well, well; sit down, and tell me about yourselves and your plans. Are you through with school, and what are you going to do next?" She drew a chair for each and seated herself in front of them.

Such a cheery-faced and bright-eyed old lady she seemed to be. They wondered that they could have known or seen so little of her. Never since that morning that she had gone out to "find herself" had they met her. She had not visited Tintuckett once, and though she was frequently called to minister near there, she had kept steadfastly to her post ; for once known, she was in great demand. At long intervals she had written, however, so they had generally known her whereabouts. A faint bell tinkle was heard, from some region near by.

"Oh, excuse me. That's my patient. That's the way he calls me;" and she disappeared in the adjoining room.

.   .   .   .   .   .

"He's just beginning to learn his first lesson," she explained, on her return, "but I've had quite a time. What children some of these sick folks are!" as she sat down again.

"Why, Aunt Creesh?" asked Mary with interest.

"It takes them so long to learn that strength and health don't come from the outside, but from the inside where God is.   They have the silly notion that I can bring it to them by dosing and coddling and fussing, or some such performance—as if I could carry it around in a bag and dish it out! So I have to teach them to get their minds ready to think health, and their bodies will soon *have* health. God is an open horn of plenty, pouring blessings upon his children and then the foolish creatures refuse to receive them.   But then, they don't know, poor things, that they can take God at His word.   Well, well; tell me about yourself, Mary; what are you going to do now that school is over?"   She turned abruptly to look at Mary, who flushed rosily with surprise.

"Oh, I don't know, Aunt Creesh—start a select school, perhaps?"

"Well said.   So the flower is so soon to send forth its perfume.   Well, that's right, little girl.   Give away all the good you can, whatever be the way."

Mary had put in words the first thought that came to her.   She really had no thought of entering upon that work, and now that her aunt had taken it so seriously she felt not a little embarrassed, but knew that an attempt at explanation would only make the matter worse. Carrol saw her discomfiture, but was not inclined to help her out. Her conscience would not permit total silence, so she added: "Whatever the way I am to work, I hope I shall always do my best." She thought this sufficient, and felt much relieved when the conversation turned into other channels.

Going home, she pondered uneasily over how she should tell Carrol—tell her what—something she knew she would not like to hear. They were nearing the home outposts. What should she do? "Oh, Carrol, I wish you would get a situation near here this winter. I dread to have you go away," she exclaimed sincerely, but hoping it would lead to something more confidential.

"Well, Mary, I am thinking of applying for a situation right here in Tintuckett, for the winter at least. I want to be with you once more."

This was too much. Mary felt guilty, and saw that the moment had come. She blushed hotly but looked bravely into Carrol's eyes.

"Dear Carrol, forgive me—for not telling you before, but I couldn't bear to—and I don't like to yet—only I must. I—I am going to marry Mr. Temple."

There—it was told! Carrol did not look surprised, but why was she so quiet?

She only said, "I know it, Mary."

"What do you think of him, Carrol? Aren't you glad?"

"I think he has won the fairest, sweetest girl in all

the world   I only want to ask you one thing, Mary. Do you love him?"

Mary was bewildered with the suddenness of this question.   "Why Carrol, of course!   He is a good man, mamma says, and I feel quite happy to be with him."

She did not mention the time when a shudder passed over her at the sound of his voice, and how she thought for an instant that it was a warning.

"But, Mary, you are so young;" protested Carrol.

"Mamma thinks it best to marry young."

"Well, but what do *you* think and feel Mary?   Is it all right in your own eyes?"

"I think God leads me."

That was all.   The answer was Mary's very own. Carrol drew a long breath, but only said, "Oh Mary!'

They drew up before the gate, just as the red August sun was setting. . . Pale pink rays of glory trailed across the sky and disappeared in the eastern horizon.

CHAPTER XVII.

"For me love played the low preludes,
   Yet life began but with the ring;
Such infinite solicitudes
   Around it cling."—*Jean Ingelow*.

O the flower was plucked. Mr. Temple took his prize home one crisp October evening, and they immediately began housekeeping in a pleasant home just across the street from the old homestead, which the absence of Madame Temple and Harry had closed.

There had been no wedding tour, because Mr. Temple could not conveniently leave his business at that time. It was a novel change to Mary, to superintend the housekeeping, be called Mrs. Temple and go about in her own carriage with her husband, as she frequently did those first weeks. In after years, memory gilded all the first happenings with a golden polish that never tarnished.

Lynn Heights had never relinquished the hope of supplying the Temple home to be with a fair hostess taken within its own gates, and when Felix Temple presumed to go to another town for his bride, especially the insignificant little hamlet of Tintuckett (anything was insignificant that could not boast at least five thousand inhabitants), there was a great inclination in Lynn Heights to ignore the intruding newcomer. However, when Mrs. Bradley, the city oracle on matters of social import, condescended to call on Mrs. Temple, the whole fashionable wave speedily overflowed the banks of restraint and called, too.

Then they commented, of course. What would a fashionable caller amount to, without her talent for talking?

It is needless to repeat their words. The general verdict, however, was that Mrs. Temple was nothing but a sweet child, and Lynn Heights pursued the even tenor of its way, with the few exceptions of those who had some personal disappointment to remember. " Nothing *to* her, simply nothing, except possibly the virtue of being harmless," said one defeated mamma with considerable asperity.

" I am surprised at Felix Temple's taste. I always thought he had good judgment faculty," exclaimed another critical dame with an elderly daughter left on her hands.

But Mary heard nothing of this. She busied herself in beautifying her home, making many dainty devices to hang upon the walls, to drape over the pictures, or put upon the mantel. Then too she sought acquaintance in a church near by, and became one of its most indefatigable workers.

Felix Temple was not a religious man, though he had never *directly* antagonized the church. His interest and energy had been almost solely devoted to making a name and attaining a fortune, hence he had never had time for thought on these questions. He had known Mary to be faithful in her devotion to her church (he never stopped to think whether or not she was faithful to the Principle that builds churches) and in a certain niche of his busy mind he had laid by a mental note, to the effect that she would soon get over that nonsense, after being with him awhile. " For the present, let it go," he had thought; " she is very crude in some things. It will take my own strong judgment to give her ballast, but she will take it all right."

He deemed it prudent to let her have her way in these matters for a time, till she grew adjusted to her new relations, and he even accompanied her to church a few times. So the winter passed.

Then he made a discovery that made him feel it was time to draw in the lines. It was on a Saturday afternoon. He had unexpectedly come up from the office, to get Mary's signature to some legal document, and found her busily teaching three or four little ragged children a Bible lesson.

In the first place it enraged him to find his aristocratic home turned into a mission school; then there was positively no dignity to a woman who did such things, and finally there was no sense in it. All this flashed across his mind as he entered the cozy sitting-room. In a few quiet words he made known his errand, and returned to the office.

Mary was putting her bonnet on for church the next morning when her husband said in a peculiar tone: "I think I will remain at home this morning, Mary."

He had not a doubt that she would immediately give up going herself. What was his surprise to hear her say in that entrancingly sweet voice of hers: "Never mind,

Felix dear; I will not be gone long, and here's a splendid sermon I wish you would read in the meantime," and she laid a copy of a religious journal in his hand, while she gave him a loving kiss. Before he recovered from his astonishment she was gone—actually gone from him! She had not only gone, but had presumptuously asked him to read a sermon!

He stared about in amazement. Could it be possible that she preferred to hear that old Drybones in the church mumble over his superstitious dogmas rather than sit at home with her newly-made husband, who had explicity stated his preference for her company?

He did not remember that he had made no request of her, or that he had not even indicated his desire for her presence. He quite ignored the possibility of her having any conscience in the matter.

All he could realize was that he, Felix Temple, a lawyer, who bent everybody to his own will, at whose eloquence criminals and judges trembled or rejoiced—Felix Temple, a man who had had his slightest will obeyed from his earliest remembrance—*he* had now been brushed aside with the most airy indifference, by a mere girl—a beautiful child.

Great heavens! Had he been looking about all these years for a sweet-tempered, beautiful, obedient wife, to be made so great a fool of at last? He gnashed his teeth with rage, and then composed himself to think.

It was not Felix Temple's policy to work openly or noisily unless it was positively necessary, and when Mary returned from the service, beyond a steely glitter in his black eyes, there was naught to show any disturbance in the home atmosphere. He was loving and attentive as ever. Mary played and sang for him as usual, and that evening, as it happened there was no service to attend, she began another week in total ignorance of her husband's antipathy to her religious vagaries.

The next Saturday he chanced home again at about the same hour as before, and found the same gathering of ragged children, and the same process of teaching carried on by Mary.

"Go home children," he said, peremptorily. "You will find a night school down on Jay street, and Sunday Schools at any of the churches. My wife has other duties to attend."

They all scattered at the first word. One little midget dropped the doughnut she had clutched so tightly, but dared not stoop to pick it up, although she cast a tearful glance backward as she disappeared through the door.

After they were gone, he faced Mary, who sat as if turned to stone.

"*My* house, Mary, is not to be used as a charity hospital. Please remember that in the future."

That was all. The rest could be reserved till it was necessary. He gravely put on his hat and left the house.

Mary remained sitting, in dumb astonishment. What did this mean, and was it really her loving Felix that had done such a cruel thing? How could he turn the little things out that way? She had never dreamed

of asking his permission, nor thought for one instant
that his house was not also hers.

Oh! was this marriage? . . . She prayed herself quiet.

Presently, she grew light-hearted and even gay,
calling herself a little goose to be so troubled. Felix,
she must remember, had not been brought up to a
religious life and its requirements as she had. He had
come from a family proud of social position, and ready
to judge the slightest action by the social standard. If
he objected to her having the children at the house, no
doubt she could find plenty of charity work by applying at the church.

So she met her husband at the door that evening,
with a most loving welcome. He received it as a matter of course, inly congratulating himself on so easy a
victory. She spared no pains to make the evening
pleasant by reading aloud, by singing, by all manner
of loving ministrations. He felt confident of his power
now; was assured that his lightest hint would be followed to the letter. He was tender as he had not been
since the early weeks of their marriage.

The next day was Sunday, beautiful and calm as a
morning could be. It was the very last of February.
A heavy rain the week before had taken the last vestige
of brown Earth's ermine cloak, leaving as her only consolation the promise of a more beautiful mantle later
in the season. And thus with her dark shoulders bare,
and all the tattered patches of her nether garments
making piteous apology, poor Earth shivered while she
waited. Then kind hearted fairies of Frostland pity-

ingly draped her with a beauteous white lace scarf, adorned with diamonds old Winter had left in his deserted jewel box. Upon all these brilliant gems the sun poured forth his flood of golden glory, till she that mourned in bleak despair the night before now stood forth arrayed in royal garb from Nature's richest treasury.

It was a morning that made worship of God the most natural of all human sentiments, a morning that might sweep the chords of a devout heart with the nameless harmony of inner adoration, and bring into more perfect attunement the lower aims and loftier aspirations of the human mind.

With such thoughts as these, Mary stood at the window and gazed upon the beautiful morning scene before her. Suddenly her husband threw down the paper he had been reading and, glancing up at her, said in a pleasant voice: "I want you to go with me into the country this morning, Mary. As it is such a fine day it will be a double pleasure to go, because I can do my business and enjoy your company at the same time."

She looked around in surprise. "But, Felix, it is Sunday! Besides, we could not return in time for church!"

His brow darkened ominously. "It will not matter. I do not care to attend any church regularly. It is better policy to go to different ones, occasionally." The words were very quietly said.

Better policy! What did he mean? Mary felt

herself growing dizzy, and put out her hand to keep from falling.

He saw her alarm, and that she did not yet understand he meant to veto her church going. He would put it in another, an irreproachably tender way. Going close and putting his arm about her in a loving embrace, he said, lightly: "Never mind, Mary darling; no one will miss you, and I want you all to myself Sundays. It is the only day we can have together, you know."

"But, but—" she faltered, "I cannot be—false to my religious duty, and oh, my husband, do not tempt me. I will go with you any other time, but not this morning." She looked at him appealingly, while her eyes filled with startled tears.

He drew himself up proudly. "My wife shall do as I desire."

"In anything but this, dear Felix; anything but this," she panted, feeling a benumbing horror stealing over her, which she could not resist.

"In this, too," he replied, coldly.

"Oh, Felix, I *cannot* be false to God, I *cannot* be false to my highest sense of duty!"

"You are neither false to God nor your duty, when you obey your husband." There was a bitter vein of sarcasm in the words that hurt cruelly and made Mary tremble with an indescribable terror.

"Give me time to think and pray over it, my husband," she pleaded.

"All the time you please. I will leave you now, and you can pray to your heart's content."

He stalked icily from the room, leaving her to recover her surprise as best she might.

What should she *do ?* What *should* she do ? It would not be right to disobey her husband; it would not be right to cease worshiping God because he commanded it. Oh, what was coming to her if this was to be her lot ? . . . . .

. . . Was she tempted to be—what ! a traitor to her conscience; a deserter worse than Peter ? . . . It should never be.

She glanced hastily at the clock. It was not yet too late ! What matter if her husband did object, in his ignorance ? She must be true to herself at any cost, and hurriedly slipping her long ulster over her dress, she bathed her face, smoothed her hair, put on her bonnet, and opening the back door quietly went to church.

CHAPTER XVIII.

" Oh ! how delightful to live in a house where everybody understood and loved and thought about everybody else."
—George MacDonald.

WHEN Mr. Temple had been out a sufficient length of time for Mary to regain her equanimity, he went slowly into the house, thinking by loving condescension to forgive and kiss her back to happiness. (If there was anything he hated, it was a hitch in the domestic machinery; it was always so unpleasant!) He even stopped to brush his hair and stroke his mustache.

With a dignified stride he reached the door of their bedroom, where he had left her. With a smile he turned the knob.

Mary was not there!

He went through into the sitting-room, the parlor. Not there! His smile vanished. He called up the stairway. She did not respond. "Really, this child's play has gone far enough," he thought sternly, and strode upstairs, resolving to end this foolishness by an unmistakable lecture.

But in vain he called and searched. At last it flashed upon him : she had gone to church !

She had directly and wilfully disobeyed him! Very well. If it was to be war on that score, so be it. He would be obeyed if it cost his life's happiness and hers too. No matter if it was a trivial thing, and as for that, he did not care enough about the church-going, to flip pennies over it, but he had said she should not go. That was enough. His word was law. Henceforth there should be no peace for her in the matter of religion. He would teach her a lesson that she must learn. His method would be such that she would unmistakably know his disapproval of these things.

She returned half an hour later, her face radiant with an inner joy. She had come from the altar clothed with the whiteness of divine love—the love that overlooks all faults, all pettiness, all shortcomings. She would take her husband with her into this illuminated sanctuary of her own conscience.

He sat by the fire ostensibly reading when she entered. Going straight to him, her eyes beaming with love-light, she threw her arms about his neck and stooped to kiss him.

He drew back coldly.

"The love that can disregard my wishes is not the kind I care for."

"But dear, ——"

He pushed her rudely from him.

"How many sinners were baptized to-day that you had to assist in the ceremony, Mrs. Temple?"

He had risen and was standing by the mantel, leaning upon one arm and looking down upon her with a cynical curl to his lip.

Mary turned white to the roots of her hair. "Dear Felix, please listen to me," she began in a trembling voice; "I really felt it my duty to go this morning, and could not think you meant all you said, ——"

"Understand once for all that I did, then."

She looked at him appealingly, and was about to speak, but he interrupted her with, "None of your baby ways now. You are no longer a child, but a woman, bound to do a woman's duty to her husband. As long as you do that I shall allow you to shine at my side, be a partner in my joys and successes; a sharer of my home you will always be, but as you now see, the happiness of that home depends on yourself."

He took his chair again, and opening his paper, prepared to read. Mary had removed her bonnet, and her hair fell about her shoulders in lovely disorder as she stood there, the startled light of surprise dawning in her eyes. Her lips parted as if to speak, but she refrained, and turning, fled to her room, where she threw herself upon the bed and cried with a childish abandonment.

Oh God! Was this the sacred tie of marriage? Was this the life she had chosen? Had God permitted her to make a mistake? . . . Oh the sorrow, the bitterness, the awfulness of it! Carrol had been right in her judgment. Felix Temple was not the—

"Mary, Mary, where art thou?" Like the voice of an accusing angel, suddenly came these words to her inner consciousness.

"Here, oh my Father, teach Thy child the right way. Let me know and be ready to do my duty. . . . Not my will, oh Father, but Thine, be done." . . .

A long time she lay there and prayed. Then she

arose, calmly made herself ready, and went down to meet her husband, but he was gone. She was left alone the remainder of the day.

He had thought best to make the lesson a thorough one. When he returned in the evening he was quite himself again, to all outward appearances. He laughed and chatted with a gay freedom, playfully drew her head down into his lap, while she sat at the piano, and in many nameless ways sought to let her know of his forgiveness. He could be magnanimous!

So things went on for nearly three weeks. Carrol had written that she was coming on Saturday. It would be the first real visit she had made since Mary's marriage, and now she was to stay a whole week, during the spring vacation (for she had succeeded in securing a fine position in the school at Tintuckett).

"Oh, what a pleasant house! So sunny and cozy!" cried Carrol in delight, as she rushed about from one room to another for inspection, immediately upon her arrival.

"Do you think so? Well, come and let me show you *your* room. I have thought of you every time I added to its furnishing." Mary led the way to the guest chamber, a large, sunny room on the second floor. Its upholsterings were pale blue and cardinal, with carpet and bed trimmings to match.

From the south window could be seen a charming view of the Perune river and its opposite banks of sloping hill-sides, covered here and there with lingering patches of snow.

"Why, Mary, it is perfectly delightful, I just wish

I could live with you," cried Carrol with an ecstatic hug.

"Of course you're to live here whenever you want to, dearest," replied Mary, warmly.

"Rest assured I will remember that and act accordingly."

Carrol began to untie her bonnet strings and throw her gloves on the bed. With all her gayety, Mary fancied she was trying to hide an under-current of perplexity.

"Dear me, Mary, it must be nice to have such a home—and you are very happy?"

"What a question to ask a bride!" laughed Mary with an attempt at being playful. Carrol did not remember till long after what a faint little attempt it was.

They went down-stairs and talked till the shadows began to grow long and thick on the walk outside.

The roast was done to a turn, the potatoes in a snowy heap of inviting flakiness waited in the best tureen for somebody to dish them out, the delicate French rolls and dainty side dishes which Mary had prepared with her own hands had been ranged upon the table in tempting array, for the small family and the honored guest, and still Mr. Temple did not appear. It grew late. At last they sat down without him. Then came the office boy with a note, saying the host was called out in the country and could not return till late.

It was a disappointment to Mary. All the week she had been planning for this visit, and this night. She had longed for the time to come, when a more genial element might be added to the little home circle. But she quickly disposed of her own feelings, and made the best of her position as hostess.

After they returned to the parlor, Carrol suddenly unburdened her heart in the old way, as Mary knew she would.

"Well, Mary, I've had a queer time since you left us. It seems, sometimes, as if I am changing to a different girl."

She gazed thoughtfully into the grate fire.

"Why, Carrol?"

"In the first place, I have been very gay and—and flippant, too, I'm afraid. With all I have to do in school, I still find time to go a great deal."

She appeared to be making a confession. Mary drew her chair close and caressed the hand that lay in her lap, while she looked at Carrol interrogatively.

"And of course Auntie doesn't like it," pursued Carrol; "and really, Mary, I've had a dreadful time with—with Ralph and Harvey." She kept her face averted, and Mary waited patiently for the rest. At last she asked, in a low voice: "Why haven't you written, Carrol?"

"What's the use to write about the snarls in one's life? They're more pathetic on paper."

"Tell me, dear," whispered Mary, with a pang of sympathy.

"I'll have to go back a little, then. You know, Mary, how unhappy I have always been about religion. Well, hearing Harvey talk so much seemed to turn me

completely against it, especially when he grew tragic
and wanted to pray for me."

Mary made no sign, except a motion for her to proceed.

"And then I forbade him to mention the subject
again, at which the silly fellow looked at me in such
solemn silence, at all times and in all places, that I
grew quite desperate and went with Ralph every chance
I could, never thinking but that he would understand.
In fact, I've been double-dealing—in order to escape
Harvey, I went with Ralph; in order to escape religion,
I went into society. Mary, I'm perfectly wretched. I
can't bear to be a hypocrite to Ralph, and yet I don't
care for him, except as a brother."

"What about Harvey?" inquired Mary, a little
roguishly.

"Harvey is *non est.*"

"Oh Carrol, you ought to be more considerate."

"Never mind, Mary, I can't; and besides, I've got
to make it unmistakably plain, in some way, to Ralph
when I go back."

She covered her face with her hand and sat with
bowed head.

"Sometimes I think the only way for a girl to do is
to marry and settle down to the usual work of women,
but I've wanted to be and do something more that I
might be better prepared for that, when the riper time
comes." Carrol spoke slowly and gravely.

"Be true to yourself at any cost, Carrol. If you
don't love Ralph, tell him so and don't trifle with him."

"I should never trifle with him, Mary. But the trouble is, he will not take a final answer."

"He must understand your true position then. Are you sure you will never love him?"

"I will never marry until I find and bring out the highest and best of my own nature, if at all. I am so far from being satisfied with myself, Mary."

"You know Carrol, *I* think there is but one way."

"But Mary, have you proven that way? Does it give such a perfect rule of action that you can depend upon it in the troubles of life?" She looked at Mary apologetically, and continued: "I know Mary darling, yours was a beautiful childhood, with its sweet faith and contentment, but is this religion as beautiful and satisfying when you are out in the field, as it were?"

There was such a depth of earnestness in poor Carrol's voice, and at her last question Mary was smitten with sudden doubt as to her ability to answer it. Could she truly say she had proven it? Had she been faithful? Conscience answered for her—No!

But here was Carrol waiting to be answered. "Carrol, I have not proven it in everything, because I have not been faithful in everything. But He will be my power and wisdom and strength to overcome all obstacles, if I hold out, and by His grace I *can* and *will*."

There was a strange intensity in her words, and Carrol withdrew her eyes from the fire to look at her. "But you have perfect faith in the possibility of finally overcoming?" she queried.

"Perfect faith. There is absolutely no limit to the

power of overcoming, if one lives in the consciousness of consecration."

"Mary, I can't believe it.   Don't think I mean any reproach to you dear, but I seem to be a born skeptic, and the way grows darker every moment.   I *cannot* stand this empty life, for it seems more and more dreary. God is nothing to me.   Why Mary, how can I believe in Him as a loving father, when he leaves poor Mrs. Rice to suffer and grieve herself to death over her lost son, at least she thinks that he is lost.   Has she not prayed earnestly or faithfully enough?"

"I cannot see why such things are, dear, but I am sure everything will come right if we trust."   Had everything come right in her own circumstances?

"But Mary, I cannot have your faith.   Surely there must be a way for the doubting Thomases, like poor me."

It was the old wail of despair, that Mary had so often heard before.

"There is a way for everybody, Carrol," was the utmost comfort she could offer, and that was built upon her untried faith.

A step on the walk at this juncture effectually put an end to the confidences.   Mary glanced hastily about the room to see if everything was in perfect order Carrol's jacket was lying across a chair.   It was scarcely hung upon the hall-tree, when the door opened to admit "the lord of the manor."   He came forward with cordial greetings.   Carrol thought he had never appeared to better advantage.

CHAPTER XIX.

" To whomsoever ye yield yourselves servants to obey, his servants ye are."—Rom. vi, 16.

"FELIX dear," Mary leaned over to kiss her husband affectionately, as they waited in the dining-room the next morning for Carrol to make her appearance. He was sitting by the fire, reading, she standing beside his chair. "You will accompany us to church this morning, will you not?"

It had taken hours of earnest praying for her to say this naturally. He glanced at her, a strange light scintillating in his eyes. Then, picking up his paper, he said with the utmost *nonchalance:* "I think we will not attend."

That ended the matter. He had made the law; it only remained to enforce it. If there ever were to be any exceptions, he would make them. His whole attitude, his silence, even the cynical twitch of his mustache, said all this and much more.

The lines were growing tighter around our sweet, untried little Mary. . . . Carrol was coming down the stairs. She even then turned the knob. Mary resolutely put back the sob that welled up in her throat.

"Good morning, Carrol!" was her cheery greeting.

"Good morning. Good morning, Mr. Temple. I

could hardly wake at all this morning. Hope you
haven't waited long."

"Oh, no; but everything is ready."

Mr. Temple chatted pleasantly, even brilliantly, and
proved himself, in every way, a most charming host.
Carrol was delighted. She began to think she had mis-
judged him sorely, and to make amends, exerted herself
to be entertaining. They talked of books, authors, pol-
itics and social questions.

"Carrol, what do you say to a little taste of Whittier this morning?" asked Mary, as naturally as she
could, as they stood on the porch an hour later, enjoying the beautiful spring morning.

"My favorite poet; but, Mary, you don't mean to
stay at home from church on my account?" and Carrol
looked at her in the greatest astonishment; for never in
all the years of their school-life had she ever known
Mary to willingly absent herself from church.

Mary's eyes fell before the searching gaze.

"We do not always go. Mr. Temple does not care
to attend church often," she said, in a low voice.

Carrol checked herself from remarking that she
thought nothing would influence Mary in such matters.
For the first time she suspected all was not well with
her cousin. An indignant thrill passed through her
at the thought of such a thing, but the next moment
they were joined by the host, who was so evidently in
love with his wife, that the suspicion faded as quickly
as it had come.

During that week Mary passed through a varied
experience. She learned the expediency of deferring

to her husband's judgment when he was present, and of making his comfort the prime object of her life. Another thing she discovered too.

Being down town one day shopping with Carrol, she had picked out a very pretty piece of soft gray stuff for a new gown, that she needed as a house dress. It was not expensive, but she found on opening her purse that she had not enough money to pay for it. She had never yet asked her husband for money, having had no occasion until now to do so.

"Can you wait a few moments with this package?" she said to the clerk. "I find I must get more change, and will call as I return from my husband's office."

The clerk politely offered to send it to the house C. O. D., but she would not hear to that way out of the difficulty. Mr. Temple had one of the finest offices in the city, and with evidences of plenty all about him Mary had no scruples in asking for what she needed; so with Carrol she walked into the elegant apartments of "Temple & Hawley," and asked to see Mr. Temple. He was in his private office and very busy, the boy said.

They waited nearly half an hour. Then Mr. Temple called to them through the open door. He was surrounded by voluminous documents of learned lore. Mary began to tremble as she walked into this place; she suddenly felt like a child that would ask a favor too great to be given, but then she reassured herself with the thought that she was only doing what any wife would do.

Mr. Temple's face expressed a single, sharply defined interrogation point. "Well, my dear?"

"Carrol and I have been shopping this afternoon, and I found I had scarcely enough money to finish my purchases, so—"

"So you came to the base of supplies, eh ?" with a jarring laugh.

"Yes, if you please."

"What do you want to buy?"

"Oh I want several things. A new dress, principally."

"How much do you need?"

"I don't know exactly." She was deeply humiliated and would have given worlds not to have this scene take place before Carrol, but there was no help for it now.

He put his hand in his vest pocket and drew out a roll of bills, carefully selected one which he tossed over the desk to his wife. In her embarrassment she tucked it hastily into her purse without noticing the amount, murmured her thanks, and turned to Carrol with the announcement that she was ready.

They went out into the spring air again. How refreshing after the warm atmosphere of the office.

"Dear me, Mary, that is a part of marriage I couldn't endure," remarked Carrol as they picked their way along the muddy street. "It seems to me too humiliating for a woman to have to ask for and account for every cent she spends, just as though she has no mind of her own, and no rights of her own and can't be trusted with money."

"You must be turning over to woman's rights, Carrol," replied Mary, trying to disown the miserable corroboration of Carrol's words that she felt deep down in her heart.

"Not woman's rights except they be the rights of humanity, but I do believe in the equality of the sexes, as they put it."

"Well, don't be a rampant, loud-voiced woman, I beg of you."

Mary must say something—as well this as anything else. She had no fears that Carrol could ever be loud-voiced or rampant.

"Here, isn't this the store?" exclaimed Carrol suddenly. "We were going right by."

"So we were. Yes, this is it."

They went in and Mary called for the package that had been laid aside for her.

"Here it is Madame, do you wish it delivered?"

"If you please."

"Your name and address?" taking out his pencil.

"Mrs. Felix Temple, 55 Temple Place."

"The amount due is four dollars," said the clerk, waiting expectantly.

She drew the bill from her purse and handed it to him, then turned to look at some laces with Carrol.

"Beg pardon, but this is only two dollars, Mrs. Temple. You handed me a two-dollar bill, and the amount required is four dollars."

Mary stood aghast! Was it possible Felix had given her this paltry two dollars for a dress!

"There must have been a mistake," she gasped. Then very firmly: "I cannot take the dress to-day."

The clerk protested his regret and still offered to

send it, but she cut him short by taking the bill and requesting the amount already paid, which was speedily handed her, and she escaped to the street again.

Was there to be no end to this week of humiliations? Oh, for a single moment alone, that she might give one little shriek of protest!

Carrol pretended to think it was all a mistake, and rattled on about anything and everything that came into her head.

" Oh, I am so glad to see you Mrs. Temple," said an effusive voice at her elbow. " We've missed you at the church lately. I just wish you had heard the sermon last Sunday. It was splendid. Had a meeting and election of officers of the Ladies' society, yesterday too. You were chosen Vice-president."

" I can't possibly serve, Mrs. Bissel. You must have them take my name off the record. Allow me to introduce my cousin, Miss Evans, Mrs. Bissel."

" Happy to meet you, Miss Evans. But I do assure you, Mrs. Temple, we can't get on without you, and really that little Dowey girl that was in your mission class (what made you give it up?), is down with measles and her mother applied for help and asked for you. I told her I'd see about some clothing for the child. Guess we'll have to have a sewing bee. They're real destitute. Well, good-bye; I see you're in a hurry. Good afternoon, Miss Evans."

Mrs. Bissel hastened on, and they stepped into the street car to go home. " Have you given up church work, Mary?" asked Carrol, as they sat down in the crowded car.

"Oh no, but I have not been out for awhile."

A mantle of silence seemed to have dropped upon both of them. Scarcely a word was spoken during the homeward ride.

A slight rain was falling as they entered the house. Carrol sighed as she took off her jacket: "And to think, Mary, by this time next week I shall be puzzling over my problems again."

"That is our life work dear, and everybody is really doing the same thing."

There was no resonant joy in the tone in which Mary said this; none of the palpitating faith that used to make her every word alive with a nameless power. Carrol wondered not a little over the change marriage had wrought in her cousin, but it was useless to speak of what she instinctively felt would be painful to both of them.

On Wednesday she returned to Tintuckett. It was a bleak gray day, with a sharp east wind blowing over the hills, and mingling with the river's icy breath. It seemed as though nature had suddenly changed her mind about letting her busy beauty children out of their close-locked winter prison. The soft tenderness of mood she had displayed but the day before, was changed to a severity uncompromising and bitter.

Mary bade Carrol good-bye at the station, and after watching the train out of sight, turned her face homeward. Somehow she had unconsciously fallen into sympathy with the spirit of the weather. The wind that blew sharply into her face was not more keen than the wind of desolation that swept over her soul. She

realized as never before the deeper meanings of life.
She was slowly awakening to the necessity of proving
the theory of living by its practice.   Small clouds that
she had thought harmless at first were now beginning
to seriously darken her sky.   She was face to face with
a problem more deep and awful than any that had ever
troubled Carrol.   Could she solve this one any better
than Carrol could solve hers ?   Yes, a thousand times
better, because she could rely on God's help, and Carrol
did not even *know* God.   Why need she tremble and
feel afraid ?   Was it not her privilege to rejoice and be
glad ?

She was turning the corner nearest home.   A blast
sharper than the rest struck her face, and with it a few
drops of stinging hail.   She compared it to the inner
storm that seemed to threaten her.   Drawing her cloak
more closely about her, she hurried on.   It was really
sleeting now, and by the time she reached the house
the sidewalks were quite slippery.

" 'Into each life some rain must fall,'" she quoted,
as she closed the street door.   "But no, Lord, I will
not murmur.   Thou knowest best.   Whatsoever Thou
hast in store, send it and Thy child shall receive a
blessing."   She took off her wet wraps and hung them
up to dry in the back hall.   The loneliness that met
her as she went into the sitting-room was something
appalling.   Not a living thing within the walls but
herself.   She had had a cunning little kitten to pet
and care for awhile, but Mr. Temple found her neglecting his comfort for that of the kitten, so he had

unceremoniously flung the little creature into the street one stormy night, since which she had not seen it.

In the long darkness that crept slowly over the earth that dreary day, Mary bravely faced her own soul, and prayed for strength to conquer its manifest short-comings.

CHAPTER XX.

"Watch and pray—the darkness shall vanish, the storm sleep and God Himself, as he came of yore on the seas of Samaria, shall walk over the lulled billows to the delivery of your soul."
—*E. Bulwer-Lytton.*

CARROL reached her destination in less than an hour, and found Ralph at the depot with a carriage. He had known the day of her return and made the storm an excuse for going to meet her. She frowned with annoyance when she saw him, but could not refuse the luxury of a ride home.

He tucked the robe about her tenderly and made an extra shawl of one end of it, which he drew around her shoulders to protect her from the stinging blast.

"Thank you, Ralph," she said laughingly. "I am sure that will be all-sufficient."

"Did you have a pleasant visit with Mary?" he asked, as he finally seated himself beside her.

"Yes, very, and it was such a relief to be off duty awhile," she returned absently.

"But what about the poor fellows who must needs be *on* duty?" with a significant glance.

"Oh we all have our turns," rather shortly. "Any news since I've been away?"

"None that I know of; hope there is some in prospect," with another significant look. "When may I come for the surety of it," he added, daringly. "I almost hinted something to mother when I was home last Sunday."

"No, Ralph, you were surely not so foolish?" she queried, with a passionate pain in her voice, and throwing off the robe as she spoke.

"Why not, Carrol? Isn't it almost certain?" tenderly laying his hand on her's as he spoke.

She sat up very straight. "Do you wish me to answer now, Ralph?" with an ominous calmness.

A sudden fear smote him. "No, no; I will wait. Forgive me for forcing the subject upon you again to-day. I really meant to hold my peace, but—" He stopped abruptly and nothing was said till they reached her aunt's.

"To-morrow night shall I come?" he asked, as he left her at the door.

"To-morrow night," she rejoined, and went into the house.

"How it would please mother if—" he mused, as he drove back to the livery barn. "Poor mother! She has had so many disappointments. If this is to be one, may she never know, but then I only hinted at a possibility."

Ralph had thought of this "possibility" five years, and so closely was it entwined into the very fiber of his life that he could not think of its opposite.

The next evening he went to face victory or defeat.

Carrol's face was pale and her eyes looked heavy as she entered the room. She wore a plain black dress, with only a simple black ribbon at the throat to break the severity of the collar.

Ralph's courage fell when he saw her, and an indefinable dread seized him.

"Tell me the worst, Carrol; I can bear it better than my black forebodings," he exclaimed as he grasped her hand and held it in both of his.

"Sit down, Ralph. I will be explicit, as well for your mother's sake as your own." She made room for him beside her, and laid her hand upon his arm with an almost maternal tenderness.

His last hope fled even before she said another word, but he schooled himself to patience.

"I allowed you to come this once, to satisfy yourself that further consideration is useless, as all my earnest thought has only brought the same answer." He would have interrupted, but she motioned him to silence. "As a dear friend," she continued, "as my brother, I regard you, but as nothing more, and that also is sufficient reason for my decided no."

"But Carrol, only give me an opportunity,—" he was saying eagerly, the old story of a disappointed lover. . . . .

"Ralph I cannot give less than the best I have to the man I marry, and as yet that best has not come forth. It would be the acme of selfishness to give a true man the husk when he gives the heart. Besides—"

"But—," he interposed again.

"Besides," she went on, not heeding the interruption, "I have other plans. I want to do so much in the world that—that a woman of family cannot do—"

"You should have perfect freedom," he cried, eagerly catching a straw of hope.

"No Ralph, it cannot be," was the firm answer.
" Tell your mother, if you must tell her anything, that
I am going to devote myself to a life of public usefulness in some direction, that is not yet defined. As soon
as school is out I intend to prepare myself for a larger
work and shall probably visit Seaton to make arrangements."

Ralph's face was pale and haggard. All the brightness had faded out of his sky. Not even the pale glimmer of starlight cheered his future pathway; but there
was surely hope in the years that he would wait for her,
whispered his heart.

"Only tell me this is not final, not absolutely final,
dear Carrol, and I will be content to wait," he replied
huskily.

"It *is* final, Ralph. I do not wish any 'ifs' or
'possibles,' to dwell in your mind for the present or
future." Her voice was almost harsh in its earnestness.
She must be free to do and be what she would. The
idea of going to Seaton had come to her during the ride
from Lynn, and the more she thought of it the more
the plan grew upon her.

"What shall I live for," asked Ralph, "if you cut
me off from even the pleasure of hoping?"

"Live for a broader, better future than you have
built yet, Ralph. Make the attainment of the highest
your aim and effort, and when the time comes for a
home of your own, some one will be found to share it
who is much wiser than I."

There was a look of weariness about her mouth in
spite of her brave philosophy.

Ralph mistook its import, and deep down in his heart he bade the last faint hope to linger yet a little longer.

"Don't mark out my future for me, Carrol. You cannot," he exclaimed, passionately.

"I wish, Ralph, you would go to Miss Allbright's 'Help meetings,'" said Carrol, suddenly changing the the subject. "I went out last night—yes, in spite of the storm," answering his look of astonishment, "and really, I was very much interested."

"Well, Carrol, excuse me, but I'm hardly up to talking commonplaces to-night, for that is what everything seems,"—drily—"I think I'll go," and he rose, a little unsteadily, but quickly regained command of himself, as he reached for his hat.

He was a noble-looking fellow, this Ralph Rice, with his broad white forehead outlined by the brown hair above, with his clear gray eyes and firm mouth. Through his own study and determination he had finally succeeded in being admitted to the bar, and was recognized as one of the finest young men in Tintuckett. The deacon's pride was somewhat mollified now that his eldest son had turned out so well. Ralph had settled in his native town because of his mother, to whom he was tenderly devoted. Carrol had not forgotten all this, and a wave of pity swept over her as she saw his white face ; but she had been true to herself.

"Good-bye, my more than friend, my brother Ralph!" she said, with a great compassion, as she held out her hand at the last.

He seized it, pressed it gently to his lips, and was gone before she could say another word.

"After all, it is best, and I am free," she sighed, as she sat before the fire watching the glowing embers in the grate; "free to do what and to go where I will; but oh, how desolate! No father, no mother, no God!" For it had finally come to the point of real agnosticism with poor Carrol. This intense desire to be busy, to be absorbed in the great world's heart of usefulness was only another way to forget the longing after a God she had never found. She thought of Mary. "Where is her Helper, her Comforter, her Protector?" she thought bitterly, as the many little signs of Mary's unhappy lot recurred to her memory.

"No, no, the dear girl is horribly deceived. She has even now begun to taste the fruit of her misplaced confidence in God. There can be no God, no loving Father, who would let His trusting child fall into such hands as Mary has fallen." . . . . . The darkness of a night, more hopeless than she had ever known, enshrouded poor Carrol. That terrible "what if" would rear its hydra-head occasionally, in spite of her sweeping rejection of belief in that to which it pertained. The visit to Mary had not been a help, spiritually; for could she not forsee the dark cloud that had even now begun to overspread her cousin's horizon, notwithstanding Mary's trust in God? The very fact of the marriage had been a great blow to Carrol's unconscious faith. She had never openly mentioned her feeling in regard to Mr. Temple, but she had hinted

at it once, just before the wedding day. They had been
discussing the bridal dress:

"I believe some men fairly charm girls into a yes,
as serpents charm their prey!" Carrol had exclaimed,
impetuously.

"Did you ever know of such a case?" was Mary's
innocent query.

"Yes, one," she had replied hastily and rushed from
the room to avoid a plainer betrayal.

All this came back upon her with a vivid memory, as
well as the many other incidents of failure she harbored
in her mind against Mary's God.

With a sigh she went up-stairs to her room to escape
the black-winged thoughts. She had learned in these
later years to shut the door of willingness to harbor
them.

The next two months she was very busy. Not once
did she falter in her determination to seek some special
work that would engage all her time and attention.
She had a school friend in Seaton to whom she would
apply for such information as might possibly lead to an
opening of some sort. All this winter in Tintuckett
she had been to Miss Allbright's but once. Thinking
of her great delinquency in this respect, and of the
various trifling circumstances that had kept her away,
she suddenly resolved to make amends by going that
very evening.

It was late twilight in early May. A rain in the
morning had cleansed and refreshed the busy earth.
The buds were unfolding their leafy banners, and the
tender grass blades had sprung cheerfully to their work

of clothing the earth-mother. Creeping green tendrils reached their loving fingers through crevices and over places where the grasses failed. The air was filled with a combination of suggestive odors, and that peculiarly fresh, growing smell of early spring. Over-arching all, a clear blue sky, paling into tints of pink and gold toward the horizon, with here and there a golden censer swinging in the far-off zenith. There was a hint of hope in the beautiful picture and Carrol was insensibly affected by it. Her cheek flushed rosily, and the dawning brightness in her eyes made her seem a part of the coming spring.

Miss Allbright met her at the door. She had seen her walking up the path towards the house.

"I am *so* glad, Miss Evans, I *knew* you would come sometime," holding out her hand with a cordial smile. "Pray come in to the fire and sit in the easy-chair."

The lamps were not yet brought in, and the large handsome room was lighted only by the firelight and the fading glory of the outer world. Such a cheery, hospitable atmosphere, such unobtrusive warmth and pervading beauty. Carrol instinctively felt more than she saw, and notwithstanding a natural diffidence, she soon found herself chatting away as if she had been in the habit of dropping in to see Miss Allbright every day of her life.

"You are so kind, and are doing such wonderful good in the world," exclaimed Carrol, with a wistful look of admiration.

They had been talking of individual abilities and how they were used.

"Miss Carrol I am doing no more than anyone can do in his own way, which may be a different way from mine, but is none the less excellent or productive of results. Every flower must wear its own dress and carry its own perfume. If it does not, it is a failure. It is when people try to do or be something other than they are that they grow stunted and unhappy. . . . I tell you, Miss Carrol," ringing the bell for the maid, as she leaned over towards Carrol confidentially, "humanity must find itself individually, and know whether it is a rose or a tulip, and then live accordingly."

The girl came to the door. "A light please, Jenny," with a kind smile.

As Jenny turned to go, a large, handsome gray cat with zebra stripes, bounded into the room with a stately air of possession.

Miss Allbright saw him. "Come here, Senator," she called, coaxingly. With dignified strides and a purr of assent, the cat came forward and sprang gracefully into her lap.

"What a pretty creature!" exclaimed Carrol, involuntarily, as Jenny at that moment brought in the light.

"Of course; the Senator knows what it is to be respected, doesn't he, Jenny?" laughed Miss Allbright, with a pat on Senator's back and a bright smile for the maid.

"Yes, ma'am, an' so does the rest of us."

Whether she meant to include herself in the category of cats, or whether she meant to acknowledge the satisfactory condition of both cats and servants, she did not stop to explain.

"You see now," resumed Miss Allbright thoughtfully, "in proportion as we recognize the bright side of existence, our sense of justice develops, and as we appropriate justice, we feel a self-respect that shines forth in natural beauty. Beauty belongs to all God's creatures. Did you ever think of that?"

"I must confess I never have, in a universal sense; and yet it must be true."

"Fact. Given self-respect and a consideration for the rights of others, there is nothing that will so beautify and sunnify—if I may coin the word—either human or animal faces."

She stroked Senator's shiny fur with a caressing hand.

"Yes; most of the ugliness of this world is caused by the ignorant and selfish scramble for what really *belongs* to the individual," she continued; "and I am so anxious to have people brought into co-operation and thus induce a mutual appreciation."

"If all could do as well as you," began Carrol, with a little sigh, as the old shade fell over her face like a mask.

"Excuse me for making a personal question, but my dear child, are you not happy in your present work?"

The tone was so earnest, and the voice so sympathetic, that then and there Carrol broke down all barriers of reserve and told Miss Allbright her life history, with all its unsatisfied longings, doubts and fears.

She tremblingly touched upon the desire to enter upon some useful and congenial work for humanity.

With intuitive insight and delicate sympathy, Miss Allbright divined at once the rare nature and character of the girl before her. She tenderly pressed Carrol's fingers that had sought hers, and leaned her cheek upon her own hand in deep thought.

Senator had curled himself down on the rug before the fire. The minutes went by so slowly, Carrol began to think she had committed some grievous error in talking so freely.

"See here," said Miss Allbright suddenly, "would you not like to assist me ? I—"

"Oh, Miss Allbright, do you not understand? I— I am an infidel! I am not good enough, and—"

"Hush, dear; you don't know what I would say. I have long projected establishing a "Voluntary Help" school or home in Seaton, and in fact have been waiting to find the proper assistant. I believe you will do admirably. Will you go ? "

"But Miss Allbright—"

"Never mind, dear. I can wait for you to grow into religious faith. As long as you conscientiously do the best you know, you will accomplish what many could never accomplish with their religion labeled, pinned and anchored to them."

"Oh how can I ever thank you for this confidence ? I will only too gladly serve the world with you, and hope I may learn to serve it half as well !" cried Carrol, with tears of gratitude.

Miss Allbright detailed her plans more fully. The

purpose was to provide an opportunity for the mental, physical and moral education of working children and girls from ten to seventeen. In other words, it was to be a sort of home for those unfortunates without one. They were to be admitted in consideration of mutual service rendered and received in the various duties of the house, and the voluntary contribution they felt impelled to give out of their individual earnings. They were to be taught the righteousness of labor, the justice of equal rights, and the benefits of sympathetic co-operation.

"Of course I will have a housekeeper," added Miss Allbright, "and another assistant probably, but I wish you to be general overseer and instructor. Will you accept it?"

Without a moment's hesitation, Carrol answered, "Yes, I will try at least."

So it was decided what her work was to be. What a sudden change in her prospects! As she stepped out into the crisp evening air, she almost wondered if she were the same girl that walked along the street two hours before. The very stars looked different, the air was cleaner, fresher and more invigorating, the round-faced moon appeared more benignantly beautiful than ever before. Oh she could do so much in this broad field, and life would surely be worth living!

With her face turned bravely to the star of hope, Carrol laid her head upon the pillow and dreamed of better things.

CHAPTER XXI.

"Not belief, but life makes a man a christian. . . . He who has Christ's life is a christian, whatever his name. 'Whosoever loveth is born of God.'"—Rev. A. H. Bradford.

IN September Carrol went to her new duties. It was not really a position of assured ease that she had undertaken, even though there were only four pupils to begin with, but she had resolved to do her best. It did not take long for Tillie, the sewing girl, to grasp the idea of co-operation and all the benefits it promised, and thus assist in interesting the other three—twelve-year-old Jack the news-boy, Kitty the cash-girl aged ten, and patient little Nina, who went about the streets selling flowers, bravely earning her daily bread in spite of her orphanage and the ugly hump on her back.

To all these lonely bread winners, the "Helpers' Home" was a veritable Providence that seemed to have been established expressly for them. How to instruct, govern or assist them or even establish sympathetic relations, was the test of Carrol's fitness for the work, and for this reason Miss Allbright left her to deal with the situation alone, merely assuring her of unbounded faith in her success.

How helpful is the sympathy and whole-souled faith of a friend! One word, and the fire of effort is alight, burning out all weakness, inability and lazy indifference. Courage, hope, faith—let us have more of the magic words of friendship and brotherly love.

"Suppose we spend this evening in getting acquainted;" suggested Carrol, that first night after Miss Allbright had left them. "Let us tell each other how we came to think of coming here to live. Come Tillie, you speak first."

"Yes, Miss Evans, I will be only too glad. I was living in the tenement house on Payne street with Mrs. Bortleson and her six children. We were all very poor like everybody else in that neighborhood, and was only getting twelve cents a day for the hardest kind of sewing in the factory. One day a lady came there to talk to us and see if she could not help in some way to make us happier. She came two or three times to talk to the folks in the tenement, and they always felt better after she had gone, so at last we began to have faith in her—you know so many ladies visit around among poor folks just to tell them about how they ought to believe the Bible if they want to go to heaven when they die, and how they ought to pray for help, and *that* I never *could* understand, and we had got so tired of such visitors that at first we was kind o' suspicious of Miss Allbright; but she was so sweet and kind every time, that we got to looking for her, and being disappointed if she didn't come, for her talks was always like a piece of sunshine right from heaven. Finally she told us about this home and asked me if I wouldn't like to live here. Of course I was only too glad, and here I am, though I did hate to leave poor Mrs. Bortleson and the baby, but Miss Allbright promised to look after them."

"She will keep her promise, too," said Carrol warmly, as she turned to Jack, feeling that he was getting a little restless. "How did *you* know about it, Jack?" she asked.

"Wal, yer see, I'm a kid as always keeps his eye open fer a good chance, 'n' one day a pleasant-faced chap what allus buys his mornin' "Herald" o' me was a stan'in' on the corner, a readin' of a bill what had fell on the sidewalk, an' he called out to me one o' the minutes I wasn't a yellin' 'M-O-R-N-I-N' Herald, News, 'Nter-Ocean, Trib-*yune*,' an' he says, says he, 'Look a yer, Johnny (lots o' folks call me Johnny), here's somethin' fer you,' an' then he read that there bill what told that such fellers as me could come here an' live if we only wanted to live on the square an' do a little suthin' to help the folks what was helpin' us. An' I've got it now," pulling a crumpled, soiled paper out of his ragged pocket, and tossing it over to Carrol as if it were the most valuable credential in the world.

Carrol took it without the least sign of amusement on her face, read it and then handed it back, saying: "You'd better keep it Jack, to remember the day you found a home, for I'm sure that is what you will call it. And now, Kitty, let us hear from you. Come, bring your chair up closer, and tell us all about it."

Carrol had a winning way about her that especially won children's confidence, and Kitty's heart had been warmly drawn towards her at the very first. She was very thin and sallow-looking, and her face was sober and pinched, as though it belonged to a little old woman, but there was a childish gleam of eagerness and hope in her eyes that somewhat relieved the look of age. She drew her chair as close to Carrol as she dared, and began.

"I'm not sure, but I think it was two weeks ago last Monday, I was runnin' a package for a lady that had a little boy with her, and the little boy—he wasn't more'n a baby anyway, but he was reachin' up to the counter and pullin' things down like a regular little mischief, and pretty soon his mother slapped him. Just then I came along with the package, an' I heard a lady that stood close by a-sayin' to the baby's mamma: 'Oh, *don't* strike the baby, he doesn't know any better,' in such a soft, sorry voice that I remembered it, for she was the very same lady that spoke to me last Christmas time when I was standin' by the door of the store cryin' cause I was hungry, an' the floor walker wouldn't let me stop to eat my lunch, 'cause they was all so busy, an' that morning I went without any breakfast, cause there wasn't enough for me and mamma both "—Kitty stopped to wipe her eyes at the remembrance—"an' mamma died the next week, an' when this kind lady heard me cry, an' saw how cross the floor walker was, she just came up to me an' spoke so nice an' sweet that the floor walker said I could go for ten minutes an' to hurry right back, for everybody wanted to be waited on at once, an' I would lose my place if I didn't hurry.

"An' then when I turned away wipin' my eyes, the kind lady followed me an' gave me some money to go an' get a nice lunch. Well, when I saw this same lady talkin' to the little baby, I couldn't help smilin' at her

an' sayin' ' I know you,' an' then she remembered me,
an' asked me all about how I got along an' if I was
happy, an' how my mamma was.   I told her 'bout
mamma bein' gone, an' she told me of this home an'
'splained how they would be a kind lady to help teach
us if we would only try to help back again, an' how as
it would be a nice clean home an' said she'd take me to
it when it opened.   So she did, this morning an'"—

"It was Miss Allbright," interrupted Carrol, with
a hint of a tear in her eye, and a resolve to succeed at
any cost for the sake of the noble woman who was
reaching so many desolate lives by her quiet, unobstru-
sive ministry of love, in the by-ways and hedges of
humanity.

"And now little Nina, where did *you* come from?"
with a gentle pat on the dark head.

Nina's great brown eyes filled with tears a moment,
and she did not answer immediately.   Such a pathetic
but patient little mouth, Carrol thought she had never
seen, but there was great sweetness and strength in the
face.   Nina had evidently suffered much and was purified until the angel side shone through.

She timidly put her hand on Carrol's, and looked up
in her face.   "I'm so glad I found you," she said
simply.

A great lump rose in Carrol's throat, but she choked
it back.   "Well, dear, *how* did you find me?" she
asked, smiling encouragingly at Nina.

"Oh, Mrs. Badger, the apple woman around the
corner, she said as what a kind lady had come and
talked to her so nice and asked her if she knew of any

little orphunts as didn't have any home, and said she was going to have one started pretty soon and would Mrs. Badger tell 'em about it and show 'em where to go? An' Mrs. Badger, she told ever so many others too, but they didn't believe it could be true, 'cause they said nobody'd do anything for ragamuffins like us, that nobody ever cared for 'em. But I b'lieved it. I believe if we only do our best, somebody or something does take care of us, just like somebody or something takes care of the flowers and birds. My mamma used to say so too."

"Flowers is mighty purty but they don't have to work, like we kids." It was Jack's voice that spoke. His freckled face wore a thoughtful expression, and his hands were plunged into his pockets as though he had come to a wall that put an end to his reasoning.

"But they have to bloom and look beautiful. That is their work," said Carrol, wondering if she could say anything he would understand.

"They can't help it, so that's no work," retorted Jack, rather scornfully.

"Oh, no, it is not work like ours, but it is use. We all have some use in the world. What we do will never change that, but it may hide it, until nobody can tell what it really is. That is the difference between us and the flowers. They do just what God intended them to do, while we grow cross and naughty, and choose to do what we *want* to do, instead of being like the flowers, contented with what we are. Just think of a sweet little rose, growing naughty and shutting its leaves together, refusing to bloom for anybody. You would say something was wrong with it, wouldn't you?"

"Oh, but they never do," exclaimed Nina, catching her breath quickly, as though the roses were sadly slandered.

"No, dear, they never do, but human beings do and—"

"What's human beings?" queried Jack.

"Men, women and children; people."

"Oh, *them!* Bet yer life they shut agin each other. I've knowed that allus."

"Well, Jack, it is *because* of that we have such a time getting clothes to wear and things to eat. We've been so busy trying to shut up, that we've lost our bloom. Do you understand?"

They all answered in the affirmative.

"So you see," she went on, "we are never really happy until we learn what we are and how to bloom for each other, and that is what we will try to do here in this beautiful home, isn't it?"

She explained to them the meaning of their work together, what they ought to attain by the help they would give each other, and aroused their sympathy and ambition in carrying it out successfully.

After each had in turn learned the use of the clean, large bath-room by a practical test of its cleansing powers, the new family retired · and Carrol went to sleep happier than she had ever been in her life before.

CHAPTER XXII.

"No longer forward nor behind
   I look in hope or fear;
But grateful, take the good I find,
   The best of now and here."

—J. G. Whittier.

BUT while Carrol was so happily employed, it was quite otherwise with some of the friends she had left behind, especially Ralph Rice and Harvey Willard. Ralph bravely kept on in his chosen work, trying for his mother's sake to wear a cheerful face, even though his heart might be heavy with its own burdens.

Harvey had a double grief. He not only had come to love Carrol with all the ardor and devotion in his nature, but he groaned unceasingly in spirit over her unregenerate heart and the wilful and continued rejection of her soul's salvation. How to accomplish the latter was the scheme of his constant thought and prayer. Willingly would he sacrifice himself in any way that would gain the desired end. He was conscientious to an extreme degree, and in many ways had displayed a nobility of character that had almost surprised Carrol into admiration, or would have evoked it had she not allowed prejudice to blind her to a fair judgment. Her remembrance of him as a child was tenaciously held to in spite of the natural development that had made him manly as it had made her womanly.

It is true there were certain expressions and mannerisms of which he was guilty in her eyes, that might have offended others also.   But they were traceable largely to his method of thought, his religious education and his narrow understanding of certain subjects.

It was not without great forebodings that he heard of the new occupation Carrol had undertaken.   He feared Miss Allbright's influence and mourned much over the broad path to destruction that his beloved had chosen, but he could do nothing except leave her in the hands of the higher Power, which he did with a heavy sigh of what he honestly believed was faith.   When Carrol went away without a word of sympathy or even farewell, he considered the matter from a religious standpoint and felt that he must quench all thought of personal love or preferment regarding her.   Such thoughts therefore were dutifully strangled as soon as they were born, so far as he could strangle them.   To succeed was victory over self and the devil.   To fail was condemnation and remorse without measure.   His own selfishness should not allow him to forget what he, as a preacher of the gospel, owed to every human soul.

The time was now at hand for his ordination, an event to which he had looked forward with warm anticipation.   It was his intention to accept a call to a pastorate as soon as possible after becoming a candidate. What was his surprise to find himself appointed to the very parish in Seaton, located near the "Helper's Home."   He could hardly realize it, and his first impulse was to write to Carrol, telling her of his proximity, but his rigorous law forbade such a proceeding.

His work was arduous, requiring the closest attention, and all the tact and ability of which he was capable. As a speaker, Harvey was earnest, forcible, and at times eloquent, though rather stereotyped in his expressions. He was considered a rising star by his denomination and his appointment to this place seemed to all who knew him the propitious beginning of a useful and successful career.

Several weeks had elapsed since his arrival. In that time he had gotten fairly launched in his new duties, but not once had sight or sound of the nameless one gladdened his hungry soul, for it *was* hungry in spite of his firm resolve.

One rainy evening he sat alone, his sermon written and a lonesome mood upon him. What better opportunity for the tempter to enter the fortress ? Be that as it may, before he was aware he found himself suddenly thinking of Carrol. He remembered her as a child, and realized, as never before, the thoughtless cruelty of his boyish criticisms and accusations. What would he not give to undo the memory of that past? Even if she needed those corrections why had *he* been the one to give them ? Why could he not, now at least, have a fair opportunity to lead her into the fold ? But the pain of those years seemed burned into her consciousness, and worst of all, he was closely connected with it. . . .

The rain pattered against the windows, and the wind roared angrily through the branches of the great elm at the gate, but Harvey knew nothing of it. He first intended only the indulgence of a short reverie, but now all thought of time faded from his mind.

He was reviewing his life ánd hers. He tried to find palliation and excuse for her skepticism and his earnestness (bigotry she called it), but in vain; the one demanded the other. She had refused to listen to the voice of the Lamb, not only in childhood, but in womanhood. Oh God, what would become of her ?

Great drops of perspiration stood out upon his forehead.

What could be done ? Could he stand idly by and see this pure soul cast into the burning ?

In his agony he paced to and fro across the room. A vivid flash of lightning, followed by deafening thunder, caused him to look without. His eyes instinctively sought the house where she lived, the roof of which could be seen from his study window. With horror-stricken face he turned to the door and rushed hatless into the blinding storm. He had seen a blue tongue of flame play upon the roof, and with a loud cry of fire rushed to—he knew not what. As he reached the door Jack bounded out screaming that Nina was killed and the house on fire.

"Anybody else hurt, boy ?" cried Harvey, clutching him as he rushed past.

"Do' know, mister, but I want somebody to help ——"

"Where is Miss Evans?" shouted Harvey hoarsely.

"Up-stairs with Nina, and Nina's ——" The words were lost as he flew down the street.

"Get help ! Quick !"

Harvey sprang up the steps with a white face. He met Tillie in the hall, the empty water pail in her hands.

"It's out," she gasped, "the fire's out, but oh! I thought the house would surely burn and Nina ——"

"Where are they?"

It seemed a century before he found Carrol, and when he saw her bending over the pale-faced child, he rejoiced to have found, not only the lovely girl whom he adored, but a strong loving woman, whose womanhood was crowned by the heavenly sympathy that beamed from her eyes.

"Does Nina feel better now?" she asked tenderly as she bent over the child.

"Yes," in a faint whisper with the rare smile upon her thin lips.

"You here, Harvey Willard?" was Carrol's exclamation a moment later.

"Yes, Carrol. Can I not help you? I live only a few doors from here," he said humbly, apologetically.

"No, there is nothing to do now, unless it be to tell those people down-stairs that the fire is out and everything safe. Nina was only shocked."

"And you, Carrol, are you perfectly well?" he could not forbear asking as he turned to go.

"Oh yes."

"May I call again and inquire after the little girl?"

A flash from the great sun of Love, the Love that takes all life and living creatures in its embrace, the universal, omnipresent Tenderness, illumined the face of each, and made them one for an instant.

Carrol remembered only the blessedness of service to those who needed serving.

"Come to-morrow, Nina will be her own sweet self again I hope."

The instant was gone; they were once more painfully conscious of Harvey and Carrol.

He scattered the crowd that was rapidly gathering, and walked forth into the wet night. He was dazed with a consciousness of something grander, nobler than he had ever conceived. The dazzling glory of the moment was almost a revelation. Vainly he sought to recall it.

Not till he reached his own room, did he realize the depths into which the tempter had led him. Had he so painfully schooled himself to forget her personality, only to bow down and worship at the old shrine the moment he came within sight or thought of it?

Long and earnestly he wrestled, not alone for her, but for himself—and when at last he rose from his knees, the light of a great, and he hoped a final victory, filled his heart. He did not go to see Nina the next day. He would not so soon put himself in the tempter's hands. The reins should not be dropped again.

With more earnestness than ever he plunged into his work, and the next Sunday preached a stirring sermon from the text "Am I my brother's keeper?" From that time his reputation was made.

Carrol meantime congratulated herself on his absence, and went on in her new duties with increasing interest. Miss Allbright had expressed her pleasure and satisfaction in Carrol's management, and proved her confidence by insisting on the opening of a Voluntary Help meeting, to be conducted by Carrol.

It was a complete success.

From a timid, self-conscious, low-voiced girl, who could say but a few words and those few brokenly, painfully, Carrol soon developed into a message bearer whose forceful but sympathetic and well-modulated voice and wisely chosen words carried help and hope and courage wherever they were heard. She was enthusiastic. She was filled with a knowledge based on experience of what a recognition of good and the mutual exchange of help and sympathy will do. She had awakened to the greater possibilities of her own soul, hence of every soul. She had lifted the veil of ignorance and was entranced at the glory that awaited her, the glory of truth that lies always behind the veil. She spoke with a true eloquence, because she was "drunk with a certain belief," as Emerson tersely defines eloquence, and thus it was, as the months went on, the tightly rolled bud expanded and unfolded until its gracious fragrance proclaimed it a half-blown flower.

After the long, weary search for something to believe in, Carrol had at last found it in this doctrine of the Supreme Good—in this ministry of helpfulness.

. . . .

Oh conscious rest supreme
That cometh like a heavenly gleam,
That knoweth naught of pain,
Or blighting grief, or e'en a grain
Of boisterous joy.

Where art thou all the years
We search and long with blinding tears
For thy sweet gift of peace,
While awful storm-clouds but increase
  Our weight of fear ?

 . . . .

In *thee*, Oh Child of Life,
Beyond the fear, the doubt, the strife,
Beyond the wave of feeling's crest,
Abideth peace, divinest rest,
  Thy birth-right true.

The power of trust, serene,
Secure and firm, fore'er unseen,
In thy true mind doth lie;
'Twill sweep all clouds from out thy sky
  And give thee rest.

CHAPTER XXIII.

"Ye are not bound, the Soul of Things is sweet,
  The Heart of Being is celestial Rest.
 Stronger than woe is will; that which was good
  Doth pass to Better-Best.

" Ye suffer from yourselves; none else compels,
  None other holds you that ye live and die;
  *   *   *   *   *   *
  " Behold, I show you Truth!

" Before beginning, and without an end,
  As space eternal and as surety sure,
 Is fixed a Power Divine which moves to good;
  Only its laws endure."
                    —*Arnold's Light of Asia.*

NO tramps fed here!   Be off about your business,
  I say!"

Mr. Temple shut the door with an angry bang and
turned back to the cheerful grate fire in the back
parlor.

Mary turned pale, grasping a chair for support.
She had caught a glimpse of a brown face and shaggy
beard, and would have opened the door with a wide welcome if she had only dared, for surely she knew that
face. It looked so much, especially about the eyes,
like that of a heart-broken mother, who had sorrowed
for a lost son almost since Mary could remember.

But there was nothing to do about the matter

except keep silent and stifle the pitying heart-throbs that so often died in her bosom.

"If it only wasn't Ned," she murmured as she busied herself about the sewing in her lap. But the thought that it was somebody's Ned haunted her. Oh, if she could but give him a word of sympathy, a hint that she knew what suffering and loneliness meant.

"Mary!" It was her husband who spoke, and though his voice was pleasant and the tone gentle, it grated harshly on her ear.

"Mary, I accepted the invitation to Mrs. Hoyt's reception to-morrow evening. I want you to look your prettiest and let me see the roses in your cheeks again."

"But Felix I have nothing to wear; and ——"

"Nonsense Mary, you will find something, don't be foolish."

Had he forgotten that her wedding dress, the one resort for all occasions since her marriage, was no longer presentable? Did he expect her to go to a party without even the tinsel of happiness? She choked back a sob, and after a moment's silence, began a second remonstrance.

"Besides Felix—"

"Besides what?" he interrupted sharply.

"Baby is not well enough to be left, and I ——"

"She will be all right by to-morrow," in a decided tone; "and now what do you want to wear?" with a magnanimous smile, as he took out his purse.

It was no use to waste words; the decree had gone forth.

Before she could reply he tossed her a roll of bills,

saying as he did so : "Go down to Perry's to-morrow and we'll order the handsomest dress in their store. I will not have my wife outshone by anybody," and he playfully drew her head down on his shoulder in the old winning way, which so well simulated love, the love she had long since ceased to expect or even hope for.

It mattered not how many necessities stared her in the face with pathetic vividness, as long as her husband did not and would not see them she must accept the shams of luxury with a smiling face and let the world go on envying "that rich Mrs. Temple who has everything heart can wish."

Mr. Temple's desire was gratified, as he expected it to be. What was the use of being a rich man with a handsome wife without an occasional display of both riches and wife ?

Baby Margaret was feverish and very restless the next evening, but the doctor had said it was only a cold that would soon disappear with good nursing, so Mary left her precious darling in Janet's tender hands and went in her shimmering robe (Mr. Temple had chosen it) to the fashionable party.

Beauty was there. Gay smiles and rippling laughter, sparkling eyes and brilliant jewels vied in attractiveness. The gold dust and silver bars, as well as steel filings of humanity, gathered by the social magnet, were placed and grouped in ever varying patterns of artistic grace or careless incompleteness.

Flowers were not lacking; neither the dainty blossoms of nature or their human representatives, for there are some people, whose face, form and manner convey the flower quality of thought and character.

Mary was one of these. She was like a delicate, white lily, and in all the shining throng the one of all most fair. And yet, no sparkling joy was hers. Quite unsuspected lurked the keen anxiety and unrest beneath her calm exterior.

Like all other women, she was an actress, for where is the woman who has not been obliged to learn this art in order to live at peace with the world? A sad statement, but true, nevertheless, and yet Mary was one of the most artless of women.

Once home again, she flew to her baby, the one ray of unalloyed sunshine she had left.

Margaret was very ill. Janet bent over her anxiously as Mary entered.

"What is it?" cried the mother, in sudden terror. "Is my baby worse?" She rushed to take the child; her white finery and gauzy draperies trailing about her as she moved.

"Oh, why did I leave you, my precious pet? There, there," in a soothing voice. "Go to sleep now, mamma's sunbeam," putting her cheek close to the little face on her bosom.

But the wide eyes gazed fixedly, without a sign of recognition in their depths, and the breath came in quick, short gasps.

"Oh, what shall we do? Run, Janet, for Mr. Temple—telephone for the Doctor. Quick, Janet! O, my one ewe lamb, surely God will not take you as he did little Carrol!"

Suddenly she put the child back in its crib, and with compressed lips and dry eyes threw aside her mantle and gloves, as she moved about in a dazed way.

Janet returned saying Mr. Temple had gone himself for the doctor since they could get no response from him by telephone.

"Watch her carefully, Janet, while I change my dress. Don't let the slightest thing disturb her."

Janet was astonished at the white agony in Mary's face. It was drawn and pinched into angular lines of suffering. No one knew how near the mother's heart was to breaking.

Janet tried to comfort her. "Is na God the Laird o' the leevin' as well as the deid?" she timidly suggested in her warm-hearted way.

Mary's mouth twitched convulsively.

"That is worst of all, Janet. I have been wickedly forgetting Him and disbelieving His promises, and—" She nervously threw on her wrapper and seated herself beside the crib once more, looking with strained anxious eyes into the face of her darling.

"But He ne'er forgets," ventured Janet again, hoping in some way to break this frozen calmness.

"Hush!" Mary turned upon her almost fiercely. "I know all those words and phrases;" then suddenly relaxing, she burst into tears of exceeding bitterness.

When Dr. Shaft entered the room, his first words were sword points. With a despairing gesture he turned away: "It is too late."

Mary, poor white lily, swayed and drooped, a withered lifeless thing. Her husband caught her in his arms and gravely laid her on the bed, while Janet brought water and sprinkled upon her face.

She revived with a heart-breaking sob of consciousness. " My baby," she gasped.

" Please be quiet, Mrs. Temple, the child is better without you now, and you must be calm," said the doctor, as he prepared a stimulant. She closed her eyes and lay so still, they thought for a moment she had swooned again. The doctor left some powders for the child, and took his departure, leaving only the bleak wind of despair to blow over the barren field of hope.

Janet sat by the dying child. Felix Temple paced the floor with an anxiety he had never known before.

Mary suddenly arose, a new light burning in her eyes, a dauntless determination stamped upon her face.

" Henceforth All or Nothing. Oh my childhood's God of love, once more I love Thee, trust Thee, serve Thee." She walked past her husband, not heeding his presence, motioned Janet away, and knelt beside the cradle.

Like a lightning flash the truth had been revealed to her as she lay there on the bed hoping, praying to die. The white germ of her childish faith had suddenly seemed to spring forth a vital reality, bearing upon its living stalk the possibility of a blossom.

" That child *must* not, *cannot* die," she said passionately. " She is my all—God is good—I will trust Him."

Silently the nurse and husband left the room. Mary prayed.

Janet with streaming eyes knelt outside the door,

her warm Scotch heart melting with sympathy. Felix Temple, a strange softness in his heart, paced up and down the long dark hall.

"Oh Thou most high and only God, Thou who gavest back the widow's son, Thou who raised again the buried Lazarus, who brought the maiden from her still white couch of death, Thou art here now, and Thou art forever the same God, the same loving Father whom we know through Thy Son, the living Christ. Thou wilt reveal Thyself to and through me, who knowing Thee still knew Thee not. But now, Oh Father, I know Thee as Thou art, the perfect Love in whom we live forever. Thou hast said: 'Acknowledge me in all thy ways.' I do acknowledge Thee now—In Thy presence is fullness of joy. In Thy presence weakness, doubt, failure, fear, sickness are consumed forever, for Thou art the consuming fire, the Love that knows naught beside Itself, the perfect, perfect Whole. . . Oh my Father, I cringe not nor shrink before Thee, for Thou art in very truth the overbrooding Tenderness, that gives to all its children its very Self. 'He that is born of Thee, sinneth not, for his seed remaineth in him.'"

"This child is not mine but Thine, and it lives with Thine own life. Naught can take Thee from Thine own, for Thine own dwell in Thee, living and moving and having their being forever. . . Father I fear not, for Thou art with me.

"Take this Isaac Thou hast loaned me. Do with her as thou wilt. . . I lay her upon the white altar of Thy love, leaving the incense of my faith to ascend unceasingly to Thee. . .

"Take my years of doubtings and their failures, their sorrows and regrets—all oh Love Supreme, I bring to Thee. Now I know that life is hid with Christ, in Thee the everloving God. . .

"Not my will, but Thine, oh Lord, be done. . . I thank Thee Father that Thou hast heard me, that Thou hearest always. . . "

All was still. Felix Temple opened the door softly and looked in. A sweet, natural sleep had fallen upon the child.

With clasped hands and closed eyes, Mary knelt beside the cradle, her face transfigured with a holy light, a divine ecstasy.

He withdrew as softly as he had come. An unfamiliar lump rose in his throat, a strange dimness assailed his eyes. There are times in the lives of individuals when the burning bush that Moses saw, flames forth in sudden vividness, and the still small voice whispers, "Put off thy shoes from off thy feet, for the ground whereon thou standest is holy ground."

. . . Mary turned to the child. She felt the soft, cool flesh, and listened to the gentle breathing. . . "I thank Thee my Father. It is finished. . . Not by might nor by power, but by my spirit, saith the Lord," she murmured, great tears of joy raining down her cheeks. Then, clasping her uplifted hands, she solemnly exclaimed, "Henceforth, Thou only. Once more a child, oh my Father. Keep me always thus. . . "

A strange stillness possessed her soul. Fear, doubt, unhappiness disappeared. The meridian of her life had come. Above her in the clear, blue ether of trust, rose the Sun of Righteousness, the absolute and only God,—divine Love, and in the radiance of its shining, clouds and shadows melted into nothing.

Love, joy, peace, like rippling waves of light, bathed her in their embrace, and kissed her into knowledge—knowledge of life and its meaning.

Once more God "whispered in her heart," and she knew the lovely truth. Oh, the joy of knowing!

There was no mistake, then ; God had never refused to answer prayer. He was the same yesterday, to-day and forever. *Now* she had proven it. Before, she had dimly believed it, and what was belief beside positive knowledge? Knowledge is certainty, fixed and absolute understanding. . .

What was this secret of becoming as a little child and entering the kingdom of heaven?

Willingness to believe in God, trust in Him and keep His commandments without selfish judgment. . . As a child she *had* believed in this way—yes, and she had entered the kingdom, too ; but when she became a woman, with the grand privilege of life before her, then what ? *Then* she had turned to the human for comfort, for satisfaction, for the food of vanity, approval of self; and when condemnation had come instead, she had still pined and moaned for that which only Spirit can give. She had suffered much ; but when the first heart-breaking agony of disappointment had come to her, when cruel words had seemed to draw her very heart's blood, when the prison doors of marital authority had shut her away from the best and sweetest deeds and impulses of life, *then* had she turned from the human to the

Divine for help or strength? Ah, no! not until the
furnace was heated seven times hotter; not till now,
when the jewel of her life was to be the sacrifice of her
idolatry, did she turn to That only which could keep
the jewel in its setting. . . Oh, this necessity for
constant acknowledgment!—she knew now what it
meant, and in the knowing, how well revealed were the
failures of the past. . . Had she acknowledged the
ever-loving, omnipresent God when the lovely form of
her first-born was taken out of her sight forever? Had
she been able to love to the uttermost her neighbor as
herself? Had she not allowed fear and tribulation and
mental anguish to be greater powers than the one only
Love that casts out such demons?

Alas, alas she had broken the commandment in
every instance. Ceasing to be a child, she had been
banished from heaven, that consciousness of the
unbroken circle of harmony which is within every soul
that recognizes the Perfect.

. . . . She had grieved and struggled and agonized
for very pity of herself, instead of speaking the truth
for Christ's sake. . . She had resisted evil instead
of recognized good. . . How could Love flow into a
channel filled with bitterness, disappointment and
rebellion?

Could any prayer be answered that went forth from
such a consciousness? Never.

. . . . "Let the same mind be in you that was in
Christ Jesus" . . . Ah there it was again, the child quality of mind—the receptiveness, the willingness to do and
speak righteously, to acknowledge the Father.

"Be still and know." To still the waves of sense-judgment, to quench unkindliness and distrust would surely be to know that in all the kingdom there could be naught but the Love that fulfills all law.

So Mary watched beside the sleeping child, and consecrated herself anew to the Highest. She had been resurrected, born again into the life of the Spirit.

A consciousness of Omnipresence filled her. . . . . From the depths of her inmost soul she awakened. . . . . Truth poured in upon her like a silver flood.

. . . .

"Oh sense unutterable by which I know Thee, in all Thy matchless majesty and supremest beauty: by which I know but to adore.

"To Thee O God, I offer thanks, above, beyond what lips express. To Thee I turn as lily turns to sun, with chalice pure, but yet unfilled, waiting for the glorious baptism of Thyself, waiting for the rich beams of Thine own translucent whiteness to filter through the tender petals of my meekness.

"Having turned O Wisdom infinite, divine, O Boundlessness unnamable, by the strange sweet alchemy of Thy great Presence understood, I find a living thread of Thine own Self woven into the warp and woof of my being, which is no longer mine but Thine!

"O wondrous miracle of mystery! The I apart, but to survey and apprehend the mighty Whole! The I submerged but to know and act again itself in Thee!

"Power stupendous, moving with slow, unnoticed tread, or quick and mighty throes of action—is but a guise of Thy almighty Self.   Perceiving this, the I shall be of Thine own Self the center and circumference, transfused into Thy great and mighty Force.

"Intelligence, far-reaching and diffusive, through all, in all brought forth, shining with a radiance different, yet unsurpassed by rarest gem of earth, known in the highest sense as boon most God-like and Divine —that, too, is but another name for thy prismatic Self; that, too, absorbed by this conscious I, is but another reading of the ' I in Thee and Thou in me.'

"Love, O rare, ineffable, all-abiding, all-residing Love! Thou art very, very God! In Thee may all alike perceive the white essence of Life; the matchless, lackless marvel of the Universe, in which dwells *All!* O Excellence supreme! O Gift divine! In Thee, may I be known as Thee! O Love, burn with Thy white flames the outer, lower sense of person and turn it into the brooding tenderness of Spirit. . . .

. . . .

. . . "Marvel not, O child, that thou art already ensconced within my heart. The uttered long-held wish is but the instrument which tears away the veil that hides the rare surpassing knowledge of my Presence.

"Yea, in the very whiteness of that wondrous Love, Thou movest. In the warm radiance of its never-ceasing fire, thou dost dwell forever, transfigured with a shining pearly light, of which thou canst as yet but dream.

"Sleep not nor dream again, dear one, of time or

place or sense where Love is not, for there thou never wert, nor aught of which thou dreamed.

" In Me are light and life unquenchable. In Me are health and strength unspeakable. In Me are peace and joy unnamable. In Me are love and power immeasurable.

" Think of Me. Speak to Me. Name Me to thyself, and thou shalt be forever freed from the turmoils and trammels of thy sense of sickness, sin, despair or bitter sorrow. Move in Me, knowing I am Power—the Power of thy moving. Manifest thy higher self, knowing thou canst manifest naught but the self of Me, in whom thou hast forever lived, from whom thou canst ne'er depart.

" Wouldst thou have my spoken words? Let them rain upon thee in the summer dew, the gentle air-breath, the tender sunlight, the ray from golden censer swung in heaven's far-off blue, the note of melody from feathered throats, the prattling music of childhood's innocence, the shifting panorama of Nature's glory-scenes: all these dear child, are whisperings of My heart to thine.

" Read them rightly and ye have the key to the other side of sunlight, the other side of beauty, the other side of harmony, the other side of innocence.

" On this ' other side ' wilt thou find aught but Me, the indivisible, the perfect One?

" Far from it ! Me and Me only shalt thou learn to know, if thou still hold the key—the magic key that opes the door of all mystery, the key whose name is spiritual understanding.

" There ! Thou hast made the circuit. " I am the Beginning and the End, the Alpha and Omega."

CHAPTER XXIV.

"For life, with all it yields of joy and woe,
    And hope and fear—believe the aged friend—
    Is just our chance o' the prize of learning love,
    How love might be, hath been, indeed, and is;
    And that we hold thenceforth to the uttermost
    Such prize despite the envy of the world,
    And, having gained truth, keep truth ; that is all."

JANET was awestruck. She had never seen "sic mys*teer*ious workin's o' Providence." "Why," she exclaimed, in speaking of Margaret's cure, "she cam' oot o' 't like the Laird Himsel' had touched her, an' I'm not richt sure but He did;" wiping her eyes with the corner of her apron.

Janet was a warm-hearted earnest-souled Scotch woman, and habitually referred everything either good or bad to Providence, for a belief in Providence was about the only real conviction she had, though her opinions were numerous and chameleon-like, inasmuch as they generally manifested the color of their sur-roundings.

The sudden cure of Baby Margaret perplexed her greatly. She had never heard of anything like it, but her great faith in Providence made it quite possible that all this was true.

"Why Janet, what's that you're saying? The Lord don't work that way now," rejoined Sarah, the extra help, who had come during the baby's illness.

"Eh, Sarah, but wha *cud* a done sic a thing but Him?" remonstrated Janet, her face clouding at such a thought.

"Who? Why the one that's always beguilin' of us into believin' in *his* ways o' doin' things, 'stead o' the Lord's."

"But Sawtan cud na lay hold o' that wee bit lammie, Sarah," argued Janet, for once able to hold her own. "He's not ower bold where baith gude an 'vairtue are, an' war na the mither prayin' i' the richt gude wull o' love an' faith?"

"Yes, an' ain't the devil goin' about like a roarin' lion, seeking whom he may devour?" quoted Sarah, severely.

"Ay, but there was nae davoorin' this time, an' I doot verra' mooch if he roared," persisted Janet, her eyes shining with zeal, as she put a cup of milk and a napkin on the tray she was preparing to take to the nursery. "Sic a wee bonnie lammie to be caught i' the deevil's paws—hech!" she mused, indignantly, her round face flushing with excitement.

"Humph! the child got well because the doctor's medicine operated just then, an' there was no miracle about it," cried Sarah impatiently, quite forgetting her religious views.

"'Twas the Laird, an' no dochtor," replied Janet stoutly, as she marched upstairs.

But after she thought about it she was a little afraid Sarah was right.

Janet had been a simple, unthinking soul all her life, doing what her hands found to do, but depending

on those in authority to supply her religious beliefs for
her. She was endowed with a natural intuitiveness
and strong sympathy, which made her continually subject to two distinct qualities of thought, without an
understanding of either. The real fact was, she was
trying to wear a garment made for the middle ages,
rather than for a woman of the nineteenth century.
Her soul was great, but knew not the meaning of greatness. Glimmerings of the true light had come to her,
but she had mistaken them for tallow dips of illusion,
and mercilessly snuffed them out of existence.

And in this, Janet was like many other poor souls,
quenching, in their ignorance, the brightest of God's
beacon lights, that wondrous intuition which alone
reveals the inner wisdom of the Holy Life.

"I maun be sairly i' the wrang," she murmured
one day in Mary's hearing. She had just laid Margaret on the bed asleep, and after an earnest contemplation of the rosy cheeks and sweet child-mouth, she
had turned away with a sigh and the foregoing exclamation.

"What is it, Janet?" asked Mary, looking up from
her sewing. She sat by the east window in the nursery, where the leaves of the great maple lovingly swept
the walls with their soft fingers, or gently swung themselves inside with a low *swish* of greeting.

"There's aye sae mony meanin's to the Laird's
worrds, it do mak' me clean distrackit ofttimes. My
hert wull hae 't that the Laird's the same for aye, an'
He'll heal the sick folk to-day as i' the time whan the
Maister walkit the airth, but Sarah do say, an' she

stan's for the Chearch, 'at it's wicked to believe i' sic a thing." Mary did not reply.

"What div *ye* think o' 't?" continued Janet.

"I know but one thing to think, Janet, after such an experience as I have had. Do you think Margaret would be with us now if it weren't for God's law of healing?"

"Eh, mem, div ye ca' it a *law* o' healin'?" with a startled look.

"It must be law, else Jesus would not have said that whoever believed would have the same power."

"Oh, but the gude Laird cud na a meant it sae!" cried Janet, dropping the towel she held, with a sudden gleam of something akin to hope sparkling in her eyes. "'Twas the followin' twelve he spake til!"

"How do you know?" asked Mary, quietly.

"Eh weel, but the Chearch says that "—

"Is the Church greater or better authority than Jesus?"

"Far fra that, Meesis Temple, but there's aye sae mony fa'se lichts, an' it's the fa'se licht that wrecks the mariner," rejoined Janet in great perplexity.

"But we can never expect to find the harbor if we do not keep our eye on the light-house."

"Ay, but th' hoose is na aye whaur we luik fer 't, an' hoo can a puir body ken th' set o' their ship whan th' fog's doon upo' 't? Hap its til th' sea an' hap til th' shore."

"But the compass we always have, Janet."

"What's that, mem?"

"'Lo, I am with you always.'"

"But hoo can that be ony help i' th' *prahkteece* o' releegion?"

"By taking it as Jesus said it, and believing that the presence of Truth will overcome all evil and evil conditions."

"But th' Chearch wull hae 't 'at ye mun na tak' but a sma' pairt o' th' sayins' an'—"

"I have just learned what I knew long ago as a child—that it is better to depend on the sayings of Jesus than what people or the Church say about them."

The bright eyes, the flushed cheeks, the low earnest voice, and, more than all, the words gave evidence that Mary spoke "with authority."

"Nae doot, mem, if a body but kens what it a' means."

"To be filled with truth as Jesus was, Janet, is to know and do what he did."

Janet shook her head doubtfully.

"Ay, mem, but ist *paw*seeble for sic worms o' th' dust t'e'en think o' oorsel's an' the white-souled Maister doin' th' same warks?"

"*He* says so, Janet."

"But th' Chearch"——

"Janet, I told you to study what *he* says, not what the Church says. What is the Church but an assembly of men and women whose beliefs are supposed to be founded on the sayings of the Master? If they have not held to those sayings they have lost their authority, and are living in the letter that killeth instead of the spirit that maketh alive; I've tried both ways, and now

I want to live always in the light of his words, which means in the spirit."

Mary's voice trembled with its burden of meaning. She plucked a leaf from the swaying branch and idly pulled it to pieces as she gazed vacantly through the window at the far blue sky.

Janet drew her breath quickly and wiped away the tears, as she asked with a dawning light in her eyes, "Cud ye be free frae sufferin' gin ye luiket till the Word that we hae for aye, is that y'er meanin', Meesis Temple?"

"Not mine, Janet, but his. He said: 'The words that I speak unto you, they are spirit and they are life.' And many other things that you must read for yourself, my dear."

"It's me hert's ane langin' come true," exclaimed Janet, excitedly. "Eh, mem, daur I hang til 't?" The light suddenly quenched again by a cloud of doubt.

"I would rather trust him, Janet, than anybody else. I trusted other people too long. No person or thing must we rely upon but the Truth which Jesus knew and lived. To be as a little child is to live in the spirit. It is the false gods we worship that bring all the trouble and sorrow. Everything fails us—riches, honor, human love—but God, the eternal Love, never fails. Oh, I have learned much Janet, since that night I stared at death for little Margaret, and now I know what it means to prove Him and receive the blessing."

A thoughtful pause ensued. Janet waited a moment, then asked slowly:

"Div ye think ye cud be temptet any mair, Meesis Temple?"

"Tempted, Janet? Even the Master himself was tempted, but he knew how to overcome evil with good; that is true strength and it is knowing his method, being of the same mind with him, that helps me so much. It is no disgrace to be tempted, Janet, but that I may be armored with his strength not mine, is my highest prayer."

"Cud ye na' mak' 't a bit plainer til me, mem what his stren'th may be?"

"It is the strength of Truth, Love, Almighty Good, any and every kind of strength, strength of mind or body; strength to say no to what is not true, strength to speak and act righteously, strength to work, walk, lift, breathe or to do whatever is necessary."

"Please mem, wull ye lat me hearken anither day? Me hert's ower full the noo."

She waited for no reply, but walked quickly from the room, and Mary went to little Margaret, whose bright blue eyes just then opened roguishly.

CHAPTER XXV.

"If there be some weaker one
    Give me strength to help him on;
If a blinder soul there be,
    Let me guide him nearer Thee."

—*J. G. Whittier.*

OVER two years had passed since Carrol opened the "Helpers' Home."

The rain fell drearily and steadily one cold evening late in May, as a thinly clad, ragged unkempt man paused on the outer steps. The blinds had not been drawn and he could see the family circle within; two boys with bright manly faces leaning over their slates, apparently studying a lesson. A placid looking girl of eighteen or twenty, with an illustrated magazine in her hands; another girl sewing, and still another—a humped-backed little creature—with the happiest face, engaged in making paper flowers. A lady presently entered, awakening cheery smiles and greeting from all present, as each looked up from his or her occupation.

In a few moments they all left the room, except the lady, who turned down the gas and drew the blinds.

Darkness and the worst of its allies, a feeling of desolation settled upon the man outside.

"It's no use," he muttered; "I will try once more to-night, and if they won't help me the saloon will."

He staggered up the steps in a weak dazed way, and rang the bell.

239

The pleasant-faced lady herself opened the door.

"If you please, Madam, have you any odd job I could do in exchange for something warm to eat?"

"Oh yes, we always have 'odd jobs' that will turn into Aladdin's Lamp if you do them right," she said, with a smile. "Come in out of the rain and have something to eat first. There is the bath-room," pointing to a door, "with nice hot water, soap and towels. When you have finished, come this way," as she opened another door and disappeared.

"Now children, big and little," she said, addressing the group around the tea-table, "I am going to ask you a question—no, not a hard one," seeing Jack's look of dismay. "Where would you rather be, out on the street with no place to sleep, or here in our snug little home?"

"Here!" all answered in chorus.

"Well, if you hadn't any home, and somebody else had, what would you wish them to do?"

"Share it," cried the girls together.

"Give a feller a chance to earn his lodging," said Jack, heartily, not losing sight of the mutual help principle.

"That is doing as you would wish others to do to you, is it?"

"Yes ma'am," cried the chorus again.

"Very well; now here is an opportunity to put your principles into practice. A poor man just came to the door, asking for supper. He looks very thin and weak. I do not like to turn him out this wet night. After he has had something to eat in the warm kitchen, what can we do for him?"

" He can have my piller and—" began Jack.

" And our quilt," interrupted little Nina, speaking for herself and Kitty.

Before Tillie could suggest anything, a faint knock was heard on the door.

Carrol put her finger on her lips. "Sh—sh, I wanted you to speak for yourselves, for all the helpers must have a hand in the work."

So saying she opened the door, and gave a sudden start of surprise as she saw the clean face and well brushed hair of a gentleman, instead of the "tramp" she had left in the hall a few moments before. She led him into the kitchen, where a warm atmosphere savored with culinary orders, was peculiarly grateful to the wanderer.

Carrol recognized him as the long-lost Ned, but made no sign. She had him remain for the night, in the "Good Samaritan" room; an apartment devoted to the common use of the helpers, and where occasionally a bed was extemporized, as in the present instance.

That night she spent in planning what could be done for the prodigal. She must first gain his confidence, and then would come reformation (for she could see his besetting sin stamped upon his face), and a return to his mother.

As Carrol let her mind wander into the dark avenues and byways of memory, she remembered the love and kindness lavished so freely upon her by Ned's mother, when her heart was almost broken with grief for the loss of her own. . . She would give love for love; she would do all in her power to make a man of Ned Rice. Perhaps this would in some measure also atone for poor Ralph's disappointment. . . Yes, she would put away all fear of the world's criticism—would not shrink from false judgments.

She would forget the experience with Magdalen Lostt, that occurred only three months ago. Why should not a young woman, with the purest and highest motives, associate with a fallen creature—man or woman —for the God-like purpose of developing that within, which had never fallen and could never fall?

Oh, the cruel, misjudging world, that seems not to conceive of anything higher than its own gross materialism, by which it judges humanity.

Is there no way of escaping its Argus eyes and cruel tongue?

"I will not think of it," she said aloud, after tossing sleeplessly till near morning. "If my own consciousness of right is not my protection, then it shall be my peace. What *should* be done shall not be left undone through any cowardly fear on my part."

Then she slept until the sun shone brightly into the room and told her it was very late.

What a morning it was! Glittering gems sparkling on every leaf and flower; the breathing earth sending forth an odorous incense to meet the golden sheet of light that mantled everything. Liquid, bubbling streams of melody pouring forth on all sides.

Nature smiled with contentment. This day was a pean of joy.

Strangely enough a Bible text that she had often heard Mary quote came into Carrol's mind; it was regarding the false and the true fast. She only remembered the substance of it, but as she looked out on the glorious day these words repeated themselves again and again: "Is this a day for a man to afflict his soul, to bow down his head as a bulrush, to spread sack-cloth and ashes under him? . . . Is not this the fast that I have chosen? To loose the bands of wickedness, to undo the heavy burdens and let the oppressed go free."

And like the rhythmic cadence of far-off music coming nearer, she heard the crowning promise: "Then shall thy light break forth as the morning, and thine health shall spring forth speedily; and thy righteousness shall go before thee, the glory of the Lord shall be thy rearward."

As one who has been dreaming Carrol suddenly came to herself. What did it all mean? She, quoting the Bible! . . . But it was very beautiful; and she began to see a meaning in it she had never seen before.

The breakfast bell rang for the last time as she hastened down the stairs.

Repeated knocks at the door of the Samaritan room brought forth no response. Later they found that the whilom guest had disappeared. But nothing was taken or even displaced in the room, as we are too apt to think must necessarily be the case under such circumstances.

It was a disappointment as well as a regret to Carrol that he had thus gone without even a word, but she was sure he would return sooner or later. And he did.

It was nearly a fortnight later, just after the children had scattered for the day's work; Carrol was working in the garden, and with a broad hat over her eyes, did not see the approach of the recreant tramp.

A low-voiced "good morning," caused her to drop the garden tool and start with a little exclamation of surprise.

"Why, is it you, N—." She quickly checked herself—"who stayed with us one stormy night a week or so ago?"

"Yes ma'am, I went away so early in the morning on account of feeling sick; and now I have come back to pay for that night's lodging—not in money, for that I haven't got, but in work, if you can give it to me."

Carrol looked at him closely. Evidently he did not recognize her.

"I am glad you came back," she said. "It is a disappointment to me when people cannot exchange a few words, even if they never meet but once. Put on your hat again. Now you may weed this strawberry bed, if you please."

He went to work heartily, and as she lingered about, watering the flowers, tying up the sweet-peas, or plucking weeds, she had a good opportunity to observe him. His face betrayed more weakness than real sin. But there was a boyishness about him still, that savored of innocence and good memories.

Carrol could stand it no longer. "Why don't you go home to your mother, Ned?" she cried at last, with such startling suddenness that he dropped the hoe and paled visibly, as he stared at her in amazement.

" Wh-what?" he asked stupidly, as if under a spell of some sort. And then added, huskily, "Are you the little girl that was with mother when—" he seemed unable to proceed.

" Yes, I am Carrol Evans," she interrupted. " And now, Ned, I am your friend ; come, tell me all about it."

Then with his face turned to the growing things around them, Ned told the story of his life.

"I ran away," he began, " because I wanted to get away from that everlasting praying and pretending, and father's cruelty, but I did hate to leave mother and—Ralph—tell me about them, please, before I go on ; for I have suffered, no one knows how much, wanting to know."

He drew a ragged cotton handkerchief from the hidden regions of his tattered coat.

"Ralph is doing nobly and has devoted himself especially to your mother, who would have died long ago had it not been for him, and the hope of sometime seeing her baby, as she always calls you."

" Does she hope yet?" he asked, faintly.

" Yes, and always will. I never fail, when I see her, to say that you will keep your word and go back to her."

"Impossible," he murmured, looking down at his clothes, dejectedly.

" No, Ned, nothing is impossible to him who truly desires and works for an end. You shall have the best chance in the world. I can and will help you. I thought it all over that night you slept here."

He made a motion of protest, but she would not

heed it, and ostensibly continued her work among the flowers.

"Now, Ned, please go on with your story, then I will tell you my plan. Where did you go first?"

She would not allow him to linger in the depressing fog of regret, nor look back to painful memories.

"I went to Cincinnati and from there worked my way to New York, where I found odd jobs on the ferry boats for awhile. I cannot tell you all, Carrol, and you would not care to hear it if I could. I kept thinking that by and by, when I had plenty of money I would go home to mother, but the money did not come fast, and what came was used in—I might as well say it—gambling and drink. Then I lost all I had, even my place. And for awhile tried to get honest work to do, but everybody shut the door in my face and called me a worthless tramp until at last I got clean discouraged and desperate. One day in a crowd (I had gone hungry three days) I managed to pick a woman's pocket, but was caught and carried to the station. They kept me thirty days, but it might as well have been thirty years;" he spoke bitterly. "I was a jail-bird from that on, and went from bad to worse. Finally one night I had a dream. . . ." He paused as if the recollection was painful. Carrol stopped picking weeds, and begged him to go on.

"Well, that dream took me back to childhood. I had done some childish wrong, and mother, with her great melting eyes of love, stood over me, just as she used to "—his voice grew unsteady—" and said, 'do the best you can to make it right Ned, I will help you;

whatever you do, remember mother loves you.' . . . And I didn't care for father's rage or punishment, or even public shame, for it was something everybody knew about; I only cared for mother's love. Then I awoke, and such a great homesickness came over me that I started that very day in the home direction. It took me several weeks to get this far, and I had walked two days with only a little bread and water to eat that night I came here first. . . . If you had not been kind to me, I should have gone to the saloon, for there, at least, a fellow can go in and warm. Many a night I walked the streets of New York without even a shelter, except those places that are always open to wretches like me. That night, although I did not quite recognize you, I had suspicions, and so got out early in the morning. . . . I had made a promise to myself, in the name of the mother . . . who loved me "—

"Loves," interposed Carrol.

"Yes, who loves me, to be honest, at whatever cost. . . I have not broken it, but there is another temptation "—

"Ned, I want you to help me; will you?" Carrol spoke in a quick, decided voice that seemed to compel an answer.

"If I can," he said, stumblingly.

"Of course you can, and I need you from this moment." Then she explained something of the work she was doing, taking care to exclude all terms that might seem to his ear to savor of religion.

They agreed that his identity was to be a secret till

he chose to reveal it himself.   He was to be known by the name of Edwin Hartwell.

And so the compact was made, and that very day he began the new life.

CHAPTER XXVI.

"Was it not to preach forth this same Higher that sages and martyrs, the Poet and Priest, in all times have spoken and suffered; bearing testimony, through life and through death, of the Godlike that is in man and how in the Godlike only has he Strength and Freedom! Which God-inspired doctrine art thou too honored to be taught; O Heavens! and broken with manifold merciful afflictions, even till thou become contrite, and learn it! O thank thy Destiny for these; thankfully bear what yet remain; thou hadst need of them; the Self in thee needed to be annihilated. By benignant fever-paroxysms is Life rooting the deep-seated chronic Disease, and triumphs over Death. On the roaring billows of Time, thou art engulphed, but borne aloft in the azure of Eternity. Love not pleasure, love God. This is the Everlasting-Yea, wherein all contradiction is solved, wherein whoso walks and works, it is well with him."—*T. Carlyle.*

I WONDER who that man is that always buys my prettiest flowers," said Nina one evening at the tea-table.

"Ain't he that feller with a grave-yard face an' a white choker what walks past here every evening?"

"How do you know so much about it, Jack? you ought to be getting your grammar lesson at that time," interposed Carrol hastily, and flushing a little as she spoke.

"I am—learning moods and tenses," was the rogue's startling reply. Like all of his class, Jack was intensely observant, and because of that fact constantly acquiring knowledge on most unexpected and uncommon matter; but his ready tongue and general good-heartedness made him a favorite in spite of uncouth ways and sometimes pert speeches.

Carrol did her best to prune off the excrescences, and while he had improved greatly, Jack was still Jack, and probably would be to the end of the chapter.

"See that you attend more to your book and less to people then, Jack. You know it is a mark of ill-breeding to notice the peculiarities of face or dress, and certainly to discuss them." Carrol said this in a tone of the most rigid reproof, which was generally all the discipline necessary. For the disapproval of Miss Evans meant the darkest cloud this household could know.

"I'll help y'er with y'er flowers, Niny," said Jack, with a magnanimous smile after a moment's silence.

"Thank you," with her rare look of gratitude, "I wanted to get the pansies all put in their new bed to-night. Miss Evans said we might work an hour before study time."

"How glad I am that we have a garden," exclaimed Kitty, who had been unusually silent.

"Yes, and everything else that's lovely," said a sallow faced girl of fifteen; "this is a perfect heaven to the home what I've always had since I went into that horrid store. I wish Letty Miles could come too."

"When Tillie leaves us for that fine place as seamstress to Mrs. Boles, you can bring Letty to take her place, Ida," said Carrol, smiling.

"Wen kin I bring them two kids what's been

waitin' since Easter?" questioned Jack, with a quick jealousy for his own friends.

"Are you sure they will work well, and not do as Tommy Brown did? Because you know we can't have anybody in this house who isn't willing to help cheerfully. That is why we call it the 'Helpers' Home,' and we must keep up the good reputation we have won. I am not sure but Miss Allbright intends to build a large addition in the fall, and if she does—"

"Oh, jolly! Won't that be a go?" cried Jack, delighted into forgetfulness of his good manners and, as usual, his correct vocabulary.

"There, now, you've got to read dictionary for fifteen minutes," called Kitty, whose turn it was this week to criticise language and call off penalties.

"All right; I'm game," with cheerful acquiescence. He only understood the laugh which followed when Kitty added ten more to the minutes of his word study. The freckled cheeks flushed, and the smiling mouth drew down at the corners into a good-natured grimace, but this time Jack discreetly held his peace.

Never mind, Jacky; I'll help you get your verbs," said the little hump-back, beaming upon him with her heavenly smile.

Jack did like the help, but he didn't like to be called "Jacky;" so he ungraciously mumbled something about attending to his own verbs.

"I am going to get my lesson 'nd then help Edwin sprinkle the lawn; may I, Miss Evans?" asked Nina, ready with another plan to help somebody.

"Yes dear; I think Edwin will be delighted," look-

ing at Ned smilingly, glad that the child was so free
with him, and feeling that she would be the best companion he could have.

Ned turned toward Carrol with a spare-me expression, but said that Nina might help him.

It was not without a terrible blow to his pride that
he had consented to take this place in the "Helpers'
Home," where he must be known as "that tramp" Miss
Evans took to reform. He forgot that no one knew
him here as one who needed to reform, but the underlying consciousness of his own weakness, like an evil
demon, taunted him with innumerable "can'ts" and
"impossibles" or mocking "if you dares."

On the other hand was his good angel, the white-
robed desire for a noble character, an angel worthy a
son of the long-suffering, patient little mother, whose
love was like the fragrance of roses that clings to the
shattered vase. Between these two, demon and angel,
he must choose, and upon the choice hung happiness or
woe. Of this he was well aware, and at least his effort
should be on the side of the angel.

Nina went with him and with an easy familiarity
and child-like simplicity talked about everything in her
world, until he almost forgot that he had ever been a
tramp.

"I always think the pansies are sweet little faces
smiling and bowing to us," she said as she directed the
hose toward the pansy bed.

Ned was tying a climbing rose to its trellis.

"I sometimes think they are too."

"Oh, what do they say to you?" cried Nina,

delighted to find some one who could or would understand her own fancies.

"I don't know exactly, except they make me feel like being good."

"That is a sign you are getting ready to understand their language," with grave earnestness. The serious assurance in the tones caused him to look attentively at her pathetic little figure kneeling beside another bed of thirsty pansies, as she gazed intently into their upturned faces. Bright rays of the setting sun rested on the shining curls and wrapt expressive face, making him forget for the moment the ugly hump that at first had seemed the only thing he could see about her.

"I will tell you," she exclaimed at last, with a joyous sparkle in the clear dark eyes, "they are singing together, don't you see how they lean toward each other?"

Ned confessed that he could not discern that fact.

"Why, it just seems as if I could hear the words; such tiny little voices too; don't you hear them now?" pulling him down beside her.

"No."

"Oh, dear! I thought I had found somebody that knows the flowers as I do. Well, never mind; I will tell you about them. Pansies sing and whisper, because they love and work together. They are not happy alone, like some other flowers—like the roses and the lovely tulips. When I sell pansies—I do hate to let them go —they have to go in companies, because their work is together; and their dear little faces tell of the joy of— dear me! what is that word that means together?—

u-union—yes, the joy of union. Miss Evans told me what it meant just yesterday. An' she said they mean thoughts, too; so they must stand for the union of good thoughts, 'cause of course they wouldn't make you think anything but good thoughts. That's why you want to be good when you look at them."

"Well, that's a splendid reason, little girl, and I'm glad you could give it. I will remember it every time I look at pansies," said Ned, more touched than he cared to show.

"So will I," said a deep voice the other side of the barberry hedge, which was the only barrier between the "Home" lawn and the street.

Ned and Nina turned in startled surprise. "Oh," exclaimed Nina, at last; "you like flowers, don't you?" with a pleased look at the stranger, whom she recognized as the man who so often bought her posies.

"Indeed I do, and because I like them so well I know *you.* Can you spare me a few of the pansies now?"

Harvey? Yes, he had been sauntering by, as was his daily custom, and hearing the childish voice, had paused to listen, as one might listen to a trilling bird song.

While she gathered a handful, Ned went on with his work, studiously avoiding the stranger's eyes by going the other side of the rose trellis; Harvey, meanwhile, puzzling his brains to know where he had seen that man, and wishing very much to know who he might be. Ned knew him well enough, for deep in the memory of the past was hidden the well-known form and face of the "goody Saint Harvey," as he had contemptuously called the boy whom the deacon never tired of quoting as the perfect model.

Harvey had not greatly changed, except that his face seemed older and wore a troubled look instead of the self-righteous, complacent expression which had been one of its strongest characteristics.

The boy, with his intense conscientiousness and blind faith, had changed into the man with a greater sense of duty added to his conscientiousness, and a stronger belief in the necessity of vigilant praying added to his faith. He was the boy intensified. A little wiser, a little gentler, a little better.

As Nina handed him the pansies he offered her the usual pay.

"Oh no, sir, not now; I am not selling flowers now. I am doing what I would like to do all day— giving them away to some one who loves them and will take good care of them. I would rather be a giver than a seller," she added, in an explanatory tone.

"Yes dear child, that is a good saying, but you can not sell what God gives freely to all. You can only sell the time you spend in taking care of and procuring the gift; and it is right to charge for the time. "The laborer is worthy of his hire."

She would take nothing from him, and holding his flowers tenderly he sauntered on.

The old longing to see Carrol came overwhelmingly upon him, and as he returned, he found himself gazing toward the "Home" with an increasing desire to go in. He had never stepped inside the gate since the night of the fire—that night which lived in his memory as the sweetest, yet the most awful he had ever passed, and in all these months Harvey had suffered much. His old experience in theological debates with Carrol warned him not to go near her on that ground; and this, in addition to the rigorous laws he had made for himself, had kept him quite away from her. He had heard of her increasing success as a teacher and speaker and occasionally read reports of her meetings, and though his heart was as hungry as ever, his loyalty to his religious convictions made him true to his resolutions not to see her, and also true to his belief that she was one of the worst of infidels. Indeed, on one occasion, having heard a statement of something she taught relative to church doctrines, he had felt it his pressing duty to publicly allude to such teachings and brand them as false. As a soldier of Christ, he could not let the enemy into the field, even if admitted by one as dear to him as Carrol.

He was sick for a week after this denunciation of heresy, but he had done his duty. So time dragged wearily on, and heart submitted to head, and head demanded of heart, until Harvey was sometimes almost demented with their contention.

. . . Now he felt himself strong enough to put aside personal feelings and labor unselfishly for the cause of the Master. Should he hesitate, when by entering into the midst of error, he might be able to overcome or dispel it? Possibly the time had come when he could say something that might turn Carrol from the "path of destruction." . . .

A line of people in twos and threes entered the gateway and walked toward the house. He remembered that it was Carrol's open meeting—"help meeting" he had heard it called. What better opportunity could he find than this? The meeting was public; he would wait a few moments longer, then go in with the throng and listen; if she taught false doctrines he would know how to meet them, and would be able to do her the more good for having heard.

He found himself in a large, pleasant parlor with rows of faces surrounding him, most of them intelligent, refined and earnest. Some with marks of suffering and pain; others with a keen unrest or fearfulness marking them with unmistakable signs.

Carrol had already begun her address. She stood upon a slightly elevated platform in full view. He had never seen her appear to greater advantage. Erect, dignified, eyes glowing with a repressed power; voice round, full, at times richly intonated, she poured forth words freighted with grander meanings than he had dreamed possible. What was it all about? He leaned forward eagerly, quite forgetting that he had intended to remain undiscovered behind the portierre.

Was it a lecture on philosophy? Was it a sermon on evil? By and by he settled down to listen intelligently. . . . .

"From the One Infinite Mind, which is God, come forth individual thoughts. Each thought is represented by an object. Man is born into the world apparently a senseless lump of flesh. Flesh is merely the expression of individualized thought. As he gains knowledge he gains power, which is active consciousness.

"Recognizing the Divinity of his real self (the real mind essence back of flesh), he turns mind—his organ of consciousness—toward his source and reflects or shows forth Divine qualities as fast as he becomes conscious of them. Hence the real man is like his Father, even as the sunbeam is like the sun from which it emanates.

"Truth, which is another name for Deity or Divinity, is like the light, positive in its power and nature; so every ray of light, that is, every thought of Truth, makes man powerful, because more conscious of Infinite Truth.

"Man thinks, and in his thinking manifests God-given power. Since thinking is from God, and in reality is all the power there is, all thoughts have power. If man through ignorance uses his thoughts in the wrong way, he produces wrong conditions or environments as these are ever the result of thought. Thus when he thinks evil, or misunderstands Life, evil or inharmonious conditions result.

"So long as wrong thinking predominates, undesirable conditions will likewise predominate. So long as man bases his thought upon appearances, he will be controlled by their laws.

"As Truth is like light, evil is like darkness; so the more he thinks of truth, the more enlightened he becomes; but the more he thinks of evil, the more benighted his mind appears.

"David said: 'I shall be satisfied when I awake in Thy likeness.' To be awake to Truth, is to be conscious of true thoughts. Hence, when man awakes, he will know himself as he is in the truth of his inmost being, will be conscious of the true and good, will know his relation to God, and knowing, will manifest truth.

"In his awakened state of mind he looks back on all the thoughts that went from his mind, while ignorant of Truth. In a sense he sees himself a creator, because the power that is creative (thought), the power that he used, or called into action, created wherever it was directed, either true or erroneous conditions, either harmony or inharmony in proportion as his consciousness was true or false.

"In the same way that light has power over darkness, Truth has power over error. Knowing this, now that he has come to a knowledge of Truth, man recognizes his great work. He must now illumine the dark thoughts of past ignorance or misinterpretation, and redeem them from bondage, thus elevating himself to a higher and clearer perception of God or Good. He must send the radiating beams of his consciousness into the vast sea of thought, must transform the evil or undesirable conditions into true or desirable conditions; he must purify and redeem every thought of anger, spite, selfishness, or whatsoever is opposite the eternal and omnipresent law of Love. When this true consciousness is attained, man will see God face to face, that is, will know Good and will reflect, or show forth, His or Its glory.

"Then it is his realization of the oneness of the Omnipotence that creates and sustains all. It is seeing himself as the child of the Good, consciously and wisely using the power that comes directly from the Father.

"This, as you see, my friends, is an open hint of

the reason for the distressing environments and conditions with which humanity contends. Let us make practical application of the truth we know. Let us adjust our power of thinking, to its legitimate uses, and so change misery, sickness, discouragement, into hope, health and courage; hatred, envy, selfishness, into love, contentment, helpfulness.

"Oh, hearts heavy with anguish; go out of your own and into other peoples' lives. Think lovely, sweet thoughts of everybody; clothe them in immaculate robes of purity; baptize them with peace and the beauty of wholeness. Uphold them with your tenderness; surround them with your charity; strengthen them with your wisdom; help them with your sympathy, and so prove to yourself and the world that you love your neighbor as yourself. Thus will clouds be lifted from your sky and the sunshine of your true thought make glad the dwellers in your world. . .

In the one immortal valley
  Bloom the lilies pure and fair,
Sending forth their royal perfume
  On the wings of summer air;
Sending forth to bless and strengthen
  Whosoe'er will take their gift,
Caring naught for answering guerdon,
  Caring only to uplift
Saddened hearts whose every burden
  May be lightened, loosened, freed
If they will but hold these lilies
  Near them in their deepest need.

Understanding is the valley—
  Understanding, firm and sure,

Of the Love that never faileth,
  Of the Life forever pure,
Of the Truth that e'er abideth,
  Of the One, the All in All.

And the thoughts most like the Father's,
  Tenderest Love that reaches all—
Are the lilies in this valley,
  Growing fair and straight and tall,
Sending forth their sweet aroma
  Till the works of hate shall cease;
Annulling fear and sin and sickness,
  Filling all the world with peace.

O, fair Lily, grow within me;
  Make my life as white as thine;
Fill my valley with thy perfume;
  Make thy radiant presence mine
Thro' each act of life's endeavor.
  Then shall God's dear will be done,
And the Now one glad Forever
  When we say, 'sweet peace is come.'"

CHAPTER XXVII.

"Until the human heart knows the Divine heart, it must sigh and complain like a petulant child. . . When we find Him in our own hearts, we shall find Him in everything. It is Life we want."—*George MacDonald*.

HARVEY stumbled blindly into the street, scarcely knowing where he was or whither he went. The cool night air refreshed his throbbing temples as he walked. Unconsciously he bowed his head beneath the radiance of the patient stars. All the pent-up intensity of his long silence seemed now to overflow. Was it really the skeptical Carrol who had uttered these glowing sentences? For a few moments he forgot that he was a minister of the gospel, with a preacher's work before him, and thought only of her beauty, her power, her success, but recalled himself with a start.

"They were, indeed, excellent words," he murmured, "but Jesus was not in them, and without Jesus they are as nothing. . . Oh, that she could be converted to the true doctrine, and use all her magnificent gifts for the glory of God. Poor girl, she is as the blind leading the blind. Without the precious gospel, what matter how eloquent her words, or even her life? To be sure she has grown in many ways, most gloriously, too, but it counts for naught without conversion." . .

Surely the Lord had guided him rightly, and he was after all to be the humble instrument through which she was at last to be saved. . . Now that she saw something to live and work for, now that she was willing to recognize the existence of God, even in this heathenish way, it must be that she was ready for the milk of the word.

He would not shrink from giving it. The Lord would provide opportunities, and—his own yearning heart should be rigidly subdued, trampled upon, crushed, if necessary. . . Unless, . . well,—unless Providence ordained otherwise. . .

So he reached his own room, and with a feeling that some new, strange work, wondrously acceptable, had come into his life, he entered into his nightly devotions.

A few weeks later he rang the bell at the "Helpers' Home." Little Nina opened the door, and after the first start of surprise at seeing the gentleman she had learned to know as the lover of flowers, she ushered him into the parlor and called Miss Evans.

Carrol received him graciously; not with the old "non-sufferance" demeanor, but with a cordiality and graceful ease that made his heart beat treacherously. She seemed marvelously changed. In place of the restless, girlish impatience, with its quick irreverent ways, she now carried herself as a calm, self-centered, well-poised woman, full of the dignity of womanhood.

They talked of the weather, the day, old friends; everything on the surface; but Harvey finally mentioned his presence at the Thursday meeting, and expressed his pleasure at the evident change that had come in her religious views.

She looked up with a flash of the old spirit which, however, quickly merged into seriousness.

"I can only say that I have entered a new life since I ceased questioning and began to *live* what I know."

"Ah, yes, that is a very great essential; but after all it cannot take the place of the blood of Jesus," he replied in the ministerial tone that had once exasperated her beyond measure.

She merely smiled patiently and looked down at her plain gold ring.

"I still have hope of converting you to the true faith," he went on, gaining courage at her silence.

"I appreciate both your desire and your effort, Harvey, and I think I understand as never before what true religion means; but I have learned that conversion comes, not through human agency, but through a conviction of truth itself, and the daily experiences of a thoughtful life."

It was so unlike the Carrol he had known all these years—this speech of hers—so gently, so firmly uttered, that it pleased while it made him anxious; and yet in all her sentiments he had discovered no flavor of the real essence of Christianity, no allusion to Christ Jesus, without whom all righteousness is but a cloak, the worst of mockeries.

A pause ensued. The evening breeze played with the curtain draperies, and through the open window they heard the children's voices.

"May I ask, Carrol, what is your idea of the Trinity? And how do you regard Jesus?" Harvey said at last, encouraged by her gentleness, and feeling it a religious duty to go as far as he could, now that the opportunity was at hand.

Her face grew reverent and tender in its seriousness, and her voice took on the low rich quality of tone that so often brought conviction to its hearers. She answered the last question first.

"I believe in him as the divine Teacher, inasmuch as he was the One God manifest in the flesh. His consciousness was the consciousness of the One Mind, hence he could say as he did, 'I and the Father are one.' God is the unexpressed Love, Truth, Power. Christ is the consciousness of Truth or God, manifest to mentality. Jesus is the consciousness of Truth or God, manifest to flesh. Holy Ghost, or holy breath, is the inspiration—inbreathing—of absolute consciousness of the Divine; and to enter into that consciousness is to be baptized of the Holy Ghost."

"Who taught you all this, Carrol," questioned Harvey, huskily, as she ceased.

" No *person.* It is simply the revelation of Truth that has come to me. Oh Harvey," she cried, with the old impetuousness, "I have often wanted you to know how differently I feel about religion now, from what I used to when you labored with me so hard. Would you like to hear about it? "

" Most assuredly, Carrol; not even your Aunt Marcia could take a deeper interest in your religious welfare than I do, and—"

"And always have," finished Carrol. "Yes Harvey, if every one would make the effort to turn people to righteousness that you did with me, and do it in the right way, the world would very soon be happier and better."

Unconsciously Harvey drew his chair closer. If he had loved her as an unbeliever, how much more might he love her as a Christian? Yet it was not the bloom and beauty of physical womanhood that attracted him, but the subtly-felt beauty of soul, the round completeness of the Ideal that glanced through her eyes, breathed through her tones and cast a radiance as of something indefinably divine about her.

"I do not suppose you will ever know, Harvey," began Carrol, after a moment's silence, "because you have never experienced the awfulness of doubt or the terror of fear; but *I* know through long, dark years of suffering and struggle. I rejected every form of religious belief from sheer inability to understand it, and, as you know, rejected it in the most ungracious manner. Finally I grew disgusted with everybody who uttered a word on the subject, with the exception of Cousin Mary. She was always lovely, but through certain circumstances in her life, which all her praying did not improve, I became more than ever antagonized toward the God she worshiped, and was in a state of indescribable despair and loneliness, when the opportunity opened for my work here. No," (seeing him about to speak,) "please say nothing about Miss Allbright, God bless her! if she had not been as wise as she is good, I don't know where I should have been today—in the insane asylum probably. However, I said to her when she proposed helping me into this work, that I was not good enough, besides being a total unbeliever in Christianity."

"And what did she say?" asked Harvey with much interest.

"She bade me stop talking such nonsense, and go to work with what I already knew. That encouraged me, as you can imagine it would. I did go to work and—well, you know something of the result, I suppose?" looking at Harvey inquiringly. "This home, with the happy inmates who are now on the road to a useful manhood and womanhood, is it not good testimony to the wisdom of that advice?"

"Yes, indeed! No doubt you will unite with the church now?" with visions of the reviving energy that might come to his church if she were only one of its workers.

"Unite with the Church?" she echoed with a sudden start of surprise. "I had never thought of it. No, Harvey, not unless I have a strong conviction that it is the best thing to do. While it is well enough to join a church, or stay in it if you already belong, I do not consider it an absolute necessity to the Christian life."

"But, Carrol," with a horrified look, "there would then be no division between the elect and the unregenerate." For a moment Carrol held his eye with the astonishment in hers. Then in a very quiet voice she quoted: "'By their fruits ye shall know them. Not every one that sayeth unto me Lord, Lord, shall enter the kingdom, but he that doeth the will of my Father which is in heaven.'"

"Yes, yes," exclaimed Harvey excitedly, "but it would never do to have no outward authority; no visible union of workers."

"Why not? Would not the union voluntarily externalize itself? And what good is mere 'outward authority?'"

"Why, to teach the doctrines, emphasize and insist upon the creeds, inspire awe and fear if necessary."

Carrol shook her head decisively. "No Harvey, the day is past when people can be frightened into Christianity. Creeds are rapidly dissolving, and the outward church has not a handful of faithful believers in creeds. It is not the creed but the *life* that saves, I tell you!" with sudden vehemence.

A benumbing horror stole over Harvey's mind. Was she so near and yet so far from the kingdom after all?

"But think," he began, not willing to take direct issue, lest he should discover a greater laxity in her views, "think of abolishing the doctrine of everlasting punishment for instance, how do you suppose hardened sinners could be converted?" He nervously wiped his face with his handkerchief. "The idea of everlasting punishment has already faded out of the mind of the majority of people, even the leading Christians," she went on, not heeding his growing astonishment. "It is no longer a bugbear except to the ignorant who do not think for themselves. Jesus never taught it. Why should the Church?"

"My God!" was all Harvey could utter. Blacker heresy he had never heard. She was not converted at all then! " God forgive her," he groaned at last, burying his face in his hands.

"Harvey, I used to feel angry to see you or any one else make such a fuss as I called it, over statements that you thought false or wicked. You may know how great a change has come to me when I tell you such things only make me sorry now,—sorry that you cannot better understand the Master's words. Take the spirit of his life for their interpretation, if you cannot get it otherwise."

"Poor girl, poor girl; it is you who cannot understand, and are blind to the awful truth," he rejoined

"The spirit in me beareth witness. Harvey, I want to tell you what came to me once when I was reading about everlasting punishment."

He made a motion of protest and moved his lips as if in prayer, but she continued : "I forget just where the quotation is found, but this is the substance of it : 'Inasmuch as ye ministered not unto one of the least of these, ye did it not unto me, and ye shall go away into everlasting punishment.' What is it that ministers ? First of all, thought, for thought precedes action. False, ignorant, wicked thoughts shall be cast into unquenchable fire, as it is called in another place. That means they shall be purified, the wickedness shall be burnt, dissipated, destroyed in the white heat of the consuming fire which is God ; 'Our God is a consuming fire.' God is Love, therefore the unquenchable fire is Love which forever and forever burns out the hatred, envy, indifference, ignorance, wickedness ; and the One

Presence stands alone in the Infinite kingdom of Itself."

Harvey had not heard or at least had tried not to hear. He was dumb with suffering for this poor soul who dallied so carelessly with her eternal destiny.

"Oh, Miss Evans come quick !" cried Nina, rushing in at this moment in breathless haste.

"Be quiet dear, what is it ?"

"Oh Edwin"—and the child stopped to gasp for breath. Carrol ran out on the lawn closely followed by Harvey.

CHAPTER XXVIII.

"'There is no other name (Way, Truth, Life) under heaven, which has been given among men, by which we can be saved.' His name, his character gives mankind a new birth, and at once perfects the entire social system. His name, his character, as it is developed, written in the forehead, written in the Book of Life, saves the world from sinning, and is the only Saviour."

—*L. J. Anderson.*

POOR fellow! he needs pity, not condemnation," murmured Carrol as she comprehended the difficulty. Ned had succumbed to his old weakness. They found him lurching and staggering about in the most helpless manner. Carrol sent the children into the house.

"I—couldn't help it," he murmured, with a pitiful attempt to control himself as Carrol drew near.

"Never mind. Go to your room now. You need not work any more to-night, and remember, Edwin, I depend on you in the morning. No one can make the fire quite as well as you, or do the morning marketing as quickly. Now—"

" B—t—I've disgraced m'self 'n—"

" Do not look at what you have done, but see what you can *do*. Be a man and step into the house with the thought that you are still a child of God."

Under cover of the coming darkness whose charitable mantle hides many a scene like this, Harvey and

Carrol together got him into the house. Harvey offered to see him to bed and Carrol withdrew.

A few moments later Harvey appeared to wish her good night.

"You have undertaken a heavy burden in caring for that young man," he said as he stood on the porch, hat in hand.

"Not so heavy but I can carry it, I hope. Just think," in a pitying tone, "the poor boy needs to know that he has as great a birthright in the kingdom as anyone else, and to hear some cheery words of encouragement, which I shall freely give."

"But Carrol, you can't afford to have such a person here to compromise your name and—"

"Jesus never stopped to think of compromising his character, why should his disciples?" with a thrill of conscious strength in her voice.

"True, but you are a woman, and the world is cruel. I know you are right, but we are told to 'avoid the appearance of evil.' At least promise to send for me when you need help again." He was in the work in earnest now, but he felt that it was divinely appointed.

"I will, Harvey, and thank you for the offer; but since this work is mine to do, I will not shrink from the doing." The echo of his own thought!

"Well," holding out his hand, "good night, Carrol. May I come again?"

"Certainly, and I wish you would be with us at our meetings occasionally," with a cordial shake of the hand.

"We are too widely separated in belief for that," he

said, sadly, and with a final good night he turned and went down the steps.

The initial step was taken and he was fully resolved now to labor with Carrol faithfully, until the Lord should bless his efforts and give her a change of heart. Oh that it might be soon, was his ardent prayer . . . A deeper, grander, intenser love than ever before possessed him, but human love should have no place before the Divine. He would seek her for the sake of her salvation first of all and he prayed for wisdom to overthrow the fallacies of her reasoning. After that, God willing, he might seek her love, her companionship, her co-operation—for with such a woman what could he not do?

The evening lessons were finally disposed of, and Carrol with a sigh of relief sat down to the study-table to write her long deferred letter to Mary. She had not yet heard of baby Margaret's sickness or recovery, and did not know of Mary's precious experience.

" I must tell you a secret, little cousin," she wrote. "About three weeks ago, a tramp came to the door and asked for food. Something about the face struck me as familiar, but—well, to make the story short, it turned out to be Ned Rice. Poor fellow, he is sorry enough for all he has done to break his mother's heart, and does want to go back to her, but must prove himself worthy first. . . I could not let the boy out into the wilderness again, so told him I needed his help here at the Home. Since that he has been working nobly until this evening, when old temptations proved too much for him. He came home intoxicated. I had company too—Harvey Willard. At first it seemed as if he ought to be turned adrift again, but what am I working for, if I cannot help a poor mortal when he needs the help? It is the hour of need that calls for action.

"I spoke kindly to him and encouraged him as well as I could, for I have learned the efficacy of the good words Miss Allbright talks so much about. Harvey helped him to bed and there he is. . . Now this sort of thing, I mean his drinking, of course must stop. Probably you will think it very foolish of me to think of such a thing as reforming him, but Mary, I can't help it: I *believe he can be saved.* Why not? Is the good not more powerful than all the evil in the world? And there is much good in Ned. He truly desires to leave the evil behind him and begin a new life. I *believe in him,* and I take every occasion to tell him so too. That helps wonderfully—more than all the preaching in the world. At first I wanted to save the boy for his mother's sake and Ralph's, but now I know he must be saved for righteousness' sake, for the glory of God.

"Does it seem strange to hear me use such an expression?

"Well, dear, a strange, blessed experience has been mine since I wrote you last. I have been converted—yes, Mary, if anyone ever had a conversion in the truest sense I have. Shall I tell you the beginning of it all? The first glimmer of it came when I entered upon this glorious work for the children, for they are all children to me. I began, desolate and heart-sick, as you too well know; but the joy of doing and giving soon turned into the joy of knowing and receiving. Life had new meanings for me. I found myself understanding the soul of things and growing more religious, or rather more capable of understanding the religious sentiment. The old clouds were dissolving, the old skepticism being displaced by a growing faith.

"You know, dear Mary, how I always longed for true knowledge, for the higher life. This desire, and my poor effort to do as much as I knew, was yielding fruit in this glorious way, I thought. But the last six weeks have been even richer with new meanings. I have been looking into the New Testament, and oh, Mary, the wonderful power of the words there has been proven to me. . . . I know the gospel is true; gloriously, grandly true! Not because it is printed in a book, but because it is 'written in the heart.'

"But you must know how I happened to read the story. Little Nina, the humpback, of whom I have told you, held some flowers in her hand one evening as we sat on the porch, and her sweet face fairly shone with love, as she said, 'I always think it is God smiling at me when I look at them,' in just the way you used to talk, Mary, and it touched a spring of thoughtfulness away down in my heart. Nina kissed me good night and went in to bed, but I hardly heard her. A thousand hidden streams gushed forth. I was back with the little Mary, who used to try so hard to tell me of God and His love, of Jesus and his wonderful sayings and works. . . A great tenderness came over me, and suddenly the veil seemed to lift from my eyes. Like faint tones of a far-off bell your words echoed through my mind, and I understood what they meant; the heavy thread of my life-long, though unconscious fear, snapped, and I knew what Christianity meant to you as a child. Then I found myself thinking some words that I thought must be in the Bible. They were: 'Except ye become as a little child, ye cannot enter the kingdom of heaven.'

"I went into the house, for I had been sitting there in the moonlight all the time, found Tillie's little Testament that lay on the study-table, and searched till I found that passage. It took me a long time to find it, but in the finding I read the gospel. You may realize my earnestness when I tell you I sat there till four o'clock in the morning. Since then such reading has been my constant solace and inspiration. It is not at all as it used to be, because now I can understand, and if this is Christianity, I want to be a Christian. I am learning to be as a little child, and to take the sayings of Jesus and his disciples for what they mean to me, not what they mean to somebody else.

"Oh I tell you Mary, it is the fear, the prejudice, the awful blindness, that make people misunderstand, and fail to *do*. Once let them begin with the willingness of a child and they will soon know the doctrine. Now, Mary dear, I know what it means to enter the new life and be born again. I have the solution of that weary problem I used to puzzle over in vain. Now I know *why* the 'Spirit is all and the flesh profiteth nothing'— why Jesus said 'Judge not according to appearances, but judge righteous judgment.' It is because God and his works only that we must recognize and acknowledge at all times and in all places, under all circumstances and conditions—but then you know all this. Why have I

not told you of my new life before?   Because I wanted
to demonstrate the power of the truth in my daily work.
I have, to a wonderful degree, and that is why I say I
know it is all true.   If that which claims to be good and
true, cannot be used in all the experiences of life, to
make us better, stronger and happier, it is a falsity.
Truth carries the possibility of its own proving, and
whosoever will may know and prove for himself, as
Jesus did.   In one respect particularly, I can see a
great change.   I used to be so critical and unchar-
itable, as you know, and no one better; but now
I find myself excusing, instead of condemning
people, and I see the grander meaning in those precious
words, 'Father, forgive them, for they know not what
they do.'   Oh, the Matchless Life and its infinite
power!   What if it were unattainable?   What if Jesus
but mocked when he said 'Be ye perfect as your Father
in heaven is perfect'?   What if he but idly amused
himself with the promise, 'he that believeth on me
shall do the works that I do, and even greater shall he
do'?   What if he cruelly deceived his followers by
telling them to 'preach the gospel, heal the sick, cleanse
the lepers, raise the dead, cast out demons'?   What if
he meant nothing at all by praying that not only his
disciples, but all who believed on him, through their
word might be one with the Father even as he was one
with the Father'?   What if—?

   "But no, these are idle questions in the face of all
the grand proof that has come to me—to *me*, Mary, who
used to agonize for one little sign that there was even
a God, . . Yes, I, the skeptic, the unbeliever, the hope-

less, despair-entangled doubter, can say to all the world
in tones that thrill with the joy of knowing : Christianity is not a dead letter, an empty dream, an impossibility. It is divinely true; its power is a reality; the
Christian life *is* possible, yes, grandly possible. It is
possible for all; and it is only by living *the life*
that we can know the truth. . . Well, Mary. what a
long letter ! It seems as though I could write all night,
but I *must* stop soon. . . . . Miss Allbright is thinking
seriously of organizing a Home and Voluntary Help
Society, in Lynn Heights. Can you not help her in
some way? In order to extend the work, and have a
Home in every town or city, she has thought of a
co-operative system by which it might be supported
indefinitely. That is, to form a stock company composed of all who desire to further the work, and
require the payment of a specified sum (say ten dollars,
if there are two hundred members), to be paid by each
on joining the company, and a yearly payment of five
dollars after that. This, with the private donations,
would be sufficient to start the Home and carry on
the work, until increasing membership and the due
proportion of wages from the " Helpers " themselves
would insure the permanency of the enterprise. It is
for this purpose that Miss Allbright wishes me to give
a series of public lectures in the fall, in order that the
masses of people longing to do something for humanity
may know the grand opportunity this work gives them.
Think of me giving a lecture in public! But then I
forget you have never heard me talk to my weekly
parlorful (I have the meeting once a week, so many

think it helpful to them). Seriously, dear, I can only say the talking is a part of my new birth, and so sacredly do I hold it as one of the gifts, that I never think of it without heartfelt thanksgiving.

"Harvey Willard, they say, is successful, very eloquent, and very earnest, as we know he has always been. Poor fellow! he still thinks me a lost sheep, although I gave him proof enough I thought, of being found. We had a long talk—the first since I could talk with him, and I begin to see now where he stands. Truly I am sorry for him. In spite of his life-long religious training, which is more responsible for it than anything else, he is in abject bondage to the letter of the law as laid down in the doctrines and creeds, which he does not seem to know, or at least remember, are simply men's opinions. . . I only wish he might see the spiritual truth and be helped as much as I have been. . . But I may be able to help him some way. Harvey is a good man and has many noble qualities of mind and character that I could not see in my days of blind prejudice. . . It is late. I *must* go to bed. Will finish in the morning. Good night." . .

But the letter was not finished, but a week later Carrol hastily added a few explanatory words:

"Good morning, cousin; I hope you will not think this letter 'stale and unprofitable' because it is slow in the accomplishment of its duty. You remember Ned? Of course, if you have had patience to read thus far. The next morning I called and rapped at his door in vain. He was gone! For three days we saw nothing of him. I was careful to have no discussion of him or his conduct before the children that would implicate him in any way. . . I knew he would return. He did, and so shame-facedly and in such a condition! He had been drinking, but was very repentant, although evidently expecting me to dismiss him. Instead, I roused his self-respect by speaking of his capacity for good, and told him what confidence I placed in him. The poor boy broke down completely and said nobody had ever trusted him that way—not even his mother, for she was always afraid he *would* do wrong—and then Mary, he poured out such a recital of woes and tribulations as boy and man, that my heart was wrung with pity, while I rejoiced more than I can tell to think I had taken him in. . . What right have we to judge anybody, when we know not the secret causes that have undermined their strength, constancy or virtue? . . But I must not stop to moralize. Ned has been lovely the last few days. Emerson is right: 'Speak to his heart, and the man becomes suddenly virtuous.'

"This letter is long enough for three. Consider that you have three to answer.

With fondest love,
CARROL."

CHAPTER XXIX.

"I must be myself, I cannot break myself any longer for you or you. If you can love me for what I am, we shall be the happier; if you cannot, I will seek to deserve that you should. . . I will not hide my aversions. I will so trust that what is deep is holy, that I will do strongly before sun and moon what ever inly rejoices and the heart appoints. If you are noble, I will love you; if you are not, I will not hurt you and myself by hypocritical attentions. If you are true, but not in the same truth to me, cleave to your companions; I will seek my own. I do not this selfishly, but humbly and truly. It is alike your interest, and mine, and all men's, however long we have dwelt in lies, to live in truth."—*Emerson.*

A WARM summer evening, the sky still rosy with the ragged fringes of a golden day's worn robes. Here and there a belated cricket singing his way to home and safety under the secret crannies of stone or grassy forest. The plaintive notes of a whippoorwill ringing out with echoing distinctness. Over all the arching depths of space with here and there a twinkling point of silver light glowing more brightly as the moments passed. Such was the time and scene as a carriage containing the Temple family, rolled slowly over the dusty road a few miles from Lynn Heights. They had spent the day in Tintuckett, Mary and the child with Mrs. Noble, and Felix Temple in the court room attending an important case.

The ride had been unusually pleasant. Scarcely in

Mary's remembrance had Felix been more amiable or tender. He was not even annoyed at the noisy prattle of little Margaret, and smiled when her tiny fingers clutched his beard. With impulsive haste Mary released the captive and was now scolding and kissing the charming delinquent in the most approved motherly fashion.

"Goo—oo" cried Margaret with a gurgling smile and a happy light in her eyes that said, "I don't care whether you scold me or kiss me, so you love me."

"What a charming day this has been Felix," exclaimed Mary, as they turned a corner that brought them face to face with the glowing west.

"Yes, it has, and I've won that case at last. No other lawyer wanted it. They were afraid to have me on the opposite side."

"Why?" asked Mary faintly.

"Oh because they knew the defendant would engage me, if the plaintiff did not."

Felix Temple smiled, a complacent smile of self approval, such as generally passed for genuine pleasantry in his case.

"That Claret is a smart fellow, and he knows where to get help. He knows very well I make a specialty of succeeding."

Mr. Temple was evidently pleased with himself. "Heigho baby, smile a little for papa; can't you now? There, mamma, I believe she has another tooth!" and he chatted and smiled with the tiny Margaret until she began to wonder what the world was coming to, that papa talked so much.

"By George!" gathering up the reins and urging

the horse into a trot. " I almost forgot that this was lodge night."

" Can you not stay away from lodge this once Felix? Baby and I would so like to have you with us," said Mary, venturing for the first time to make such a request.

" Couldn't possibly. Very important meeting, and I am one of the officers."

" We'll take revenge sometime, won't we Margie?" rejoined the wife in a half playful tone, as she buried her face in the snowy neck.

" See here Mary," said Mr. Temple suddenly remembering something—" I saw that Miss Allbright on the street to-day, and she asked me about getting a lecture hall for her in Lynn Heights: said something about starting some kind of society there, and hoped you would help her. Now I want to warn you beforehand, not to have anything to do with it. I will not have my wife turning crank and riding a runaway hobby horse."

A strange light glowed in Mary's eyes. She listened quietly until he ceased. A sense of largeness and freedom filled her. What she had longed to say a thousand times before, she felt could be said now.

" Felix," the tone was very gentle. " *Why* don't you wish me to help Miss Allbright or join her society?"

He was amazed. When had she questioned his motive before?

" I told you," was the curt reply. " I will not have people pointing you out as a crank."

"What is a crank?" Her calmness surprised him into answering.

"A –a crank? Well, a person who has unpopular ideas and parades them in public like a Punch and Judy show."

"And you are afraid I would do such things?"

"A woman's place is not in public, nor are her capacities fitted for grasping subjects outside her legitimate field," evasively.

"And what is her legitimate field, Felix?" persisted the calm voice.

"Confound it all! What's got into you Mary?"

" He looked at her angrily, expecting to see her quail and shrink into silence.

"Nothing wrong, I hope," was the unfaltering reply. Then clasping the sleeping Margaret close to her bosom, Mary met her husband's gaze with one so full of dignity and fearless power that he was impelled to listen as he never had before.

"I have something on my mind that must now be uttered. For five years I have lived with you and never until the last few weeks—since we regained our baby from the grave itself—"

"Stuff and nonsense! She would have got well anyway."

"From death itself," Mary repeated with the same calmness. "Never have I known the shadow, much less the real substance of marriage, and now that I do realize it to a degree, I know that it does not mean the growth or freedom of one, to the detriment or exclusion of the other. True freedom is that which removes all bounds in one's own horizon, and all desire to dominate over those in another's. I have never been able to assert my freedom, consequently I have never had it."

"Confounded nonsense!" muttered her husband, but the low firm voice went on.

"Now husband, I know that it is an injustice to you as well as to myself to allow dominance in any particular; to you because it restrains and puts aside those noble qualities within every true man that enable him to be the complement of a true woman ; to me, because it dwarfs and deteriorates the real woman, substituting in her place a slavish menial, who dares not claim the right to an individuality."

"What in the name of common sense do you mean ?" demanded Felix, explosively, too much astonished to compel her silence, according to his usual fashion.

"I mean simply this, Felix dear. I am an individual with the power of thinking for myself, and thereby governing my own actions. I claim the right of an individual. If I—"

"So !" he cried, hotly, "you mean to say if you want to become a crank or anything else, you will do so regardless of my will in the matter ?"

"Not at all. I mean that, as I must breathe for myself, so I must think for myself ; and as I think, I must express. *Expression is life ; repression is death.* I am no longer dead but alive." Her eyes glowed with a growing brilliancy.

"And you, dear husband," she continued, "will find me a better wife, a wiser mother and a truer woman than I have ever been in the past. My own judgment must, at least, have the final right to decide what books I am to read, what companions to choose, what work to do. Not that it will be necessarily sufficient of itself, dear, should you wish to suggest or consult upon those or similar vital points. True marriage is a blending of individualities so that each is the complement of the other, and the union is but a rounded whole in its outward expression of completeness."

Glorious as she looked, sitting there like a goddess, clasping the sleeping child in her arms, gazing at her husband with the burning soul-light in her eyes, he still could find it in his heart to sneer.

"So you think, forsooth, you've been repressed because you've never joined secret societies, or gone brawling over the country giving public lectures or stump speeches, and consequently we are not truly married ?"

Only a deeper wave of crimson surging over cheek and brow told of the sharpness of this weapon of sarcasm that never dulled by use.

"Be still my heart," panted Mary inwardly, "God *only* will I acknowledge even at this moment, for He *is* my strength and my tower of defense." To her husband she said, "I have repressed myself by allowing another's judgments, opinions and desires to be expressed instead of my own. Like the fungus on a tree, I have clung to and absorbed the juices of the tree, until I wear its clothes, partake of its hardness, and am indistinguishably swallowed up in its personality."

"And is not that the very blending you spoke of?" a gleam of triumph in his cynical smile.

"By no means. That refers to the mutual exchange of building material, of giving and receiving of sympathy and silence."

"And now that you have this exalted ideal, may I ask, Mrs. Temple, what you intend to do with it?"

The goddess was suddenly transformed into a real live woman, with real tears trembling on her lashes.

"To love my husband better than ever, and respect myself as much as any one else in the world."

Bravely said, little woman. Who can know the nights and days of anguish and longing that besieged your troubled heart in its impulse to declare itself? Who would dream of the quivering efforts, the choking sighs and ceaseless prayers that were the prelude to this victory?

Not Felix Temple, and yet a strange thrill of pride in the little wife flashed through him. He had never seen her in this *rôle* before, and it was not uninteresting. In fact he rather admired the new exhibition of fire and fearlessness, but it would never do to let it run riot. . . Trust him for that!

Outwardly he made no sign, and in silence they neared the home where Mary had found her womanhood.

Dusky night with her sparkling jewels and caressing breath now reigned queen of the passing hours.

In the stillness of that memorable midnight, the gates of wisdom opened wide to Mary's awakened soul:

"Thou hast done well to declare thyself, for now

shalt thou see the dawn of a new day. Thou art one of
the chosen, and by chosen is meant one who is ready to
enter the higher path. I would have thee know the
mysteries of wisdom. I am thy higher self and will
teach thee all things if thou wilt but listen and obey.
First of all, conquer thyself—thy mental, thy physical,
then thy whole kingdom shall be well governed.

"Thou shalt be the *light* of *thy* world. Live well
what thou knowest now, so shalt thou know more and
still more of the infinite All, and knowing, live.

"Keep thine eyes well set, looking for that which
shall bear thee a message. Keep thine ears open for
sounds of the heavenly. Keep thy tongue ready to speak
and thy hands ready to do. Be unmoved by words or
acts of others. Their good is thine own, their evil is as
not to thee. Good is harmony in unity. Evil is broken
consciousness of good. Learn to center thy thought
upon the good only, so shalt thou see and know the unbroken unity of the whole.

"Many and beauteous are the things awaiting thee
when thou canst guide thy thought like a well-manned
ship straight to its goal. Over high billows and deep
waters shalt thou glide with fearless majesty, gathering
whatsoe'er thou wilt from the crystal store house beneath
thy sails.

"Man well thy ship, O Mary, for thou hast a long
journey before thee, but one which thou hast eagerly
longed to take. The time is come.

"Keep thine eye single and follow that light which
is set before thee—thine own consciousness of God. . .

So far thou hast done well, but thou may'st do better.

"Remember, thy will is helmsman—thy conscious will, which is but a part of the Universal Will, is the power that shall guide thee whithersoever thou wouldst go. Thy will the governor, guide, master—consciously one with the Divine, may overcome all things—is that to which thou must give the place of honor and power.

"How shalt thou install this master in thy ship of life?

"I will tell thee. Listen, O Mary, and heed well.

"Look about thee. Did I not tell thee to use well thine eyes and ears?

"Naught else?

"Aye, all. Thine every sense and faculty must be used for the searching and the knowing of the One. Look about thee. What seest thou? Beauty, use, purpose, everywhere. Majestic mountains that reach with towering greatness toward the boundless blue, are treasure-houses of untold use. Life, strength, everlasting steadfastness, are pictured there. In the wind that sweeps across thy cheek, thou hast a symbol of that pulsing Life, that breathes through all, in all, and above all. Then comes the message of sound—breathing, sighing, rippling, rushing, roaring sound, that tells of mighty force—force that moves and lifts and shifts and slides with a mightiness that belongs only to that One which rears mountains, creates watercourses, guides the eternal stars, peoples worlds, breathes in all things, speaks through all voices and lives in all lives.

"And when thine every sense shall bear thee witness

of this One, then shalt thou discern that mighty Will which exists only to Be and to Do. Then shalt thou know that thy will may be but the One Will working in thy conscioneness, thy doing but the Divine Doing.

"What then shalt thou seek after?

"To know the One, speak for the One, *live* the One. Then shalt thou work with the mightiness of God, for it shall be God only working *through* thee, and thy will shall be merged into the Divine. Thus shalt thou attain individuality.

"Knowest thou now what is meant by saying that will must be the helmsman?

"Ponder well and thou shalt know—and do."

CHAPTER XXX.

"Be no longer a Chaos, but a World, or even World kin. Produce! Produce! Were it but the pitifullest infinitesimal fraction of a Product, produce it in God's name! 'Tis the utmost thou hast in thee: out with it, then. Up, up! whatsoever thy hand findeth to do, do it with thy whole might."—*T. Carlyle.*

AS the Temples returned from a drive one evening, Janet met Mary at the door. "Gie me the bairnie, Meesis Temple," holding out her arms for the child who was still asleep, and pointing her thumb over her shoulder towards the sitting room, "ye hae a leddy to see ye. Wha she maun be, I dinna ken, but she's braw an' herty like wi' mony a gude worrd i' her speak."

"Who can it be," thought Mary, as she hastily bathed her face and brushed her hair before going in to the visitor.

"Oh, I know! It is Aunt Creesh!" suddenly laying the brush aside and rushing impetuously into the room with the exclamation on her lips.

"Of course it is," responded a well-remembered voice, as a tall, portly figure, with outstretched arms, advanced to meet her.

A long silent embrace, a quiet survey at arms' length, and they were ready to subside into more quiet talk.

"But how you have changed Mary! I should hardly know you!" exclaimed her aunt after a prolonged scrutiny, an hour later.

Mr. Temple had gone to attend his lodge, and they were to have a quiet evening together.

"*How* am I changed, Aunt Creesh?"

"Can't say. The blossom is not the bud, but it's what the bud was. The fruit is not the blossom, but it is the heart of the blossom, and a little more added, to account for the sunshine, the rain and dew, the wind and heat—which are all a part of it."

"And I suppose we all get what we need to make us ripen," said Mary, with a faint smile.

"Exactly; and, now I think of it, that's how you've changed, child; you've ripened." Aunt Creesh turned her head for a closer inspection.

"I believe you are right, auntie; I have been conscious of that very thing since the night Margie got well."

"How's that?" asked her aunt, as she took the familiar knitting work out of the old black bag.

Mary told her of that night, and of the agony, the despair, the prayer, the revelation and Baby's wonderful recovery. "Since then, auntie, the world has been very different to me, because I know God is everywhere."

"So, ho! That means you've found the secret of happiness, which is the only thing that *does* ripen humanity, talk about experience as much as they will."

Aunt Creesh took an immense white handkerchief out of her reticule, blew her nose violently and resumed her knitting.

"I—I don't quite understand you, Aunt Creesh,

about the secret of happiness," Mary ventured to remark.

"Don't, eh? You ought to. I was saying you'd found it when you began to think of the Almighty instead of yourself. Most folks are miserable because they think of nothing but their precious selves, no matter whether it rains or shines; and, of *course,* they're green. It's taking in the All-Something that ripens and rounds human kind." She paused a moment to take a fresh supply of yarn around her little finger.

"But what do you think of Margaret's cure?" queried Mary, longing to hear the forceful opinion Aunt Creesh would be sure to have.

"Think of it? Why it's all of a piece! The Lord has always said 'look unto me and live,' and 'look unto me and be healed,' or words to that effect. It's meant to be taken literally, and then what?" Aunt Creesh laid down her knitting to be more impressive. "Why," she continued, with a sweep of the hand, "you know all your burdens and cares and sicknesses are gone, consequently you're not unhappy nor worried nor doubled up with pain; you're just taking your natural place and knowing what the Lord intended you to know from the beginning, that He was your Father and would take care of you as long as you'd stay at home."

An infantile wail from the upper regions announced the awakening of Margaret. They could hear Janet's voice soothing her to sleep, but Mary would have rushed upstairs, notwithstanding, had not Aunt Creesh restrained her with a remark.

"What's the use of distrusting the Lord for even a minute? Don't you s'pose the maid can do as well as you can? Stick to the thing you're at, and don't fly off to something else unless you've got your dismissal from the first duty."

"Well, Aunt Creesh, you're the same old general you used to be, are'nt you?" laughed Mary, sinking back in her chair again.

"Mary!" lifting her forefinger and peering the other side of it as if it were a tree. "Mary! there's nothing that will make a general, but common sense, and plenty of faculty to distribute it, and, thank the Lord, people can have it if they only use what they've got to begin with."

"Aunt Creesh, I wish there were more people who could distribute as well as you can. Why, even the majority of Christians would think it terribly wicked for me to say Margaret was cured simply by trusting God. I know, because even the few I've told are horror-stricken, and tell me God does not work that way—that He does not make Himself known by signs now, as he did when Jesus was on the earth. But I have learned that very few understand the sacred things that your own heart tells you are true."

"Right, my girl," responded Mrs. Briggs, with a skillful lunge after her runaway ball. "The things of the Spirit can only be known by the Spirit. Self is a stranger to Spirit, and the people who think they know everything and have to advise the Lord besides, are the ones who know self and not Spirit. . And where is their judgment? Simply nowhere, because it's nothing at all. . . But look here, Lucretia Briggs, speaking of judging, what are you doing?"

She had suddenly addressed herself in this abrupt fashion as she often did when alone, quite forgetting for the moment that she might have a listener.

"Judgment belongs to the Almighty—"

"But auntie," interposed Mary, not willing to drop the matter just here; "why do some of the best Christians call it presumption to take the words of Jesus to be true? For instance, they say there is no healing done in these days, because the time of miracles is past, and—"

"So 'tis, child, so 'tis, Do you s'pose God's laws are only weathercocks to be whiffed around whenever the wind blows?"

Mary looked inquiringly at the speaker who continued energetically. "Law wouldn't be law if it could be changed. But there is law natural and law spiritual. Jesus understood it all, because he kept himself so at one with the Law; consequently he knew how to let the Law be expressed through him. His life was an open secret that all can read if they choose, or they can cover themselves with the veil of self till they think they know everything, and disdain to look outside their veil."

"Then you believe we can all know and do these things?" questioned Mary again, a wave of satisfaction showing itself in her countenance.

Aunt Creesh looked at her keenly an instant. "I believe the Lord works through every good instrument, for He is no respecter of persons, and I believe Jesus

Christ represents the possibility of humanity—if we take any stock in his life or his words. Come, come, Mary, I want to hear about Carrol, and your husband and all the rest. S'pose we change the subject."

It was only Aunt 'Cretia's way, when she was most deeply in earnest, to be the most abrupt. Mary knew her of old and pretended not to notice the furtive use of her aunt's handkerchief, or the increased speed of the knitting needles.

"Well auntie," she began, "they are all well. We found mother and Ada busy with the fruits, and Ada, dear me, how she's grown! I never realized it so forcibly till I went home this time and found her preparing for a special visitor—"

"What! You don't mean she's thinking of marriage?" cried Aunt Creesh aghast.

"It looks very much like it, I'm afraid," laughed Mary. "She has been corresponding with Mr. Fernlow for several years—you remember him don't you?—and this summer he is coming as one already fortunate."

"You don't say! Land alive! How *tempus* does *fugit!*" exclaimed Mrs. Briggs, with a retrospective gaze on the rug at her feet. After a short silence, she resumed: "Ada's pretty sensible, but there's one thing: I hope she won't lose her head after she's married, and allow her individuality to be swallowed up in that of her husband. If there's anything young women need nowadays, it's education on that very point," and Aunt Creesh knitted away as if her very life depended on it.

"But do you think they will learn by precept? Will it not rather be the lesson of experience?"

"Land alive ! I s'pose it will," sighed Mrs. Briggs "but the poor things wither into nothing, before they know what is the matter, and then haven't strength enough to assert themselves as a rule. Why, it stands toreason," she continued, raising her right hand with its impressive forefinger and shaking it dramatically; "it stands to reason that a woman can't give away her birthright for a mess of pottage, without losing that which makes life a great and grand privilege."

"What do you call her birthright, Aunt Creesh?"

"The individual power of thinking, acting and living—that which makes an independent human being with independent powers of self-government, and the recognition of a direct relation with God. That's what I call a birthright, and any woman—or man either— who gives that away, robs herself of all that makes life worth living—yes, deprives herself of the privilege of building the greatest thing on earth or in heaven—a God-like character."

Mary's eyes filled. It was so unexpected to hear Aunt Creesh expressing the very thoughts that had been her own greatest inspiration.

"The individual must find union with the Universal, in order to express individuality in its highest sense," she said, quietly.

"That's certainly true, child. Until we stop leaning on this or that person for comfort, love or satisfaction, we are ignoring the birthright."

"Do you think, then, that human relations will change?" asked Mary, with a hint of alarm in her voice.

"Certainly not, only to become purer and better."

"But do you not mean that we will cease to find satisfaction in the love of our friends?"

"Of course not; land alive! But when we realize that it is not the *personal* love of our friends that satisfies or helps us, but the Universal—the God love—which they express, we will find ourselves able to be satisfied and happy whether they are with us or not. In other words, Love, Comfort, Wisdom, will be with us whether we are with friend, lover or husband, or whether we *have* friend, lover or husband."

"Oh I see! You mean we must learn to depend on the Infinite for love, comfort or wisdom, and—"

"Exactly. How else could we develop the true individuality, which is nothing more nor less than the consciousness of oneness with the Father, and the consequent expression of that oneness, in thought, word and deed?"

"How would you define personality? So many times the words personality and individuality are used interchangeably."

"Ah Mary, you're a thinker after my own heart, and I perceive you have already answered these questions in your own mind. Well, I've never put into words the distinction between personality and individuality, but it's clear enough." She paused a moment with her knitting needle pressed against her lips and her eyes half closed in meditation.

"Personality," she said slowly, "is that which constitutes or pertains to a person, and person is the corporeal manifestation of a soul, the outward appearance.

while individuality, as a distinct combination of qualities inhering in the One, relates to Spirit."

"Oh Auntie, how clear that is! Where have you
learned all these things?" sighed Mary wonderingly.

"By thinking, child, by thinking; although I learned
most of that definition from Webster.—Yes, thinking
and proving, and I've been at it nigh onto thirty years."

For an instant a shadow flitted over the face of Aunt
Creesh, but it was gone as quickly, and she began asking questions about Carrol.

"Carrol is very happy in her work at Seaton,"
replied Mary. "You know what she is doing, don't
you Aunt Creesh?"

"Teaching a charity school, aint she?"

"Hardly that, because it is a mutual help affair, but
in one sense it is the broadest kind of charity."

Mary went on and told all about Carrol's work.
"She feels that it is a grand success, so far," she concluded.

"I always thought that girl would come to something good, but land alive! how unhappy she used to
be!" mused Aunt Creesh, putting in a fresh needle.

"If you could read her last letter, you would see a
vast difference between then and now. I don't know
but I have that letter in my pocket. Yes, here it is."

"Read it then," was the laconic request.

"I will, just what she says about her conversion, for
I am sure she would want you to know."

Mary drew closer to the light and opened the letter.

"It touched me," said she, "because it is so in line
with my own experience. She knew nothing of Mar-

gie's cure, and the fact that she perceives the possibility
of salvation in every detail, as I do, only proves to me
that we are right, and now that your ideas are the
same, I am more impressed than ever."

"He puts His testimony into the mouths of many
witnesses, or words to that effect," ejaculated Mrs.
Briggs, solemnly.

"Aunt Creesh, don't you believe these are the days
in which 'the Spirit is to be poured out on all flesh,'
according to prophecy?"

"If most people should ask me that question, I'd
tell 'em it didn't concern me whether they are or
whether they ain't, but you, Mary, shall have my private
opinion, which is that we are entering a more spiritual
age, a new dispensation, which means the pouring out
of the Holy Spirit, the consciousness of truth—"

"And the consequent adjustment of our life problems," added Mary.

"Exactly.   Suppose you give us the letter now."

"Why, to be sure; I'm forgetting all about it,"
cried Mary, unfolding it and reading the earnest words.

Aunt Creesh listened, motionless, needle in hand.
"That girl's struck the right key," she exclaimed, as
Mary finished the reading. "It is the *doing* that brings
the knowing. Talk about Christianity being a failure,
indeed ! Not to those who have tried it in the right
way, and there's a right way to be a Christian as well as
everything else. What's all this hue and cry about
heresy and infidels that fills the papers nowadays?
Simply an exposition of the failure to be as little children, instead of the failure of Christianity; for the

world is anything but a child in its own precious estimation."

"It makes such a difference whether we want to teach or be taught," sighed Mary, remembering some of her own experiences.

"Exactly. Land alive! The Spirit never fails; it's only the letter that kills the law."

Mary shrank from such bald statements, but she knew the straightforward earnestness of her aunt's character, and felt all the more desirous of hearing her opinions.

"What is your understanding, Aunt Creesh, of the difference between the letter and the Spirit?" she asked, after a momentary silence.

"Well," mused Mrs. Briggs, scratching her head meditatively with a knitting needle, "letter means according to rule, form, law, custom, creed. Spirit means according to that within which bears witness to what is right, whether creed says so or not. Christianity, as Jesus taught and lived it, is very different from the dogmatic hash and wafered practice, served in twenty-minute courses from the pulpits of to-day."

"That is the secret of all this talk about failure, I suspect," remarked Mary, thoughtfully, folding Carrol's letter and putting it into her pocket again.

"Yes, and an open one at that," was her aunt's reply, as she returned to her knitting, with renewed vigor.

It was late. A click in the lock informed them of Mr. Temple's return. . . In a short time the lights were out, and all was quiet in the Temple household.

CHAPTER XXXI.

"The essence of righteousness is right thinking. Here is the true following. Every one who is upward bound, receives the direction, 'Whatsoever things are true, pure, lovely and of good report, think on these things.' When this command is strictly obeyed, right action is the natural consequence."

—*Mrs. Myron Reed.*

THE summer months passed quickly. August had come. Carrol still found herself too busy with her duties, to leave long enough for her promised visit to Mary. Several changes were to take place in the Home. Jack was soon to begin his work at Wise & Flightman's who wanted just such a quick, thoughtful boy to assist them in their store. Tillie was preparing to go to Mrs. Rice, as Ralph had written to Carrol to see if she could not send someone to help his mother.

Ned had done splendidly and expected to go home soon. Carrol's words and daily living had renewed, strengthened and healed him, physically and mentally. Not that he was beyond the old temptations, but with his new knowledge he was able to overcome as never before, and every day he felt the dignity and privilege of manhood.

"When you are tempted to drink, smoke or anything else, Ned," she had said in one of her helpful talks to him, "refuse to fellowship with the temptation. Hold yourself above it by declaring yourself a spiritual, instead of a material being. Say aloud over and over in your own secret chamber, 'I am free from all desires of the flesh, for I am satisfied with spiritual truth. I am filled with all completeness, for I am a child of Infinite Spirit.'"

And Ned tried it the very next time the enemy assailed him. He was amazed at the result. He tried it again and his confidence grew. The third time it took three days of almost ceaseless struggle, but he would not yield. "She trusts me, and I *will* prove myself," he groaned the third night as he paced back and forth in his room. He *did* prove himself. The enemy surrendered, and Ned felt himself a free pure man with the possibilities of life before him. He was eager to fly to the dear mother, but he could not go empty-handed. Through Miss Allbright's aid he succeeded in obtaining a position for a few months in a vinegar factory.

Matters stood thus when one evening Ralph came striding up the walk with his well-remembered gait. Ned could hardly restrain an exclamation, and fearing recognition from his brother, got out of the way as soon as possible, but Ralph was pre-occupied.

With beating heart and rising hope he had come, not alone for his mother's sake, but for his own as well.

He had loved silently, but none the less intensely for two long years, and he felt impelled once more to put his fate to the test. He rang the bell. "Is Miss Evans in ?"

"Yes."

"Tell her an old friend wishes to see her."

He would note the first look on her face. It seemed strange to be in her house with the evidence of her taste and the subtle impress of her presence all about him.

"She is coming, my own, my sweet;
    My heart would hear her and beat
        Had it lain for a century dead,"

he hummed inaudibly, with love-lighted eyes, as he heard the rustle of her garments.

Was that Carrol, that tall, stately woman, with the calm face and the soulful eyes? Yes, there was the old smile, the cordial welcome added to the new dignity, but no quickening flush that told of pleasureable heart-beats; nothing but a frank, sweet sisterliness that was unmistakable. Ralph's heart sank like lead, but he compelled himself to talk, listen, smile and acquiesce, as if the passing moments were not like needle-points of pain.

Carrol, with a woman's keen intuition, discerned his suffering and divined its cause. . . She succeeded so well in her effort to divert him that he soon caught the fire of her noble enthusiasm. Then she sent for Ned. Ralph glanced indifferently at the entering stranger. A second glance and he sprang to his feet with an exclamation of sharp surprise. . . The brothers met.

Carrol quietly slipped from the room.

In the hour that followed, Ralph heard the story of a life of weakness, struggle, failure, of final hope and the assurance of victory through the saving charity of a woman who dared follow the dictates of her own conscience, regardless of the world's opinions. With glowing eyes and quickened speech Ned bore witness to the patience, goodness and wisdom of his benefactress.

"She has taught me the meaning of life, Ralph; I never could go back to the swine, and thank God I know now what religion means, and I believe mother will understand too. Oh, I tell you, Ralph, I have learned what it means to eat the husks. Carrol has been a perfect revelation, and the work she does is wonderful. It is the Lord's work if there is any such thing . . . and I ought to know." . .

Ralph had listened dumbfounded, but the meaning of it burst upon him at last, and he then and there renounced all claim to Carrol, and consecrated himself to a life of effort for the betterment of his fellow men.

Another beacon fire was alight now, and its glow would soon reach into the far valleys of ignorance and weakness.

Ned went with Ralph and Tillie the next day to the heart-hungry mother.

Carrol soon received the letter from Miss Allbright bidding her prepare for the proposed lecture tour.

"You are perfectly competent, my dear Carrol," she wrote, "and I feel that we ought to set people to thinking on this subject. If it is really the reform that my twelve years' experience proves it to be, the world ought to know it, those working so hard in the interest of reform as well as those needing the reforming impulse, or the opportunity for educational or moral improvement. You are prepared to do this work now because you have proven it, and one experiment continued long enough, is the possibility of all. Therefore, my dear girl, throw off all fears of inability, diffidence or doubt, and resolve to depend on that alone which giveth strength, wisdom, eloquence, or whatsoever you may need.

"On one point I wish particularly to impress you. Do not think in going before an audience that you must necessarily have an elaborately prepared manuscript. If you have something to say, hold yourself to that something and the expression will take care of itself. Be as free as though you were uttering your thoughts aloud in the privacy of your own room. The great heart of humanity throbs as one; if you speak to yourself, you speak to the world.

"Do not be anxious about leaving the Home. I have found some one to take your place. Be a good girl now and go forth to carry the good news you have so nobly proven true. I will be down to see you shortly and make more definite arrangements."

"I can if I must, and I must if I can," murmured Carrol ruefully, as she finished the letter.

CHAPTER XXXII.

"The question of the honest Thomas is ever answered by the proof needed, and the convinced mentality exclaims, 'My Lord and my God!' Beloved, we are in One place of One accord in One mind, Taught by the invisible Spirit of Truth. This certain perception of knowledge manifests the Power and Wholeness of Love, and the fullness and completeness of the Good Life that is in, through and around us, is indeed manifested in thought, word, deed, condition. Back of all expression throbs the great Heart of Love Eternal. Conscious oneness with this is the atonement."—*Mary D. Fisk.*

WHEN Harvey Willard héard of Carrol's intentions he felt deeply disappointed. He had been in the habit of dropping in to the Thursday evening meetings, and not infrequently called privately to discuss the points of difference, for now that he had set himself to make good her conversion, he conscientiously sought these opportunities to hear her arguments, that he might refute their fallacies. He was honest enough to admit that occasionally he received help from her reasoning, and once or twice he had even asked her advice concerning certain parochial problems, for at times he sadly felt the need of a woman's judgment. Why did he not go to some lady of his congregation, you say?

He did as a rule, but Mrs. Dilbow, president of the Ladies' Aid Society, who considered herself the proper advisor in all church difficulties, was very positive in her opinions and conclusions as to the right method of doing things, and sometimes Harvey found it difficult to adjust himself to her decisions, or even her voluble suggestions. Mrs. Dilbow was a martyr to duty wherever it placed her or whatever it exacted of her. She had taken great responsibility when she used her influence to have the parish vote for this young minister, and she felt in a certain sense obliged to sustain him personally, she therefore freely gave advice whenever and wherever it was needed, looked after delinquents in church discipline, gave pointers for sermons, criticized the minister when necessary, and in fact made herself generally useful. Of course she had allies, as every worthy general should have, and between them all they assisted the young minister to the extent of their ability. The first year of his stay with them, these worthy sisters had generously turned their attention to the work of finding a wife for him, but to all their hints he seemed deaf, and instead of falling in love with the various maidens so cunningly placed in his way, he enlisted each and all of them in the Sunday school work, thereby supplying the long-felt need in that direction.

Finally Mrs. Dilbow had concluded that "poor Mr. Willard" was not of the marrying kind, since which conclusion there had been a sudden cessation of church fairs, festivals, socials and such like—something "poor Mr. Willard" rather enjoyed, since it gave him greater opportunity for long walks, evenings away from home, and occasional calls.

Mrs. Dilbow hurried home from the Ladies' Aid Society. She must stop on her way to see the minis-

ter, as it was very important he should go immediately
to Benny Ballard, who was not expected to live, since
the boiler explosion yesterday, in which he had been
terribly injured.

On her way to the parsonage, she passed the Helpers' Home, from the door of which, as she could see
through the shrubbery, Mr. Willard was just departing.

"Aha, young man," muttered the general under
her breath; "we need not wonder any more where the
heterodoxy in the last two sermons came from! And
now we may as well believe what Meg Brant said about
your going so often to look after this Home, as if it
were suddenly put on your list of necessities. . .
Aha, so he is putting his finger in this pie," she continued, keeping up a mighty thinking, and for
the moment forgetting her errand, as she slowly followed him to the parsonage. She had once attended
one of the Help meetings, where she heard the statement: "There is no reason why the healing of the sick
should not be done to-day as in the days of Jesus of
Nazareth. In fact I know," continued the speaker,
"of several remarkable cures performed through a
recognition of the power and presence of God, and
the acknowledgment 'it is the Lord, that healeth
thee.'" . . Carrol had just learned through a long
letter from Mary of Margaret's cure, upon which, in
addition to several striking experiences of her own,
she had built an earnest and inspiring address.

Out of the hour's discourse, Mrs. Dilbow had heard
but the one statement, which colored all others for her.
She went home raging over the blasphemous teachings

taught at "that Home, where they pretend to teach pure Christian principles! why," she exclaimed in righteous indignation, "it would be better for those poor waifs to be homeless and shelterless, rather than be under such heresy as that!"

Whereupon the Ladies' Aid Society had quite agreed with her, and Meg Brant, a professional nurse, declared she had seen the minister go there a number of times, and that he had sometimes walked by the house. Meg Brant was only a letter member of the church, and had been in town but a short time, and to think that this important news had come through her, and up to this late day had been unknown to the one who should have known it first, was a hard blow to the general.

She had resolved to wait however, for a little more evidence, and now, as she slowly sauntered along behind the minister, she was congratulating herself that she had it.

Just as he entered his gateway, she overtook him.

"Good evening, Mrs. Dilbow; will you come in?" said Harvey cordially enough, but with a preoccupied air.

"No thank you, Mr. Willard. I just stopped to ask you to go down and see Benny Ballard. You know he was fatally injured by that boiler explosion. The doctor says he can't live till morning."

"How shocking! I will go at once," said the minister, stepping to the sidewalk.

"Do," she urged, "and I do hope you can save his soul. He's never been converted, though he's lived well enough. Never heard but what he's always been kind, really kinder than young men commonly are, to his mother and sister; but then that won't save him, poor boy, if he doesn't believe in the blood of the Lamb."

She had talked on unceasingly as they walked, for his way lay towards her own home.

"Has he expressed a desire for salvation?" he asked, plucking a leaf as they passed under the arching trees.

"I don't know exactly, but somebody proposed to send for you and he didn't object."

Harvey did not reply, but walked on rapidly, as if he had quite forgotten her presence.

"Stop in as you go back, and let us hear how the poor fellow is," she called as she turned the corner.

"If it is not too late, but do not sit up for me; I may remain with him."

The young man was indeed in a sad condition. Burned, bruised and internally injured, he lay gasping in agony, his heart-broken mother and weeping sister whose sole support he had been, standing near the bedside.

"Here's the preacher; come away, Dolly," whispered the mother, as she went forward with mute courtesy to welcome the visitor.

"Oh, sir, save his soul afore it is too late," she begged, with a heart-breaking sob. "He's never professed, an' I can't abide to let him go to—to—"

Dolly led her weeping from the room.

The preacher knelt down and prayed. When he finished, the poor, pain-drawn face was turned away from the visitor. The prayer had not smoothed the anguished brow or brought one ray of light to the dull eyes.

"Would you like to make a confession of repentance and be baptized into the Church, my brother?" asked Harvey, in a low voice of sympathy.

A stony silence, with no effort to even make a sign. Harvey was not sure whether it was from disability or disinclination.

He would try again. "Do you realize the mighty Love that sent Jesus into the world to die, in order that my sins and yours might be washed away with his blood?"

No response save a shudder of repulsion. Harvey mistook it for one of fear.

"It makes no difference, brother," he resumed, "what our sins of commission or omission may have been, if we accept the Saviour, God so mercifully provided, we are washed white as snow in the cleansing Blood."

Still that stony silence, broken only by the labored breathing, and at intervals, an irrepressible groan.

The preacher prayed again, this time, if possible, more devoutly. His heart was heavy for the dying lad. He pleaded earnestly. He poured his very soul into the words of anxious exhortation. This work must be done, and now every moment was precious. The Lord could save to the uttermost.

"Send repentance to this waiting soul," he pleaded. "Let him not go down into the miry pit, but let Thy saving presence be a light to his dimming eyes, and a comfort in his distress."

The minister was so transported with his theme that he did not hear the door open nor know of the entrance of a lady, until he felt the touch of her dress as it swept past him. He looked up and saw, to his amazement, that it was Carrol. On the pallid face on the bed dawned a glad look of recognition like a morning dimmed with clouds.

"Yes Benny, you know me, don't you?" said Carrol's well known cheery voice. "I have brought you some of Nina's flowers. She sent them with a message of love, and we know that Nina's love is the sweetest gift you could have, for she trusts God so beautifully, that she gives you her own faith."

Harvey had risen from his kneeling posture, and handed a chair for Carrol, who acknowledged the courtesy with a slight bow, as she sat down by the bedside, and laid her hand tenderly upon that of the sick boy. A silence followed, broken only by Benny's painful breathing. And as she sat there, Carrol overflowed with a silent song of praise—praise that welled forth from a soul new-born into the Kingdom of God. She forgot everything but the supreme fact of life, the life that ever is, was, and shall be. She thought of Benny, not as sick, suffering, dying, but as the spiritual son of God—one with the perfect Mind. She radiated a divine, a healing tenderness, by her warm God-filled thought.

"Praise God for fullness of life, praise God for the perfectness of peace," she cried, in her mental ecstasy. "Praise God for allness of Love, the Love that blesses with the gift of Itself. The One Love, the One Life, the One Spirit, that is now and forever shall be manifest. . . Peace, peace, peace, be unto this house.". .

The boy slept. Peace had fallen upon him like a mantle. When he opened his eyes some moments later they were bright with a new light. His breath came more regularly and with an exhilaration not manifested before.

"Benny," said Carrol again in a low, thrilling voice, "let us speak the word of reconciliation—at-one-ment —this moment, so that you may prove for yourself, the blessed saying, 'ye shall know the truth and the truth shall make you free.'"

Another query in Benny's eyes, which Carrol answered by saying: "The truth, Benny, is that which is always true of our spirit, because, as Jesus said, 'the spirit is all, the flesh profiteth nothing.' Now, the spirit must be exactly what the Father is, because the Father being omnipotent and omnipresent, being infinite and indivisible, is Himself dwelling in us, as we live, move and have our being in Him. That means, Benny, that we are spirit like God, and therefore must be well and strong and whole in every way. Do you understand?"

The lips as well as the eyes assented.

"That, then, is the Christ or Truth word, for Christ is Truth, and if we speak it understandingly we shall find how true it is that we have been given the word that makes us of one mind with the God-Mind. . . . Now, Benny, don't think of your body, just think of your spirit, and acknowledge the power, presence and perfection of the Spirit, the Love, the Father, that is over all, and in all and through all.   We will close our eyes so we can shut out every other thought but this."

Dolly and her mother had quietly slipped .into the room, and now stood with awe-struck faces, a little back of Carrol. The silence of a sacred moment was upon the group.

A pallor as of death crept over the face on the pillow, the breath grew shorter and weaker, until it seemed to the mother, who had not been able to keep her eyes shut, that the fatal moment had come, but she did not leave off thinking, " Benny is Spirit ; Spirit can't be sick, and Spirit is perfect like God." They were the only words she could think of, in her confusion and increasing fear, but she would be faithful.

Presently she forgot to think them as her wonder grew at what she saw. Harvey also gazed with amazement indescribable.

Slowly they saw the miracle (if eternal law be a miracle) of God's presence manifest itself.

A crimson tide of returning color crept into the pale face. The breathing grew deeper and stronger. Benny opened his eyes with a flash of joy too deep for utterance. " I am saved!" he exclaimed, the first words he had spoken since the accident.

" Yes, body and soul. I knew it, Benny. . . Let us give thanks," and Carrol wept with the rest, for all were in tears, except Benny, whose countenance glowed with a radiance too bright for tears. . . . : .

" I am well, I tell you. The pain is gone. Oh, thank God." . . . .

Harvey knelt once more and prayed. . Such an

outpouring of praise, of thanksgiving, of sincere meekness, and longing to know the Father's will more and more clearly. It was a prayer that made one better for the hearing. . . . .

"Yes," murmured the grateful Benny, "thank God, I know now what salvation to the uttermost means. . I am well. I am well. Bring me something to eat, mother." . . .

When Carrol called the next evening to see Benny Ballard, she found Harvey there before her. Benny was sitting up cheerful and jubilant. "I am all right now," he exclaimed, and "Oh Miss Evans how can I ever thank you for saving me?"

"It was not I, Benny, but the one Source of all life, the only Power that can heal. Give that your thanks."

"But you did *something*," he persisted. "Please tell me what you were thinking about, for I cannot get beyond the feeling, that it was something you felt or thought that helped me."

"Do you remember the very last time you came to the meeting, Benny?"

An eager sign of assent was given.

"We talked about the healing Truth that Jesus showed us so beautifully how to prove, did we not, Benny?" she resumed.

"Yes," wonderingly.

"I am going to tell you something that I know you will understand, and that will help you very much."

She took a rose from her bosom.

"You see the beauty of this flower, don't you?"

"Certainly."

"If we grow better by looking at the beauty of an inanimate flower, can you not imagine the help it would be to contemplate the beauty of a perfect human life? You have heard me say, how much help the perfect life has been to me, Benny, and I know, by the way your face always lighted up, how great a help it was to you also."

A glad affirmative.

"Benny, I was reading in the precious story, a few days ago, and a great wave of new knowledge came to me. The chapter I read first was the seventeenth chapter of John, which gives the tender prayer of our Brother, before he went away. . . Oh, Benny, it is beautiful ! . . And in that prayer he prays that his disciples and all they who believe may be one with the Father, even as he is one with Him. . . Benny!" with a rising joy in her voice, "Benny ! that *means* something ! Listen now, for I want you to know it as I do. To be one with the Father, as he is one with Him ! Think of it ! Think of the health, the tenderness, the power of Jesus. And when they questioned him about it, he said, ' It is not I, but the Father that dwelleth in me.' " . .

Benny breathed a little easier, and he turned his eyes, full of eager interest, upon the speaker. Harvey stood by spell-bound at what he saw and heard, not able to tear himself away.

"I read the references to oneness, and atonement," she continued, "and also read the first, third, sixth, fourteenth and fifteenth of John, and kept trying to find the connection, until at last I turned to the fifth chapter of second Corinthians, and there I found the key to atonement, as Jesus meant it, and as Paul understood it. . . Why, Benny, it is wonderful, and when we understand, we are healed!" . .

Both eyes and lips were trying to question how.

Carrol laid her flowers down, and looking at the eager face, very earnestly, said: "Listen carefully, now, and I will tell you. In this fifth of Corinthians Paul says: 'Henceforth know we no man after the flesh, not even Christ who came to reconcile the world unto God '—never mind if the quotation is not word for word; you will read it when you get up—'and he gave unto *us* the *word* of reconciliation!' . . There it is, Benny! The whole secret of Jesus' life and teachings. That explains *how* he was one with the Father. By thinking the thought (Phil. 2:2), and speaking the word of God! By *living* the Truth. The word is Truth, and through the word we are sanctified; through the life, made whole ; which means, made to recognize and *express* the oneness, as the Master did."

"I see, I see," cried Benny with moist eyes, "now I know what the atonement, at-one-ment means, and why the thinking and the living must go with the healing. Oh, yes, and how grand it all is !"

"Benny do know what goodness be, even if he never joined no church," interposed the fond mother, wiping her eyes with her apron. . . . .

Out into the calm night with the moonlight silvering everything, walked Carrol and Harvey. Neither spoke for some moments. Harvey was full of solemn questioning.

"Where did you learn it all?"

She understood and answered with simple directness: "From the spirit of Truth, Harvey; 'the light that lighteth every man that cometh into the world.'"

"Yes, yes, I know; but it seems so vague and—and different. Did you really gain all your spiritual knowledge by reading the Bible?"

"I have gained most of it by being faithful to what I understood. To know the doctrine, one must do the will, I find."

"Very true, but the atonement—it is so wonderful, in this way. I want to hear more about it, for surely God sealed your words with a witness of His power."

"If you wish, Harvey, you may come in to-morrow morning, and I will explain all I can to you. I am only a child in understanding, but it is all the more impressive, that the truth is revealed to me directly, without personal teaching, and yet, why not? Is God a 'respecter of persons'? Not if He is Infinite Love."

They stopped at her gate. Carrol stood turned to the east with the full radiance of the moon upon her face. She looked more than human, Harvey thought, with her great dark eyes flashing forth a veritable inspiration, and her rich voice thrilling with the majesty of a divine consciousness.

"Good night," he said at last, and, pressing her hand in brief farewell, he turned hastily away.

CHAPTER XXXIII.

"In one of the inspired moments of the prophet, when he apprehended God as a God of Love, he cried out, 'I have desired mercy and not sacrifice; and the knowledge of God more than burnt offering.' It is mercy,—it is the knowledge of God, the word of truth, that will save, and the only sacrifice is the sacrifice of self which makes the atonement possible."

—"*The Right Knock.*"

BUT he did not return the next morning, nor the next. It was nearly a week before Carrol saw him again, and when he appeared one evening, she looked at him with a shock of surprise. His face was haggard and pale. Deep half-circles under his eyes, betokened sleepless nights, and wretched days.

"What is the matter, Harvey?" she questioned impulsively, after they were seated in the cool, pleasant study. It happened to be recreation hour and the children were all out.

"What is the matter?" he repeated. "I wish you would tell *me*, Carrol," as he wearily took out a handkerchief and wiped his brow.

"Are you ill?" with ready sympathy.

"No, only in soul. . . I will tell you, Carrol. Ever since that night I saw you last," he gave her a significant look, "I have been thinking, thinking, thinking over all the problems you have brought up in my mind. Points that I thought infallibly settled have crowded in upon me with overwhelming force, and I have pondered day and night. To make the matter still harder, Mrs. Dilbow knew of my visit to Benny Ballard, and the very next morning called to ask me how I had left him. Of course I told everything just as it happened at the bedside and the marvelous result of your visit with the young man. It was like touching an avalanche." Harvey spoke hesitatingly, as if undecided whether to continue. "It seems that certain members of my church have noticed my visits here, and because of statements they heard you make, whether connectedly or not, I cannot say, they—they pronounce you unorthodox, and therefore a—a—an infidel, which opinion, I assure you, the cure of Benny Ballard, wonderful as it is, only corroborates."

"Well?" she smiled.

"You may wonder why I tell you all this," he resumed, "but it only explains what I started to tell you about my own tribulations."

"It must not dishearten us if the whole world frowns. How can the criticism of ignorance affect the faith of one who *knows?* The question is not whether other people think we are right, but whether we *know* we are right, ourselves."

"True, Carrol, true," assented Harvey, thoughtfully. "Perhaps that is the best thing you could say to me, although I knew it well before. But I find myself in a trying position. My church is now thoroughly aroused to the necessity of inquiring into my views upon certain points, and they unwittingly found me making the same investigation in private," with a faint smile.

"In fact, Carrol, as I said a moment ago, I have been thinking, and thinking desperately, over certain things that have almost undone me."

"There is only one way to do, then," remarked Carrol, quietly but forcibly, "and that is to face the facts boldly, and deal with them as God gives you wisdom."

"God knows I want to know and serve Truth only," he replied, straightening himself into an uncomfortably upright position, as he continued: "Your talks, although always impressive, because of your earnestness, never swerved me one iota from my life-long convictions, until that night by that dying boy's bedside (for he certainly was on the verge of dying)." . .

A long pause. . . . .

"To think," resumed Harvey, "that to all my earnest questions—for they were as earnest as yours, Carrol; to all my heart-felt praying, he did not respond so much as to lift an eyelash, and when you came in, at the last moment it seemed, and began talking on the same subject, to see him revive, awake to intelligence and finally declare himself well, before my very eyes, was a miracle—not less than a *veritable* miracle, which actually stunned me into thinking, and the first text that came to me was one that impressed me no less than the subject it confirmed—'By their fruits ye shall know them.' Now Carrol, for the sake of the truth I know you love as you love your life, for the sake of the God we both serve, I want these questions answered." His voice was husky with emotion, and it was some moments before Carrol made any reply.

"In the first place, Harvey, there are no miracles."

"What!" he exclaimed, hoarsely; "do you not believe that Jesus raised Lazarus, or the widow's son? that he fed the five thousand or walked on the sea? that he rose from the dead?"

"All these things were done through the understanding of God's law—the spiritual law which the world would like to believe does not exist, but which Jesus and many of his disciples have proven, and which our God-given reason and divinely born faith *will* prove if we but use them together, instead of cruelly divorcing them every time we want to study religious truth."

"Oh, I see now how you arrive at such conclusions," said Harvey, pondering deeply.

"It is the only way we can attain to any knowledge —by this use of the faculties of intuition and reason."

"But tell me again your theory of the atonement. It is so totally different from what I have been taught."

"But Harvey, it is clearly taught in the Bible, and when you understand the connection between Jesus' life and his sayings, you will see that there is no other way in which to understand it."

"Well, what, in brief, is your idea of the atonement?"

"Atonement means agreement, concord, reconciliation; at-one-ment is the state of reconciliation, of harmony, isn't it?

"Yes."

"Then the word that brings us into harmony with God must be the word of atonement, or reconciliation. When Jusus, the perfect son, that is, the expression of the perfect Consciousness, spoke words that proved his oneness with the perfect Consciousness, he expressed the at-one-ment, the true Atonement.   But more than speaking the word, is living the life.   Ah, that is what brings concord, salvation."

"But what about the healing?" queried Harvey, still mystified.

"Recognizing this oneness as did the Master, are we not acknowledging the One, and thereby making ourselves the expression of Oneness, or Wholeness? Harmony expressed is health."

"I think I see what you mean by atonement, and I must admit there are passages of scripture that bear out your explanation, and it is something to be thought upon—yes deeply."

He shook his head sadly. Another thoughtful pause ensued.

"What do you think of prayer?" he asked, looking up, suddenly.

"If we recognize the Omnipresence of Spirit and the impossibility of getting beyond or outside of Spirit, which, in itself, is Sufficiency, can we not see that in the absolute sense we are already supplied with everything? To the Spirit—God—Christ-consciousness—there is no need; hence, we can truly give thanks that we have already received. To the sense, or man-consciousness, there are desires and needs without number, and it was to this sense-consciousness Jesus spoke when he said, 'When ye pray, Give us this day our daily bread.' To the disciples he oftenest uttered the truths born of the Christ-consciousness. To the masses who followed to gather the crumbs of his wisdom, he was obliged to speak from their own plane—the sense-consciousness—in order to lead them to the higher understanding, of which, at that time, they were not capable. 'Give us this day our daily bread,' spiritually translated, would be, 'Give us this day Thy righteous thought, Thy righteous word,' which is the bread of life. Prayer means the recognition of God first of all; then, if we recognize God as He is, we shall not beg, petition, entreat. We shall simply say, as did our beloved elder brother before accomplishing his greatest work, 'Father, I thank Thee that Thou hast heard me.' With the sense, or man-consciousness, we shall continue to implore. With the divine self, the Christ-consciousness, we shall give thanks and praises forevermore." . .

It grew late, and Harvey rose to go, with a weary air.

"I am very grateful to you, Carrol, for the time you have spent, and the explanations you have given. I can see how, to you, they seem absolutely true. For myself, I do not know."

He put his hand to his head in a dazed way. "I pray God will lead me out of this wilderness of doubt. I can only say I want the truth, be it what it may. I will try to dispel prejudice if there is any. There has been in the past as you too well know, but we are continually learning something new in God's school as we are in the school of the world, if we are willing to be learners."

She felt a sudden pity for the minister. Her thoughts flashed back to the conscientious struggles through which he had so often passed. Before this they had been for others, now they were for himself and there was a pathos about it that touched her strangely. She had been so glad to talk with him, and to know that he was tolerant enough to listen to her precious experiences, that she had scarcely remembered how she had unwittingly encouraged Ralph, in order to escape the possibility of a certain declaration from Harvey.

Of late a glance of the eye, an unconsciously tell-tale expression in word or act, had faintly warned her that she was on dangerous ground unless—but the hint was so vague, and so evidently unintentional as far as Harvey was concerned, that she had put it out of mind, whenever it presented itself, as unworthy even a thought.

To-night, as by a sudden revelation, the unnamed suspicion grew to a certainty.

Could she have known of the constant and terrible repression he had compelled himself to suffer, the awfulness of the problems, which through her had confronted him, the depths of misery through which he had passed in his grand effort to be faithful to his highest conception of truth and duty, she would have read the secret of his pathetic helplessness even better than she did.

Her talk after this discovery was constrained and conventional. She was to leave the Home in a few days. but instead of the frank, sincerely natural good-bye she had hitherto given, was one strangely quiet and cold.

CHAPTER XXXIV.

MISS ALLBRIGHT had come and gone, not wishing to stay till the very last, lest Carrol's courage should falter. The new teacher had arrived. Carrol had gone with her over the programme for the daily routine, had publicly praised the little Helpers' virtues, and privately excused their shortcomings. Now the time for departure was at hand. Her trunk waited for the hack that would call in a few moments. Carrol stood before the glass in her pleasant chamber, putting on the pretty new bonnet Miss Allbright had surreptitiously left in the top of her trunk, to be dis-covered when it was too late for thanks.

For the third time Carrol took off the veil to wipe her eyes and wash her face. "Oh how can I be thank-ful enough or good enough?" she murmured softly, as she finished her preparations for the journey.

But the moments moved on; there was no time for sentiment or even conjectures as to the future.

Little Nina, the only one of the children at home to say good-by, hastened up the stairs to say that the car-riage was waiting.

"Yes, but it is hard," whispered Carrol under her breath, as she snatched up her gloves; "it is hard to leave this little nest, where I was hatched, nurtured and taught to fly."

"Please, Miss Evans, kiss me once more to grow on," pleaded Nina, trying hard to be brave and not let the tears have their way.

"Of course I will, sweetheart, a dozen times if they will make you grow any better."

"They will; my garden is watered with love," whispered the sweet lips, while the dark eyes were quite hidden under the white curtains, that just then drew down very suddenly.

"Train leaves in half an hour. We must go, Miss," called the driver.

Then the door shut with a bang and the carriage whirled away, leaving the new teachers, Nina and the "Helpers' Home" in the fast receding distance.

At first it was a hard thing to go before a public audience, wholly trusting to the spirit of Truth to give her utterance, but with a consciousness that she had a message for the people, Carrol held to her resolve to deliver it, no matter how simply. And she was successful, marvelously so.

Throngs of hungry truth-seekers, who had long ago wearied of the husks of the misinterpreted and misunderstood religion, gladly listened to the gospel of the Good, and the history of its practice in these latter days.

Many a tearful face and hope-thrilled voice bore witness after every lecture to the need of such a gospel, and the ready soil into which the good seed fell. But it was not so easy to establish a "Helpers' Home" or even a "Voluntary Help Society." So new a movement must become respectably known before it would do to take hold of it in a public way, said those whose ample means would have allowed them to do as Miss Allbright had done. The poorer classes, "the common people," listened gladly. However, there were grand exceptions to both rules, and Carrol felt, after three months' labor in different places, that important work for the future had been accomplished. It was mostly through previous arrangement by Miss Allbright that the first six weeks were so fully occupied. After that nearly every mail brought letters asking for special appointments. Sometimes Carrol stopped in a place *en route*, generally finding a ready audience after one or two announcements in the paper, and especially after the first lecture. Her subjects were: "What will help us," "The need of to-day," Practical Christianity and its Possibilities," and similar topics.

One evening she was to give the last named lecture in the town of Ashurst, one of those small sleepy places so often found in the Eastern States. The audience was a responsive one, but one face especially, hungrily drank in every word Carrol uttered, and inspired her to the utterance of great things.

It was a strong, thoughtful face, with deep lines of sorrow around the mouth and brow. The dark wistful eyes kindled with awakening interest.

"Oh, friends," concluded the speaker, earnestly, "let us rise into the grander, higher life, by putting behind us the petty worries, the failures, the sorrows and the heart-broken hopes. Let us put out of mind the differences that have separated us from God or man. Let us recognize the untrammeled freedom of the children of God and live above dissension, difference, or even death itself. We are one family. What if this person or that person is still a child in his knowledge of right living? Deal with him as with a child, gently, patiently, tenderly. Wait until the understanding of his relation and duty to God and man bursts upon him in the full glory of a new day of life and light and beauty. Take it for granted that every one is doing his best to know and to live. Through this divine recognition of the unity of effort you will become co-workers, co-partners in this everlasting kingdom of the Good—the kingdom of eternal Love. You will prove the possibilities of Christianity as taught, lived and proved by one who at all times recognized the One-ness of all Being, all Goodness and all Life."

The meeting was over. Warm words and warmer handclasps betokened the tender chord that vibrated in sympathy with the words that touched it.

Among others Carrol noticed the face of the young woman who had so attracted her in the audience.

"My name is Helen Ward," said the stranger, with a warm, clinging grasp of the hand. "I can never thank you enough for your words to-night. I would like to talk with you. Will you not be my guest?"

"From that moment," wrote Carrol to Mary a week later, "we were friends—such friends as only the soul can find. We gazed into each other's eyes, and knew that both had longed and striven and suffered. We seemed to understand without words, and yet words were not lacking. I went home with her—my Helen, I have already learned to call her—and that very night she told me her life story; a sad, sad, minor, with an awful crash of conflict and inharmony at the last. She is a widow now. It was not lack of love or appreciation or sympathy from her husband that made her unhappy. Oh, no. He so grandly loved her that he laid down his life in agonizing efforts to convert her to religion; for he was a preacher, a majestic, noble soul, the like of which is seldom found. Helen believed in the love and justice of God, and could not see how the profession or non-profession of belief in a creed could change that love or justice. John Ward, or John, as she lovingly calls him, awoke to the fact that he had been beguiled through his affection for her into too long silence concerning her unbelief; and when the deacons of his church demanded that a session be called for, to administer church discipline, or 'deal with her,' he wrote her while she was away on a visit, that she must not return to him until she had found the truth, until she could believe in everlasting punishment, for since, through her own heresy, non-belief in that doctrine had spread, so through her conversion and consequent effort she must repair the wrong she had done. In the meantime he would pray for her. . .

"Helen could hardly tell this part of it, and I could only guess the end when she said 'he prayed to the last.' She did not say much about his death or the final suspense, but Lois, her cousin, told me how his own remorse and the agony for her salvation proved too much for physical endurance, and how he gladly gave up his life, feeling that the sacrifice would insure her eternal welfare.

"She saw him but once, and that when the end came. . . Think, Mary, what she must have suffered, and with no hope of seeing him in the future, either."

"'Why, Helen,' said I when she talked about it, 'you who know so well the meaning of love, must surely know its eternalness.'"

"She looked at me in a quick eager way, and then I told her of that which had convinced me of eternal life. The love I have ever felt for my mother, always intense, has never waned through all my years of doubt and darkness; and within the last year (I believe I never told you this, Mary), it has quietly taught me the lesson of immortality.

"I put it to Helen as it had come to me; 'Love is a spiritual fact,' said I, 'and all that makes us rejoice in our friends' presence, or yearn for their companionship is the love that responds to our own; that response makes us one. If my mother's love claimed me before she was deprived of the body, how could it relinquish itself, for if we were spiritually one, could there be a material separation to a spiritual reality?'

"'I see, I see,' she cried, her white face flushed with its eagerness,' 'you mean that the love, sympathy, wisdom, incarnated, so to speak, in a human being must still have its individual consciousness, and therefore be as much of an expressed reality as it ever was in the flesh?'

"'Yes, because consciousness of individuality cannot be annihilated any more than love can be destroyed, burned or swept away.'

"'Oh, if I only *could* believe it,' she moaned, clasping her hands, with a passionate heart-hunger burning in her eyes.

"'You can if you are willing to use faith, reason and patience.'

"'Yes, yes, anything that is true I want to believe, God knows.'

"'Do you suppose John's struggles, hopes or prayers were nothing but vain bubbles on a play-ocean? One might think so if body were all there is, but we know that Spirit, Love, Life, Goodness are verities that cannot be lost or destroyed. Therefore, because love is a ceaseless, changeless reality, because my love for mother has never died, I know her love for me still lives.'

"'And you think John still loves me as I do him?' she murmured brokenly but joyfully.

"'Yes.'

"'But is he still distressed because of my honest doubt?' a cloud of pain sweeping over the sky of her new-born hope.

"'Wisdom must be added there, as well as here, because wisdom, too, is another side of that One which cannot be broken into parts. His deep earnestness and intense effort must bear their fruitage and doubtless he knows now, that your noble honesty, and hard striving after the better life, will be the means of bringing you to the truth.

"'Yes, but not what he thought was truth; that can never be,' she cried with a sharp accent of pain.

"'The truth, Helen, is no respecter of persons, and will prove itself to every earnest seeker in this life or the next.

> 'Truth crushed to earth shall rise again,
> The eternal years of God are hers;
> But error, wounded, writhes in pain,
> And dies among her worshipers.'

"She was very thoughtful after that, and the lines of sorrow were less deep than when I met her first.

"Lois says she never saw anyone change as much as Helen in the last few days, and she is very glad. . . Helen is going to Seaton with me to learn all about the method of carrying on the Helpers' Home.

"She is more and more satisfied with this explanation of Christianity, and often says if she had only known the meaning of religion she would not have broken John's heart, for she thinks he would surely have believed it too. But Mary, I do not think a person of his firmness of opinion would permit himself to listen long enough to learn. That is the reason so many are kept out of the bliss of proving—because they are afraid to look back of established authority. Oh, when *will* they learn that ' the spirit itself beareth witness with our spirit,' and that it is not what any person or church says, but as the voice of God in our own souls. .

"Your letter of October 15th came yesterday. One item of news surprised me greatly; that is, that Uncle

Maynard has accepted a position at Lynn Heights, and that he is so changed from what he used to be. I wonder if he has ever corresponded with Miss Allbright. I heard her speak of him once as though she knew him. Of course I do not know; and, in fact, hardly remember him, as I have never seen him since we were children. I would like to see him now, for no one can appreciate better than I what the change from darkness to light means!

"Well, Mary darling, I have written this long letter because I knew you would want to hear something of my work, and a hint of my line of thinking. Am so glad we have always kept up this confidential habit of exchanging views, and more than all, glad that we are growing into a knowledge of the same truth.

"Make room in your heart for Helen Ward. You cannot help loving her. Good-bye, dear, with a kiss for Marguerite.

"CARROL."

CHAPTER XXXV.

"You are pure in heart! Having left the chrysalis of self and arisen on the wings of faith, you are conscious of the Life that now is and ever has been world without end. The completeness of life is yours. You are receptive to the brooding Spirit of Love. You are filled with the fulness of God—the Life of goodness. . . . Because *I am*, thou art, and all that I have is thine. Thou art crowned with the Consciousness of Life. See that no man taketh thy crown."—*Mary D. Fisk.*

NEARLY two years have passed since Carrol's letter was written. Helen Ward remained at the Helpers' Home in Seaton until the next September, when she returned to Ashurst, accompanied by little Nina. Together they were to begin another "Home."

One by one the original "helpers" had gone, but the house, now greatly enlarged, was filled with other waifs and workers who well responded to the trust reposed in them. Ned and Tillie, who had been married several months previous, at Miss Allbright's urgent request, were now installed as housekeeper and overseer of the Home.

Mrs. Rice had grown much stronger after her long-lost son's return, and was now well and happy. The deacon had received Ned sullenly at first, but grew more satisfied as he saw the quiet determination of the boy to prove himself worthy the respect of the world. Ralph still remained at home, the comfort of his mother, and one of the strongest allies of the "Voluntary Help

Society." When a good man's strength or help was needed, Ralph was the one to whom they appealed first; and never in vain.

Miss Allbright now lived at her Home in Lynn Heights, much to Mary's delight. Aunt Creesh had been prevailed upon to take charge of the one in Tintuckett, and a most admirable matron she made, with her cheery ways or unexpected sallies of wit or wisdom.

One bright afternoon in October, Carrol sat in her room busily working and thinking—working over some pretty bit of fancy sewing for Mary's Christmas, for she was to spend the holidays in Lynn Heights after a six weeks' tour of public speaking—thinking just now of Harvey Willard. During the two years past, she had heard of him but once, and that was when he left Seaton. He had written of his long, hard struggle with faith and reason; of the final union of both ; of his trial by the church and consequent expulsion.

"And now Carrol," he concluded, " here I am, turned adrift from the old moorings, but rejoicing to know the blessed truth, which I am preaching in my own way to an audience eager to listen, and not without results, I have reason to believe. But it was hard to have the door of my own home shut in my face, for such, as you know, the Church has always been to me. I loved it, worked for it, and lived for it. . . I can work anywhere, and worship God anywhere, but the Church will always be a sacred temple, and her ceremonies, forms and communion more precious than ever, because now I see a meaning in them I never saw before.

It is 'the spirit that maketh alive,' and now I realize the truth and power of spirit." . . .

Carrol rejoiced in his noble stand for truth, and admired his honesty and earnestness more than she was aware, but her reply to his letter had been short and cold, notwithstanding her congratulations and hopeful words.

Just as she finished tacking on the last bow of ribbon, the door-bell rang.

"Another applicant for the Home," she thought.

No, it was a caller. Reverend Harvey Willard, was the name on the card.

"Show him into the parlor; I will be down soon," said Carrol.

Scarcely thinking what she did, she arrayed herself in a pretty red gown of some soft material, that was exceedingly becoming. With a white rose in her bosom, and the hint of a red one in either cheek, she went down.

Harvey had actually grown handsome! Tall, broad-shouldered, erect and dignified, he was a type of perfect physical manhood. But, more than all, Carrol noted the change in his face. No longer the severe outlines of self judgment, or unconscious fearfulness, but peace enthroned. The eyes were clear and deep, with suggestions of the fire of enthusiasm, or the benevolent gentleness they might express.

. . . Harvey staid a long time. When he went away there were tears in Carrol's eyes, but they were not tears of sorrow. . . Yes, something had happened she never dreamed (?) *could* happen. It would change some of her plans, but her life work would be the same.

Oh, Carrol, Carrol, have you forgotten the bitter things you used to say and feel? Can you forget the unhappy days of childhood, and—yes, for love, the white magician has changed ignorance into wisdom, bitterness into joy, cruel judgment into tender recognition of good."

At Christmas time a feast of good will and rejoicing is held at Mr. and Mrs. Temple's beautiful home in Lynn Heights.

Janet bustles about with huge importance. "Th' wull o' th' Lord is pruvin' itsel' i' this hoose," she muttered as she dusted a china cup for the third time. "Wha 'd a thocht th' maister 'd be a plannin' an' prepairin' for 't a' wi' as mooch hert as th' wifie. But sic a change i' his face, an' respec' intil his voice, whan he luiks at th' sweet boddy. Hesh! but th' glory o' seein' sic gran' gude livin' is more nor I iver expecket!"

The soft dust cloth whisked about in the most lively manner, sometimes to the apparently imminent danger of the china cups and saucers, the delicate plates and vases.

"Eh, but his natur' is richt bonny noo he lats th' self o' 'im shine oot," continued Janet, still thinking of the master.

"An' to think it's that wonnerfu' boddy's ane doin's wi' her sweet ways o' smilin', an' thinkin' til hersel' no matter hoo ill a win' blaws. I wonner what she thinks, but happen it's what I foun' her sayin' ance upo' a time, not long sin' whan 's auld spel' o' hatefu'ness was show-

in' itsel' like the de'il's ane tracklets a' over 's face.
I foun' her off i' her ane room, whaur th' bairnie was
sleepin', a-sayin' til hersel' i' that trustfu' way o' hers.
'He is *na*' ill wulled. Felix is gude an' kin' an' lovely.
I wull na see, nay Lord, I wull na ken onythin' but th'
gude o' him. He *is wise* an' patient i' 'is God-like-
ness.'"

"An' that was her way o' acknowledgin' the Lord
o' heaven an' airth aboot th' true o' Felix Temple, an' I
doot not it's th' richt way to warship, for gude wull
(good will) an' kin'ness to a' is th' rule o' this hoose. ."

"And to think Mary we should be learning the same
wonderful truth in such different ways," Carrol was saying in the lovely south room where the warm sunlight
touched floor and mantel with its Christmas brightness.

"And yet they are not so different after all. We
have both found that 'the secret of the Lord is with them
that love him,' or live his life. How blindly I suffered
those first years of my married life, and I know now it
was because I ignored the truth I perceived. I did not
manifest my oneness with the Father, which I innately
knew was my life. I knew the truth that would have
freed me from bondage, but failed to apply it in a practical way."

'Yes, Mary, I have often wondered that those who
know the life and words of Jesus so well, should fail to
find the comfort and freedom he promised. Now, when
you were a little girl you had the sweetest conception of
religion, and I remember how helpful your thoughts
often were to me, saving me from unhappiness when
nothing else could."

"I was certainly happy in my childish faith, and cannot see why it left me when I needed it most."

"It seems to me *then,* you listened to the voice within, and gave forth that which was so real to you without let or hindrance. When you grew older and associated with those whose habits of thought were different, you ceased to hold mentality in the receptive attitude through which you received instruction from the Father, and turned to the *human* for help and happiness, protection and guidance; but the human failed. How could it do otherwise? We have both learned dear, that Spirit is our sufficiency. Having found our lives hid with Christ in God, we *know* that we are complete in the Christ consciousness."

"The Law which fulfills all conditions, is the brooding spirit of love, ready to answer or meet every demand. Yes, it has been my greatest comfort, Carrol, to know that I need not and should not depend on any human being for help or happiness—that *person* is nothing, that Spirit is all. With that recognition, I have been comforted, strengthened, and helped as though I had leaned on the breast of a mother. . . It was not an easy lesson to learn though," she added with the hint of a tremble in her voice. . . 'For thy Maker is thy husband,' (thy helper,) she quoted, after a momentary silence; 'the Lord of Hosts is His name, and thy Redeemer, the Holy One of Israel.' . . Oh, I cannot tell you Carrol, the help that text and its accompanying verses have brought me. It has been the key to many victories."

The dinner bell rang loud and long.

A rosy face with a golden aureole of hair, raised from the snowy bed and a piping little voice said, "I'se weady."

"So you are, my precious," replied the fond mother, lifting the little Margaret in her arms. "Come Carrol, we will not keep them waiting."

Around the Christmas feast with Felix and Mary were gathered Carrol, Harvey, Mrs. Noble, Aunt Creesh, Ada and Richard, Uncle Maynard and Miss Allbright. The faces were illumined with something more than Christmas sunshine. To Mary came a joy too deep for utterance.

"Aunty," said the small queen at Carrol's side, as she smiled in the most bewitching fashion, "I love ev'ybody. Does 'ou?"

CPSIA information can be obtained
at www.ICGtesting.com
Printed in the USA
LVOW09s2315121216
517005LV00024B/773/P